On
FOREIGN GROUND

A True Story

of a Wild Soul

On
FOREIGN
GROUND

A True Story
of a Wild Soul

INGEBORG VAN ZANTEN HAYES

Copyright ©2022. Printed in the United States of America

Cover art: Ria Huijgen
Book Design: Mary Meade

ISBN 978-1-957468-05-1

Dedicated to my mom, Christa; my foster mom, Enny; my dad, Marinus; my late husband, Toby; and our children: Christa Savannah Maria, and Patrick Henry Marinus Van; to their spouse(s) and my grandchildren: Reece Emerson, James Dalton Marinus Van, Auguste Henry, Marina Rosa, Anna Maria, and Brooke Grace, with special mention of Sister Margaret Byrne who deep-ened my Spirit with her unconditional love and wisdom for more than thirty years. Bui Tuyet Minh and our friendship deepened my love for Vietnam and its people. Indeed, all my teachers of the light and the dark who made for a beautiful journey in search of love.

Happy is the person, who feels the connection with all living things, and therefore loves life and people

—ᘒ—

Glücklich is der Mensch, der den Zusammenhang mit allem Lebendigen fühlt und deshalb das Leben und die Menschen liebt

—ALBERT SCHWEIZER

Disclaimer

Few chapters on individual countries contain a brief fiction as an introduction to place. I share my father's stories to the best of my memory as he shared them with me and others in the family. The teachings of the medicine people are my accounts and interpretations of what I experienced.

The accusations and suspicions that occur throughout the book reflect my search of identity and spiritual path. These thoughts are intended for insight and not to debunk the people mentioned. I'm grateful for my family, friends, and teachers—my memory and experience may differ from theirs. Some names are changed because of that.

ACKNOWLEDGMENTS

MY GRATITUDE TO MEMBERS OF the Houston and Bozeman Gypsy Rhythm Writers Group, Lee Standing Bear Moore of The Manataka American Indian Council, Timothy Tate who gave feedback into my shadow delving, and Jerry Mernin who shared several hours editing my bear story. I credit my perseverance and trust drawn from words of Thich Kien Nguyet of the Truc Lam Thay Thien Temple in Hanoi, Vietnam. I'm thankful for Laurie Smith Small Waisted Bear, her friendship and input/editing the first chapter. Richard Hite contributed his teachings and process of a new belief system during my life. Fred van Zanten my cousin, in Rotterdam, rekindled memories from Rotterdam. Ria Huijgen, my cousin in the Netherlands, painted the cover. Laurina Lyle gave humor and friendship. Jan Elpel honored my writings, deepened my ownership, and took on the task of editing while maintaining my Dutch in it all. Without her this book would probably not have been published. Friends Susan Morgan and Zuzana Gedeon listened to my stories and gave me feedback.

CONTENTS

Introduction / *xv*

Invocation / *xvii*

I. THE GREAT GIVEAWAY

A Shift in Identity / 29

The Collapsed Scream / 34

II. WHO AM I?

Putting Myself Together Again / 59

Birth of a Cross Cultural Child / 62

In Love During the War / 75

Oma's House / 100

Life in Overschie / 110

A Foster Mom From the Dutch East Indies / 119

Skating on Thin Ice / 133

Pray for This Baby to Die—
My Brother Henk / 145

Sister Ilse / 158

The Old Hospital / 162

Holidays / 164

Stepping into Freedom / 168

Providence / 179

La Vie Est Fragile, Le Traiter
Avec Tendresse / 205

Snakes / 210

The Great Boa Constrictor / 214

III. LEARNING FROM THE INDIGENOUS

Standing Eagle, an Apache
Medicine Man / 219

Visit by a Hungry Ghost / 237

Chief Hidden Wolf,
The Second Medicine Man / 242

Gray Woman / 277

Lakota Zintkala Oyate,
38[Th] Generation Medicine Man / 283

Earning the Name
"Standing Bear Woman" / 291

IV. WORLD CITIZENSHIP

Uncovering Culture Shock—
Voices of Iraq / 315

East Kalimantan, Borneo Indonesia / 335

Karma in Vietnam / 355

Re-Awakening the Heart of Tolerance / 391

Oneness / 400

Author's Note / *409*

Selected References and Bibliography / *411*

Recommended Reading / *412*

INTRODUCTION

"GO HOME TO YOUR COUNTRY, Mof," our downstairs neighbor yells in fury as Mom and I hang our laundry off our balcony on the second-floor apartment. It is summer 1953. We live in Rotterdam, the city of my birth. Anger and despair drench this recently bombed out city. The insecure void of an end to a barbaric World War II moves everyone forward.

Mom is stateless and rejected. She has been made a non-being inside and outside. I ask myself: Am I Dutch or German? A native of Holland I become part of a massive rebuilding. Ancestral vibes linger from a humanity who attempted to destroy itself. Our vulgar twists of mass ignorance, greed and power have resulted in suicide and genocide for millions. I taste the aftermath of hate, intolerance, sacrifice and hard work. I realize how war infects people, families, and countries for generations.

I love my German Mom, yet Germans are still the enemy even though the war is over. The alliances who freed us are my family's alliances, too. "America" becomes my icon for freedom.

Being born into two cultures then rejected by one challenge my identity. I feel no anchor. The situation comes to a climax after my American husband dies. I am thirty-four and do not connect to any place or people. The absence of a distinct cultural persona and its psychological complexity culminates in my breakdown. I end up in a psychiatric hospital. The divine guidance of a Mexican psychiatrist who cared for me invoked healing. It becomes my breakthrough.

"On Foreign Ground" chronicles my cultural and spiritual quest to gain identity among Indigenous medicine people in the US. They rekindle my connection with the Ancestors, the earth, and identify my weaknesses. The cultural values and beliefs I encounter living in Guatemala, Indonesia, and Iraq, as well as a stay in a Buddhist temple in Vietnam, also birth a new sense of unity.

My transformation cherishes the Oneness of humans. It embraces world citizenship. A land, a special spot on this earth to fulfill my destiny and purpose, calls my name. It's about creating footprints of inner and outer freedom.

"On Foreign Ground" may serve as a mirror for those who wish to strengthen their potential view and identity while living in a culture other than their own. It is about generational pain and loss in the heat of living. It touches on embracing our wounds and creating something new for the next generation.

INVOCATION

A NARROW TUNNEL MOVES HUNDREDS of people in both directions under the muddy Maas River in the center of Rotterdam. It is wet, noisy and stinky. A "Rotterdammer" would not complain about such minor things. No one stands still. There is no room.

My memory dredges up a time in Rotterdam. My parents and I are taking the thousand-meter steep escalator. What was my dad thinking to take my little Mom and I into the dark bowels of this harbor? Fear glues Mom's feet on the step of the escalator. They each hold their bikes down under the Maas River to visit the Southside of the city.

My body frozen, I'm sitting in a child's seat on the rear of my dad's bike. I'm lightheaded. No sound comes out of my mouth. Dad's bike slants sharply down. He turns the front wheel sideways to keep it from rolling. My hands clutch the cold metal that surrounds my chair. Dad has moved his body in front of his bike's black leather seat. His blue eyes penetrate from under his hat. They check Mom and then me. Slow, as if in trance, I move my head back to see Mom too. Her green eyes lock on her bike. She and her bike stand a few steps higher behind us. She looks pale. The escalator, packed with people and their bikes, transports us downward into obscure lights of a tunnel. Mom is in a stupor. She knows letting go could smash her bike down into me, then my dad and the dozens of people in front of us holding their own bikes. It would be a big pile up with sirens and ambulances and people screaming.

At the dark bottom we step off the old escalator on solid concrete. I breathe, "Because who doesn't want to fall will not learn to walk." The bikes at our sides, Mom and Dad move hurriedly as behind us more continue to step off the escalator.

At the end of the long tunnel, we step on the up-moving escalator. Again, our front wheels sideways and Mom yelling for Dad "Marinus, Marinus ich schaff das nicht." Pa doesn't answer. It's wrong to speak German in this bombed out city. He moves closer to me and reaches back. He grabs Ma's front wheel. Dad is tall and strong, if an animal he'd be a tall buck with a huge rack on his head. The weight of the bike and gravity pull all of us backward. Will I fall out of my seat? My fingers hurt.

Coming up into the daylight I inhale the cool harbor air. It smells of oil, tar and Eastern spices. Strong seafarers run the cranes. They load and unload ships that are around us. It's a noisy place. A soft drizzle falls on us. I'm happy and I'm sad. I am alone. My Mom is lost, shivering like a shy bird in this culture that hates her. And Dad, he's alone, too.

Part of me has not surfaced from that tunnel just now, a part fell off the bike. Something seized it, while I held my breath as that three-year-old. I bet for the first thirty-four years of my life some slice of me has been living in captivity in that dark and moist Rotterdam tunnel, as over time thousands of people walked by.

"Child, you deserve a statue." I tell myself.

There have been numerous dark blobs that kidnapped my artistic outbursts. Pulled them through mud, tied them to a boulder and sunk this caboodle deep, very deep. Laurina, my friend, suggests my Muse may be selling cigarettes at a market corner in Rotterdam, or just being a lazy bum somewhere. I do not like this dragging motion. My body feels as if I'm under anesthesia and needs to wake up. With all my might I gather energy for a different mode: I run. I stomp. I push myself to exhaustion. I drag my being into the fresh air, change my surroundings.

Now artistic flow pours out from me, until the day my creative manifestations come to a screeching halt. I inhale fear. Yet sunbeams try to reach in like ships steaming by on the beaches in Hoek van Holland. A pilot guides them towards the open North Sea, where they head for England.

I like the Dutch beaches where I pick up shells. Nonetheless, these shells are empty. No one is home. They remind me of the Zadkini monument found at the Rotterdam harbor, a desperate muscular man who throws his hands up in the air. In the spot where his heart is supposed to beat is a hole, signifying the bombing and burning of the heart of Rotterdam. I'm drowning in sadness.

My book feels not complete; Does it hold the flavor of being wild and adventurous? I remind myself: A Dutch person doesn't allow anyone to eat their cheese off their slice of bread.

"Voicing my uniqueness; is my birth right. I love to bring cultures together, to heal, exercise, write, paint, plan, sing and get closer to the earth. Yes, to go out of my head, dream and wake up again.

Pushing the edge puts me in the moment. Strengthens me.

"I will give them my Rotterdam harbor wild soul."

ONE

THE GREAT GIVEAWAY

She got a force she got horsepower. A warrior crossing the Serengeti of life. Summoned she's prepared she is enough to herself. She creates the energy needed to birth other warriors of passion, gentleness, and fierceness. Laughing and crying as she rides till the finish line. It has not always been this way.

T HE NOISE LEVEL OF YOUNG people overwhelms me. I sit on the first floor of a coffee shop in Bozeman, Montana. It is loud, darn loud. I found a corner far away from the crowd. Among my paperwork, an old letter written by my foster mom in 2005 surprises me. "My sweet foster S. L. Rose," she begins in beautiful italics. Then she praises me for my work. "Daughter, continue your path in this manner. I'm proud of you." The four pages she wrote are on a World Wildlife Fund paper. Typical, always putting the animals first. This organization is what she lives for. Her letter triggers memories of a time in Indonesia. We, my husband Toby and I and our two children, lived in the jungles of East-Kalimantan. I was pregnant with our third. I found a local boat driver with long black hair to charter us in his blue and red thirty-foot wooden boat. This created a way out of the dense surroundings we lived in. A breather for a few hours out into the sea. The boat had an improvised wooden rooftop. We helped each other to a couple of benches. Thus, the Indonesian driver sitting at the back end of the boat, his hands on the manual motor, moved us to the longhouse a mile or two out. It's hot, hot like it is hot every day.

Thirty or so young kids ran toward us with smiling faces. "Me please, me please miss…" they begged while happily greeting us at the wooden dock of the floating small village. The high tide made it easier to climb the ladder onto the wooden planks.

The children wanted to make some money. Carry stuff. One or two of them pushed and shoved themselves forward and got our attention. We hired them for the couple of hours we planned to be there. They carried the goods we bought. Not far from us an Indonesian man squatted on the wooden planks. A traditional brown sarong wrapped waist down around his body. He wore the traditional black narrow cap. In front of him on a piece of cloth were a few pounds of leeches, an Indonesian fruit. I stopped and could see the water through the cracks below me. With a knife he partly peeled off the red strawberry-colored leathery peel and handed me the fruit. Its white flesh had a distinct feel and taste on my tongue, which asked for more. The simple surroundings, the water beneath me, and this man sitting in front of me with his fruit would be carved in my mind. I asked him to fill the bag I brought. Somewhat further a person sold gold at a small area cut off from where a family lived. We found some groceries, too, with cleaned bamboo shoots drifting in buckets of water. I eagerly bought some to make lumpias, the Indonesian egg rolls, once back in our house.

Suddenly, noise rose not far from where I stood. I noticed that down to the right of the longhouse people threw rice at some of our group. They, the locals, were furious with them for being too loud and trying to barter prices down to unreasonable lows. It's culturally raw and inappropriate to be loud in Indonesia. It's almost the equivalent of hitting someone.

My mind spirals down to my childhood as I remember the encounters with my foster mom. She came from Java, Indonesia.

Where did your gentleness come from Aunt Enny? Was it that so much happened to you? Was it your culture? Was it your dad, your mom? The maids? How did you develop your calm, your gentle presence, your tuning into my emotions? Your compassion for *All* the animals. I feel raw and wild today—like your Ingeping—from yesteryears. I need the higher tones of your presence in my life. I know they live within me. Surely, they rooted in our fifty years of foster. Something in me smells your Indonesian food. You are sitting close now and next to me. Your soft voice talks about the animals that are presently living with you. We need to take care of them Ing. Come with me and volunteer for the World Wildlife Fund. They need us. Do you feel better now *Meis?*

I scan the folks around me in the coffee shop. There are even more people now. A crescendo of laughter by a group of young people at a round table fills the area. There is music, too. It's loud, so very loud. A fog rises in my mind. I go back in years as if watching myself change in a mirror. I see a young Dutch woman standing in her vulnerability as if naked in the cold. She has been stripped from her persona by the ambiguity of possessions. She is orchestrating a big giveaway. "You better go back to Holland to your parents," Toby, her husband, had uttered briefly before his final breath and departure to the other side.

I wanted to follow up and sell the house in Houston, Texas. His death had pushed me into bewildered grief. My mind created a false sense of justice. I didn't want to make money on the house. Buyers, a couple from England, eagerly accepted. The sale of the house required an inspection and the man that came to the house to do so pushed me over the edge.

For most people, I believe, it's easier to give than to receive. For most I say, because the exchange of energy as it occurs in nature and as it must be in all our relationships is a foreign concept to the majority. Humanity still needs to return home and create balance on this giving earth. Maybe then we shall be free to howl with the wolves.

"I can contact him, you know." Fragile to no end, I was curious and accepted his connection with a dark spirit world. This house inspector, a young scientologist, fucked with my brain. He showed me some strange credentials that I didn't understand.

My body quivering, I sat at the living room table and sobbed. Was it him or was it my own dark side he had tapped into? He knew about people that I knew, messed around with my head and was out to get stuff from the house. He picked up a washer, dryer and TV the following day for his "spiritual services." My body and mind vulnerable after the death of Toby, I wondered: Did I just have a visit from the devil himself? I drove myself to the Cenacle, a Catholic retreat house. My confidante, Sr. Margaret, planned to report him to the Better Business Bureau. The damage was done.

The experience with the scientologist on top of dealing with Toby's passing had jolted me into chaos. I began getting rid of things, Toby's clothes, the bed. I couldn't stand our king-size bed. I smelled my husband and the hospital in it. It reminded me of our last months together at home. He and I both were anxious about his heart. Each night, I would put my ear on his chest to hear and count the beats. During the day we were together like two hon-eymooners—love and gentle laughter filled our house. Each after-noon when our two children came out of school, we had tea and cake. We sat around a big table in the living room area—created this way like the Dutch do. I called a Catholic priest to please haul off Toby's clothes and the bedroom area furnishings for use at Casa Juan Diego, a shelter for mostly Guatemalan then. Further mem-ories of our marriage triggered thoughts of purification. "I have sinful possessions." I therefore set out to discard these objects my mind saw as being wrong.

Derogatory thoughts raced through my head: "You were on the wrong track in Indonesia, gathering this stuff. You didn't achieve anything." I hauled the antique vases we had collected outside. By the end of the day some $50,000+ worth of goods (the life I had shared with Toby) stood next to the garbage can. A woman from across the street went through all the books I had discarded. The garbage men drove up. "We'll come back later and pick it up, Madam." Later that afternoon the garbage truck returned. They had placed black blankets in the back so not to damage the huge antique ceramics they were about to haul off.

I even tossed the graduation ring Toby was so proud of into the garbage can. My distorted mind connected it with the military and Texas A&M University, where he had received his engineering degree. In my mind, the ring recalled Toby's hard times during the war, his encounter with the wounded girl in the Philippines.

It was all a big soup in my head. Thoughts hammered deep into shame and worthlessness.

Then there was my jewelry. I gathered the beautiful things he had given me, valuable bracelets, silver from Iraq, gold charms from Guatemala.

"Where has your brain been," I lambasted myself. "Is this going to bring him back? Why did you invest time in gathering these possessions? You could have used the money to help others. Why do you have all this and people on the other end of the world have nothing?" The guilty verdict clobbered my head: "Where is the fairness in that." A ferocious force of black thinking, much like a meteorite hitting the earth and scourging that which it touches, conquered my mindset and belief system.

"I'll take care of it," my neighbor said as I handed her the jewelry. "I know someone trustworthy who can help you with that, sell it for you. The money will end up in Africa like you want." I felt relieved. My dear friend kept and guarded it until I was well and could think clearly again.

On the flip side, during a visit to Louisiana in those early months after Toby's death, I noticed a poor black woman holding a child in the doorway of a wooden shack. This image burned into my mind. A current with a dark destiny of not being able to provide for my children took possession of my life.

In the meantime, as a young and Catholic mother, I attended Mass in Livingston, Texas, close to the cemetery where my husband had been lowered into the ground. I dropped $500 in the basket. During my hospitalization I gifted a patient who had a sad story half a grand. Later living in Holland, I gave money to a collection drive for a faraway country. I was young, a widow and bleeding from the heart. I couldn't say no to those who asked, nor did I have any desire to keep the money from the house I sold that I needed for the children.

A SHIFT IN IDENTITY

Life betrays us at times, pushes us down into the mud. I try to fight back, play possum, or dissociate, freeze like a deer standing on the road seeing headlights, or go out of my body. Yet what's needed is love, forgiveness and surrender, all the while cutting the bull shit around who I think I am, or society dictates I must be. Believing in yourself requires standing up, brushing off the dirt.

I N THE HOSPITAL, WITH THE help of Dr. Blanca Diez, a Mexican psychiatrist in the form of divine intervention, I embarked on the hard work of learning who in the heck I am after all. My persona had shattered. No longer the "wife" of Toby, no more that Dutch woman, that younger one who had married an older man; a father figure some individuals judged. No more the lover of a powerful yet gentle man, an engineer. What stood was a mother of two children with no career. A woman with weak boundaries whose projected support, yes, the main part of her identity and protection had been her mate. He had kicked the bucket—as he had said shortly before he died. In my anger I thought, "Toby, you chose death over me." Guilt hammered my mind for even thinking that. I needed to learn to love myself and others unconditionally.

We lived in a country that was not my childrens' own yet. Christa was born in Guatemala and Patrick in Germany—none of us knew which piece of ground we belonged to or who we aligned with culturally. A scenario had repeated itself. I came from parents with two different nationalities and now our kids, too, had inherited two brand new cultures from a Dutch mother and American father. The only person in this world who I truly knew loved me, that rock who loved me for who I was and who I was not, had vanished, snatched away. This man's love branded my heart a "Hayes." He had reached each cell of my body. Still standing, I stood now, but alone, alone with our two young children, six and eight years old, in a country none of us was born in. A flash of gratefulness beamed through my head realizing I had two and not three children with the pregnancy loss of the last one. Should I follow my husbands' advice and move to Holland?

Unable to consciously receive love from anyone, I was good at giving it. My father's authoritarian presence, his angry outbursts had shrunk me down at an early age. Like a punch in the gut, it had silenced me, took my voice away and made for shallow breathing. "You are hysterical" and taking me by the hand he'd put me in the bathroom. His critical stance and emotional unavailability with his hard work to bring our family forward after WWII, had rendered a wall that became higher and higher. This mindset and environment created a child-like presence for me with men. It created a path for powerful lovers, a dangerous falling in love with everyone who'd give me attention, presence and kindness. Ultimately it would require maturing, redefining what's the true meaning of being powerful in a mate. After all, my mind had to perceive a male, a healthy male and mate. The first step in that direction began at that psychiatric hospital.

I had snapped. Societal judgment, including that of my own, had to be confronted later. It felt embarrassing not to be allowed to move around or go to lunch by myself. No visitors in six weeks, not even my children except Nancy, my stepdaughter, and a pastor who came once.

All activities I could possibly sign up for, I began. Blanca, my Mexican psychiatrist, introduced goal setting and various affirmations. She navigated my sexual perspectives now being single again. Soon I would discover a new freedom. Blanca suggested certain food combinations, natural sleep medicine, physical exercise and therapies. These included creative therapies as well.

They took my Bible away. It held two recent letters from Toby. "We'll give it to you with approval of the doctor," the technician said. The Bible signified a mystery of spirit, my longing for Toby. Later, in my sixties, a monk asked me, "Why don't you like it here? Why doesn't your spirit enter this earth completely? There is so much beauty here, many good people." The truth of that question unsettled me deeply.

At thirty-four I had not found a way to trust, to trust the universe, to trust the people around me, or to trust myself. And dammit, I had not found it in the Bible either. I tried off and on, no, it was not my destiny, my calling. In fact, religion at times made me a bit crazy and I had to withdraw from it all. I'd feel as if I had overdosed on something that did not ring true. Or maybe it reminded me of my zealous dad during my youth. And that alone would throw me into rejection of it all. The "Who am I" and the "I am" were rivers, roads, maybe stars apart.

Yet in that hospital, seeing the loving person Blanca was, a role model of caring, I embraced her compassion. As her patient, she entered my consciousness at some point. I noticed that she gently touched my arm while trying to make a point. And that touch got me to give double attention. Blanca's voice sounded gentle, her face non-judgmental. Nobody had touched my arms before, not my father or mother, brother or sister, ever. Yet my Toby had. Touch had been something foreign in my family. I experienced and received Blanca: "I care about you and want to help you to get well." In her wisdom she prepared me for life in the present, the rebuilding and strengthening of my inner core to move forward with life and the children. How lucky I was to be there with her and internalize her caring heart for years to come.

"Make a list of those who love you, put me on it," Blanca said.

I did make a list, but my heart couldn't feel it.

"Why would she care for me?" I wondered. "It's just something she says to make me feel good." But I complied since I'd have to show her the list the following day.

One day yellow flowers arrived with a card from Sr. Margaret. "I love you". And, for the first time I felt it. I felt some joy, a sparkle of love. Something had shifted inside of me.

Still, I remained suicidal. I knew how I could do it, even there. It gave me a sense of control to know that I could do it, to know how I could do it, and with all their searching and taking away of my possessions in the hospital, I'd still find a way. Except, there was also a piece of me that wanted to get well, a part of me wanted to reunite with the children. I missed them terribly. "Six weeks…I want to see them."

"I'm having suicidal thoughts again," one of the patients mentioned.

"Geez, I have had those for decades wanting to drive my car into a wall or off a ramp when I was young," I reflected. Not that I would do it; no, I wouldn't. I just had those damned thoughts.

During one of my daily consultations, Blanca took off my wedding ring. This symbolic gesture evoked inner anger. "She doesn't have a right to do this—I'll put it back on later. Taking off that ring doesn't mean anything; it's my marriage, Toby's and mine that has meaning." Yet, a glimpse of reality had entered my confusion.

"You need to raise your gut level, you are single now," Blanca declared repeatedly. And thinking of my children, wanting to get well and be with them, I applied what she said over and over again. Every time I feared something, I would confront the fear with what she had said. Not at once, I did it after I realized I had acted out of fear. Then I would readdress it, walking straight through the fear. Thus, I became a witness of my emotion of fear. With the psychiatrist's assurance I did raise my gut level inch by inch. I began to trust Blanca. "Her deep care, love and belief in my sanity is real," I reflected.

"Blanca, look at that patient; will he ever be well again?" I'd ask pointing to a person who had lost all sense of connection with others hospitalized." And very lovingly, without any doubt, Blanca assured me that she could help him, and again my trust expanded. A sense of recognition of my doctor's love, her faith in me, and my strength, entered my heart. It gave me the vigor to raise that gut level.

Hospitalized for depression and medicated with a temporary quick fix, my insistence to control decreased. My turning point arrived when I surrendered.

"People don't get well the first time," other patients told me. "It's a revolving door here. Some come here many times."

"Not me," I assured myself. "I hit bottom the first time."

THE COLLAPSED SCREAM

A Dutch canal runs from Overschie, a part of Rotterdam, to the city of Delft. In the old days along that canal a narrow path had formed. Horses towed boats forward with ropes attached to their harness. A slow and enduring process. The boats delivered their goods from one town to the other.

Many of us carry a load with us from the past. It reduces our daily energy. It jumbles the cells in our body, our immunity, our thinking process therefore our relationships and our health.

T HERE ARE THREE OF US in the Texas Spring Branch Hospital's intensive care: my husband's spirit, his body and me. The intensive care ward is formed of tiny, quiet white rooms separated by curtains. For days now I sleep on a loveseat in a visitor's room off the hallway, from which I see through a window the ICU entrance ten feet away. I hardly eat any more. No appetite. At night an occasional pine tree roach, those black and long ones, rushes through the hallway. Time passes slowly. Mexican custodians clean the hallway. Visitor's hours are restricted. Toby and I are separated by their rules. The light above the large door at the ICU entrance turns green. I walk in and see my large Toby laying on his back with an oxygen mask over his face.

The smell of Lysol mingled with medications becomes a part of me with each inhalation. Fear plunges me into obscurity. I feel numb. Toby's lips are blue, his nose is blue, and his feet are purple and cold. Double blankets don't help anymore. Standing next to his bed my legs and arms weaken, and my breath slows down with his. Silent we stay present to each other; no words can capture this. I keep a little distance and touch the rail of his bed. Both of us imprisoned in a bubble of transition. I have no inkling that what happens here is the rupturing of our Oneness. And I do not fathom that his dying will throw me into a deepening of who I am, that the gift of his life will propel me. Unmoored, the two of us become lifted into the unknown.

He leaves me in his country, the United States, once my dreamland. Together with Christa and Patrick, our children, we live in a house on a road named Friendship in Spring Branch, a suburb of Houston. We arrived here a year ago from his last engineering assignment, a petroleum project in the heart of the Amazon on the Orinoco river of Venezuela.

I had a strange dream there about the sun shaking in the universe. The dream unsettled me to the core.

We couldn't do it, that destruction of jungle in the Amazon. Instead, we returned to the US with the intent to bring a different focus on our life and work.

This gentle man is the one who recognizes the core of my being and the longings I have. With him I am a child and a young adult. I adore this six-foot-tall dark tinted Texan with brown hair and green eyes. This good man with high integrity. One who sings for me "Deep in the Heart of Texas," who always puts his arm around me. Lifts me up as his Goddess. At the beginning of our romance the song "Top of the World" by The Carpenters captured us. It resembled the constant flow of peace in our life. Neither one of us sees the foreboding in these words or connects them with the dream I had before leaving Venezuela.

"The only thing you need to be jealous of in our life together is my work and books."

His worldwide engineering projects are huge in structure. They tire him out and books become a remedy to fall asleep. We differ by twenty-five years.

"You love people also for their faults." he tells me. I trust him, never imagine him kicking the bucket—as he said and dying this young.

Christa is seven now, almost eight and Patrick is six years old. A few days ago, I brought them into the hospital. They had not seen their father for days. It scared them to see all the gadgets in ICU, more so their mute father. Patrick cried and was afraid. Christa observed him in silence.

"Did I do right?" I wonder while driving them home.

No time to think, I leave them with Sister Mary, a Benedictine nun and friend from Guatemala, who had come to help us. I shower, wash my hair, things I cannot do at the Spring Branch Hospital. I rush back.

Upon arrival at Toby's side, the numbers on the monitor next to his bed fall. Then, for a while, they rise. I catch my breath and wait for the numbers to reach a safe level. I touch his arm through the sheet and repeat, "The Lord is my Shepherd" from Psalm 23.

"I'm going to make it darling. I can handle this. I can handle our children. It's going to be all right." Not familiar with the Bible, the psalm was recommended to me by someone from St. Jerome Church. These words of surrender and my words of letting him go releases him.

The red resuscitation equipment on a table stands about three feet from the end of his bed. Images how that might work panic me each time I pass it. Will they have to do that on my Toby?

Another device next to him beeps. Oh no, I hold my breath, the numbers plummet. His heart rate, it's falling. I look from the monitor to Toby, to the monitor again and yet again to Toby. I hold my breath. His eyes roll back, he gasps and then he breathes out for a long time while I wait for the in-breath to come. It doesn't come.

I think he's dead.

But then as if from a crater deep in his body … he pants for breath with a groan. This colossal moan encompasses his spirit, my Toby's spirit, his essence. A tear rolls down his cheek, just for me and us, his final gesture of goodbye and his unfathomable love. And I … I can't even receive his outpouring, this unpronounceable tenderness between us. I can't capture his, "Darling, I love you," with this tear. I am in the claws of terror, this unfolding terror.

"Go and build a house for us. A gorgeous house and come and get me when it's ready," words spoken to him from my mouth a few minutes ago. "Sing then our song, our favorite song: Hey good-looking …, and I will come." And then, and then and then… I knew he was dead forever. Nurses run to the heart shocker in front of his bed. As if that will bring him back now. I turn away, don't look or listen. Instead, I tell myself, no, he has gone to a better place with music and people, his family. I saw and heard them. No, forget about that shocker, his life here is over.

I walk away and smell tobacco: "G*d forgive you nurses smoking only a few feet away, right there in Intensive Care. But then I think, "Hey, you might have liked it darling, you smoked all your life lighting one with the other."

Toob, I should have taken you home, to be with us, to die with us, Christa and Patrick. This sterile place without a window disconnects us from who we are. It doesn't connect with our life in jungles, our love for plants, fresh air, the river and sea, the thunder beings that excite you. But we are in a jam; your older children, our little ones at home, the divorce, all the tension in the hospital and I, your wife, are drenched in fear instead of courage to take the lead.

Now at his passing, after his final breath, while standing next to him and the bed, when I knew he was gone for good, something strange and beautiful happened. It pushed aside my fear and rendered a reassurance for the rest of my life. After Toby's third final breath, with a loving tear for me and the children I saw in my mind's eyes a group of people welcoming him. They celebrated to a depth I cannot explain. No, I could not have made that up! Family and friends happily welcomed Toby when he died there. Welcomed him on the other side. This celebration of Toby's arrival there in the new world flashed by and disappeared in the depth of my being. Then there is nothing but emptiness.

I needed to scream, scream hard, loud, to scream the whole hospital together because I knew Toby was gone. But instead, I walked out and calmly told his older children that he had passed. With no words, nor feelings, Father Tom, Toby's friend, and my sister-in-law Irma look at me and understand he died. Each put their arm in mine on either side. Step by step the three of us moved as one body out of the hospital, eventually closing the gap between us and our parked car. We drove homeward. I shoved my death scream so deeply inside it was beyond retrieval. For that I would pay dearly.

—ᴡ—

Why do humans no longer scream? What is so admirable and honorable about staying calm when horrific things like death happen around us? We all admire Edvard Munch's painting, "The

Scream," but we repress our own primal emotions. All of us should have that painting somewhere in our home, to remind us that it is okay to scream our pain. But I didn't know that then as my own death scream festered. Without anchor I floated through days of funeral preparations.

"Toby once told me he wanted to be cremated, to come back as a Mayan Indian in Guatemala," I told Irma his sister.

"Oh no, we need a funeral with flowers," she said. I complied.

Choosing of the casket seemed funny to me as I entered a room full of different woods, colors and prices. "Death a business?" We buried Toby in a small Baptist cemetery in the woods of Bold Springs near Livingston, Texas.

Days pass

I miss Toby,

Must keep calm at the funeral

I could reunite us all.

Where was he?

I want to be there.

These are just thoughts.

But I could make it right.

Make us whole.

Together once more?

I need help.

I could not live with the reality of being without Toby. My thoughts became preoccupied with strategies to reunite our family. I lived in Houston and Toby had left us for the beyond—wherever that was. I wanted to be there, make it right again, make us whole again, be a family once more. Dangerously, my thoughts plummeted, exploring ways to kill myself and our two children just so we could be together. My emotions had gained control over my thoughts and destiny. I don't believe I would have ever done it, but the compulsive thinking and the awareness that I had floated the ideas prompted me to see the family doctor. "G*d forbid I'd do this. My emotions jump all over the place. One moment I'm singing, the other minute I fall in despair. What will I do, stay here in Texas or move to Holland like Toby had told me to do? My thoughts are racing, childlike uncontrolled.

Since the age of two I had learned to shut out my feelings and emotions. I had learned to see what triggers and could provoke another epilepsy attack for my brother Henk: Don't laugh too loud, don't cry too hard, stay calm, keep everyone happy. Oh, Dad is angry, tiptoe. Focus on Ma—what can I do? Keep the house clean like Ma wants. Everyone needs to be happy. Never disagree. With this loss of my Toby I am far from stable—I cannot control any of it. He had surrendered and I had not. Psalm 23 worked for him but not for me. Disciplining of my thoughts had not come into fruition yet. I didn't trust myself and allowed old traumatic behavior to take over. I'd freeze, dissociate, go out of my body.

Throughout our marriage, I blamed myself for Toby's divorce. "You are responsible. You should have waited till their divorce was final," My conscience berated me repeatedly despite Toby assuring me that this was not so. Divorces are terrible messes. And the culmination of it all, beyond my comprehension at the time, broke his heart. "Guilty beyond reasonable doubt. It's your fault." I sentenced myself. Never mind the aneurism of his aorta, his years of smoking, no exercise, coffee all day long, a year of being out of work because of the energy crisis and a re-entry with the family of his first marriage. The church too added a shadow over our Love. A love that stands infinitely. That's how love works. A love not to be dimmed, which stands and grows stronger with each generation it touched.

I would discover the mystery of the human heart in future years. Statistics informed Dr. Benjamin Siegel about emotions and disease. Major stress and upheaval be it work, family or living environment, of around eighteen months before the onset of a disease seems to be a link.

We found ourselves in Indonesia at that time. Toby, worked for a US company, directing the completion of a major plant there. He had stopped the payment of a considerable bribe involving the government and companies. He refused to sign the contract. Therefore, almost at completion of his work there, he was fired. His company appointed another person willing to sign the contract and the building continued. So, it goes.

Western medicine and research are challenged to consider alternative approaches to healing that existed thousands of years. I celebrate these collaborations and wanderings into the body, mind and spirit. Especially when experts discern old trauma. Learning to deal with our emotions on a personal, collective, and governmental level is a never-ending responsibility. "Take Heart." Where does this leave me? I began to dig, dig deep into my life thus far.

My inability to say no in life had cost me. Like fear, some men can smell one's lack of inner strength a hundred miles away. Did this vulnerability seize a part of my soul? If I had known who I was, I would have said NO! No to the rapist, to the anti-German teacher, no to the Anti-German Dutch, and most importantly, no to myself. I didn't know where I began or where I left off. I noticed everyone else's feelings first. Only sometimes did I feel my own. Otherwise, I buried any emotion, especially since after Toby died. However, the yearning for freedom began when I was nine years old.

During an outing with our class in elementary school and attending a ceremony to remember all who had died during the war I felt confused and wanted to cry, cry hard, but did not. Children around me did not express these emotions. It left me with a sense of not belonging, being different. Who was I among them, Dutch or German what was I supposed to feel? This awareness and confusion induced by the place where I lived and grew up, built up over years. A feeling of wanting out—wanting freedom began to emerge. These feelings of wanting out were the same when I called on the family doctor after Toby died and were often repeated in my life.

"We all have crazy thoughts sometimes. Thoughts are just that." My family doctor said.

"But let's gear on the safe side. Why don't you rest for a few days? In the hospital is a special department. Get some help there." That afternoon, I found myself in a bed on the third floor of the same hospital my husband had died in a few weeks earlier.

"You need to be hospitalized in a psychiatric clinic for a while, it will help you but being Dutch you'll probably be too stubborn," this shrink told me there.

"Damned right I'm too stubborn. What does he know about the Dutch anyway?" So, I returned home, but it wasn't long before I was replaying ways to kill myself along with the entire family. In desperation I called Sister Margaret at the Cenacle.

"I need help," I said. "Please come to the house."

Details were quickly arranged. Christa and Patrick ended up with Donna, Toby's oldest daughter. Angered, I signed the paperwork which would admit me to a psychiatric hospital in Houston. Dang it.

Dismissed from the hospital six weeks later and ready to move on with life, time had come to leave the US. Welcomed by my Dutch family, the kids and I found a house in Holland. My focus of getting well again, together with the move to Holland took all my energy. At the time I had no idea what my hospitalization right after Toby died could have meant to our two children. This would take years and be engraved in their psyche. We began a new life. The Dutch Airlines had some fun hospitality work. At times I picked up groups of businesspeople at the Schiphol Airport and toured them around Amsterdam on behalf of the Dutch Airlines. I joined group training with an American Jungian Analyst living in Scheveningen, Holland. In Antwerp, Belgium, an hour's drive from where we lived in Holland, I began theological studies. These courses shed light on the dogmatic ideologies of both my father and the church. They explored a Oneness of love and a new world of faith. The experience of trust, trust in my true self, had to wait many years.

"Theology and psychology, you can't make it on that," my dad repeatedly argued. And soon I began to long for Texas, for the place where Toby had grown up, where his older kids lived and where the cemetery was located. A Belgian priest who also taught at the university generously offered time and dialogue. We discussed during visits once a month over two years what would be the best for the children and where I was called to be: Holland or the US. However, while in Holland something unexpected happened. I met Ramon on a flight to and from Texas to keep my US residence. Ramon was my opposite. Unlike me, he could say no and didn't do anything he didn't want to do.

"I'm from Mexico City and visit my daughter in Belgium," he said. We exchanged phone numbers.

Occupied with the children, I had forgotten about him when one day a woman called from Belgium. "Hi, I'm Adriana, my father Ramon, is here and would like for us to meet in Antwerp, visit the Reubens' museum and go out for dinner," she said in Dutch. Nervous to no end, I accepted the first invite by a man after Toby's death. Ramon and I soon began dating.

"You better know what you are doing," my father warned when I brought the children to his house so I could spend time with Ramon alone. Know what you are doing—doing what? I argued in my mind.

Ramon had the ability to be present to my story, Toby's death and my subsequent hospitalization. He listened empathetically and cried with me. My family had avoided any talk about that since I returned to Holland. They feared it would trigger me to go nuts again. How could I shed this unaccepted societal stigma of psychiatric hospitalization?

Meeting with Ramon increased my sense of joy. We laughed and our intimacy and relations with the children flowed. It flowed fast.

"Let's go with the children to Maastricht," Ramon called. You can all stay with my daughter across the border in Belgium. We can go to the circus." I fell deeper in love with his pointing to the stars, observing how he played with the dog, and his intrigue with movies on account of him being an actor.

 Ramon eventually returned from Belgium to Mexico. "We can all live in the big house here," he called. I couldn't decide to marry Ramon. It would mean that I had to uproot the children from Holland to Mexico. Despite that, I moved forward with a trip to Mexico to see where he lived.

On my way to meet Ramon in Houston instead of Mexico, as I requested, I began losing ground. I loved him yet couldn't do it. He wasn't as peaceful as Toby. He gambled yet loved me. I loved his artistic side, his emotional presence, his laughter, our fun. We were attracted to each other. He was good looking, and had humor; he was generous, playful with the children. I had seen him with his daughter … he loved his daughter the way I think a father would. He embraced her, played tennis with her, cooked with her. Something in his eyes reminded me of my grandfather.

But he was divorced. Divorces were complicated, I knew that much. I had seen his aura with my mind's eye. It had a piece missing. Maybe he still loved the woman he broke up with, I explained to myself.

—⟋⟋⟍—

The decision to marry, to live in Mexico City, to move into the house of Ramon's former family, uprooting the children again and placing them in yet another country and culture became too much for my brain to process. Our love had not yet established a peaceful anchor and compared to my marriage with Toby I did not feel an inner peace. Ramon is there for me, emotionally present, loving, yet so different from Toby. How will the relationship unfold with the children? I felt protective of them. My mind became a battleship. Not able to think clearly, I began losing ground and the second round of my hospitalization had been triggered. Ramon flew in from Mexico City, settled into a hotel, visited museums, and came to see me each day. Christa and Patrick stayed with Toby's cousins.

"Inge, mi Amor, I brought you a Picasso." He chose one of those with the cubic faces.

The Picasso, a woman's face, printed on a silk shawl, seemed strange. I didn't know if I should be insulted or what. That Picasso expressed my head, my snapped mind. I decided I liked it.

"You are beautiful," Ramon said with a smile. He held my face between his warm hands and then went down and squeezed my arms up and down. Felt my muscles. It made me feel the ground. Ramon, the Mexican doctor, and I, met several times. Sometimes we spoke English and then again Spanish. Blanca, the doctor, assured me how deeply Ramon cared and how much he had to overcome culturally with me in a psychiatric hospital. But it was all too much for me, Ramon, the children, the healing, the grief overwhelmed me, and I didn't get clear in my head. Instead, I had episodes of lightheadedness. This scared me. I worried about that spot, the area of the third eye, an energy center, where I literally had felt a snap and a twist in the psyche when I captured that scream deep inside of me when my Toby had died.

"Ramon, you better return to Mexico, my forehead is all light-headed again. I have to concentrate on getting well and return to the children." He put the palm of his hand on my forehead, pressed it and held it there for a long time.

I loved feeling his warm hands there, on that spot where my mind had cracked.

"Why don't you ask permission to get Christa and Patrick? They haven't seen you for two weeks now. I'll keep them overnight with me in the hotel, so we can all go to church.

And that's what happened. After signing some paperwork, the hospital allowed me to leave for a few hours that night and again the next morning.

"Honey," I said while tucking Christa in the bed next to Ramon's in the hotel. "We will all go to Mass tomorrow. Ramon will come to the hospital with you and Patrick and get Mommy."

The fear in Christa's eyes at nine years old is something that stands for the rest of my life. Patrick, I think was doing better. I may be wrong about that. My children were void of guidance and love for them at a critical grieving period. I couldn't be available to them. They lacked this during the first round of the hospitalization and now the second.

The next morning Ramon picked me up with the children. It was too late for church, but we went out for dinner. Ramon, nervous that it would get too much for me with the kids there, snapped at Christa. She'd never forget.

Again, I insisted he go back to Mexico so I could focus on my healing and be with my children again. He agreed. At that point, our relationship shifted. The children came first. Ramon's love became one of non-marital commitment. After he dropped me off at the hospital doctors began a different approach.

"Something in the chemistry of your brain is missing: You need salt called Lithium." So, they put me on that, and for the first time I had one thought at a time in my head. A quiet of mind came over me, but my hands didn't feel right. With the medication, writing became hard, and my mouth was dry. "I'm not going to keep taking this," I told myself.

My calm did not remain and after Ramon left, faced with the empty future as if being in freefall, I panicked. Fear conquered big time. And because of my erratic behavior I found myself on the bed in my hospital room surrounded with nurses, Blanca, and doctors they had called in.

"If you don't get it together, we will have to put you in Intensive," they threatened me. I had enough! I didn't know where to go or what to do. I just gave up. *I surrendered.*

"Do with me what you want G*d," I angrily thought. I was furious with this darned situation. I didn't even fear the Intensive and that straitjacket that would be used to keep me from hurting myself. I surrendered to it all. I didn't give a damn.

This deliverance would carve a compass for the rest of my life. It kept me from going into the Intensive care part of the hospital.

In only three weeks of my second hospitalization I gained clarity. I convinced Blanca I could face my life and fly back home to Holland.

"I know a couple in Holland. They are natural healers. They can give you Vitamin B shots at regular times," Blanca said. Encouraged, I returned to Holland and visited them.

"What? She put you on Lithium, that poison?" they exclaimed. "That is so unlike her. You need to wean yourself off it and take the vitamin shots instead."

The two of them stood next to me. Loudly they asked me: "Who are you? Who are you? Who are you?"

My thoughts were: "G*d, they are nuts. Who has this Blanca sent me to? I can get these Vitamin shots elsewhere."

But their question "Who are you?" lingered in my mind. I still didn't know who the hell I was and that made me mad. They made me furious with that question. I had not a clue.

—◊—

Restlessness took over. Life in Holland was not what I was used to anymore. My life had been all over the world, in jungles, in deserts with different peoples, climates and cultures.

"There is an institute in Antwerp, the Pastoral Institute of Theology. A group of us are going and you might be interested to join us," my pastor said. Together with two others, each week. We trekked to Antwerp, and I learned new thoughts that were way beyond me. Process theology—realizing all in the universe is connected and in constant change. It got a hold of me. "It's all right not to understand they encouraged me. Keep at it." Slowly my infantile conceptions on religion began to change. My spiritual belief shifted from childlike notions to adult perspectives that had a healthy dose of my own views. I noticed some people valued my opinions, which included spiritual and cultural integrations through my life abroad.

One professor talked about love and the turning point each person has of knowing love for the first time, often in their mid-thirties. It got me excited, I felt joy. After Toby's death I began to realize the depth of love I had received from him that I couldn't fathom during the marriage.

These repeated insights came with days of depressions. I often wondered if I'd fall back again, back into a psychiatric hospital. During my visits to Brussels to discern if we should stay or move back to the US, I'd walk in the busy streets there. People hurried. They seemed disconnected. "And they think I'm mad? I'm the sane one." And while I had become familiar with the notion that you better watch out when you think people around you are crazy— you might be the one, I distanced myself from that stance. "This is a crazy world. I have to figure out who I want to be and where I want to go and what gives me meaning on this bizarre planet."

It's testing to be depressed, to deal with it. It's a challenge to doubt your own sanity and to live with the fact that you have been hospitalized in a psychiatric ward. It's also tough for people around you to accept, let alone understand. It's an avoided issue in society. Who wants to hang out with me, my grief, my fears, and distrust of life? People fear these shadows. It could mean they had to face their own.

"I'm not happy here," I thought. It's time to go back to where I belong to Texas. It will be a better life there. Better job opportunity, Toby's family, his older children and my sister-in-law … I can go back to school.

It became time to reconnect with Blanca. Unknown to me she'd become a beacon of love at crossroads in my life. I wrote: "I'd like to go back to the US. Do you have some suggestions?"

"Come back and settle in Clear Lake. There is a university there where you can study, and I have a job for you. I'm starting a new hospital." Her words gave me strength because she expressed belief in my sanity and capability. I approached Dad with the news that once again I'd leave for the US. Within three weeks the two children and I settled in a nice house in Clear Lake. The job with Blanca fell through, and I applied at the university and began my career and continued my studies. To compliment my regained sanity I planned visits to a retreat center.

On a monthly basis, together with Sr. Margaret, the Cenacle sister, I faced my psychological wounds, and found space and quiet to search for the forgotten parts of who I was. That helped me re-image a new way of being. Memories, images had to be kindled and come to the surface to grow. After my psyche had scattered, splashed to pieces by fear, and uncontrolled emotion, my ego had enough strength to gather myself up.

Many depressions came, however without hospitalization. With each low I pushed the norms of my existence, my belief system a bit further. All the while, Sr. Margaret listened and cared without judgment. She stood next to me, went down with me into the depths of my being. I could trust one more person again. Trust her with my story, my fears, my longing and my shame. Bit by bit we expanded my sense of joy.

During one of these visits, I received a very special gift from her. "Here, this is the only thing I took with me at the time I entered the Cenacle as an apostolate. I received it from my mom. I want you to have it." The brooch consisted of a small black onyx cross with two golden threads where Jesus would have been … Still, while I treasured her gift, I only recognized the suffering on that cross, not the joy of the love that had been conquered through it, the love that

Toby had conquered for me. This would take time. I'd wear that cross when going to Mass, not sure of what to expect from those golden threads at the intersection of the beams of the cross, there where Jesus' head once hung low.

Our lifelong friendship deepened as did the awareness of her unconditional love for me. She believed in me on a personal and professional level. It deepened my faith. Her wisdom grounded me repeatedly. The stability built through our friendship, the deep knowing I could count on her, made me long for a component that created this stability for myself. Not only that, but I longed to be able to pass it on to others. Later I began training to become a spiritual director, a companion to others.

Society had created an environment that weakened bodies and exhausted psyches. Technology filled our minds and immobilized our bodies. It made everything easy. I comprehended this. A new way of living had to be invented with different norms and pillars. The new and balanced life had to be my own road, no matter what other people thought or judged. It had to be authentic. However, I did not realize this road would be a never-ending repetition of ups and downs encompassing a longing for freedom, authenticity and meaning.

"You need to look at balance, lest you'll fall back into hospitalization," I told myself.

"You don't have that choice anymore. You now have a wall to lean on," another Cenacle sister asserted. I needed serenity between the mind and the heart. Growing into a ruthless honesty to myself and others, I began the process of a conscious lifestyle. I'd concentrate on the body as well. The integration of movement and good nourishment would take a long time.

I focused on getting a job and expanding my creative side, aware that excessive ego and shaming myself tempted me to enter the control mode. And the end station of control is suicide, I learned that much. I integrated calligraphy, sculpting and writing. The arts changed something inside of me. It kept me in touch with my feelings and subconscious. It brought me into the moment, away from the grief of Toby's loss. Work kept me grounded and part of society.

Without creativity I found it hard to be in the present. Our modern Western world exhausted my mind. Through meditation or time in nature I gained freedom and peace. I yearned for a natural flow of energy—less control. The notion that the whole world is connected, that humanity is the same all over began to grow. I understood the gift of Toby's marriage. Not only did we have two beautiful children, but all of us had also expanded our horizons while living across the world surrounded by different cultures, values, art, and languages.

The universe sent me people to deepen this path of Oneness. Among them Indigenous medicine people of various nations, therapists, and, most of all, Sr. Margaret, who, as a beacon, loved and trusted me to come to my destiny and to live through its Providence.

"I had this strange experience with a Native American," I explained to the spiritual director at the Cenacle. "Ah, you met a Shaman," she said listening to my story. "I'd love to learn from his spirituality."

She encouraged me. This trust and space to share my thoughts, dreams and challenges primed me for the meaning of life, for giving back. Conquering my wound of not feeling loved had to become a cornerstone. I had to return the spiritual direction I received to guide me throughout the years. It had to be returned for the sake of furthering love, unconditional love. This freedom, that comes with love rooted in the heart, not in dogma, became my goal. The experience of living in many countries of the world gave me insights in the Oneness of humanity and creation. It demanded the need to give back that gift, pass it on.

What then has my spirituality to do with my hospitalization for depression, my breakthrough?

Through receiving regular spiritual direction, I began to reflect on how honest I was with myself. I conceptualized the crossroads in my life and the consequence of my choices. I questioned the reason for marrying an older man. Love is love, age and gender do not matter I concluded. This honesty traveled from the mind to the heart. It became insight after insight. Yes, at the Cenacle, in that space of unconditional love, I began to discover who I was and where I wanted to go.

Sometimes I worried about going to the Cenacle for a retreat or spiritual direction. Scared I'd end up confused, that it would unlock something in my mind. Their rooms at the time were dark. And darkness reminded me of the darkness of the attic where I slept as a child in Holland. It weakened my psyche. Slowly I learned about what was good for me and what was not. Clarity of what I wanted around me and courageously taking charge unfolded. A current of writing began to flow. One letter after the other went to my spiritual director. These described my feelings, my fears, and new edges of Shamanism I explored. In time my longing for the Native American's spirituality required me to take a stand, to let go of more child-like beliefs and dogmas from the past. I began taking risks, one after the other.

My despair lessened; my worthiness expanded with my growing new identity. Each small depression assisted me in that growth, took me to a new edge. It took courage to say "yes" to whatever came up in the natural river of life. I needed patience and more of Blanca's raising of the gut level to allow life to fall in place without manipulating the outcome. I walked a road through darkness, recaptured light, and discernment. It challenged my spiritual side, to enter pain and receive joy as it came. In gratitude I sang:

Thank You Lord

Thank You Lord

Cutting the chains of fear

Entering the heart

Cutting the chains of fear

See the Christ

Be a child

Cutting the chains of fear

Entering the heart.

And just for the hell of it, I changed the words around at times: "Be the Christ, see the Child—cutting the chains of fear. Made sense!

Repeatedly I had to cut those chains of fear, one by one. It meant I had to take time for friends, get to know them better. I had to become vulnerable with those I trusted and share pain and joy. I also detected control issues in myself and others. I had to re-surrender to the unknown and trust a Great Mystery to love me through it. It took voicing my opinion. Through dance, I felt and recognized the child in myself and others. Art pieces like that of Joseph Jankovich with various body parts hovering on canvas enlightened me. Buried parts of my own body needed to become one in my body, mind, and spirit. The work of realignment had begun.

As a next step I chose calligraphy and music to stop the thinking. Connecting with others in kindness got me out of my brain into my heart. The more creative I became the easier life unfolded. I opened the path to conscious receiving, trusted and added some of the humor I inherited from my dad.

In the process I found solitude is my sanctuary: a place where intuition fears no boundaries. Freedom is my medal of honor earned in that dark valley of pain and depression. They are gatekeepers of my heart's surrender and grounding of body and spirit.

TWO

WHO AM I?

PUTTING MYSELF TOGETHER AGAIN

T O FIND OUT WHO I was and my life's purpose after Toby died required a journey back in time to Rotterdam, my port of entry.

A Taste of the Harbor City Rotterdam

"Ladies and gentlemen, the train from Dordrecht to Rotterdam is delayed and will arrive at 5 p.m. on track 4." Waiting on the platform for Trudie's arrival this announcement aggravated me. Verdomme, when the government controlled the rails, we could count on trains rolling in like clockwork. They thundered into the station trailing airstreams that were cold as ice. "Koffie en Chocolade," someone yells further down from me. I thank G*d for the snack cart delivering hot food and drink to the waiting people and to the people on trains rolling in.

Trudie and I had planned to meet at our old stomping grounds Chalet Suisse. Instead of awaiting her train I now head for the harbor.

I extract my black Oma bike with a high steering bar from hundreds of bicycles packed like sardines outside of Rotterdam Central Station. Jumping on the bike, I avoid the dozens of departing trams. My eyes focus on the rails thinking my tires could get stuck in them. I pedal alongside the traffic lining the narrow street that leads to the harbor.

Modern buildings monopolize the horizon. I am glad to leave them behind as I enter the historic part of my city.

Raindrops flatten my fine, blonde hair. At the harbor, I lock my bike against a lamp post and inhale the musky scent of the harbor. The black cobblestones are slippery, and my attention is drawn to the docked riverboats and the steamers tugged by pilots.

Toooooooot! Startled, I spin around.

"Hey Blondie! Where are you going?" I see a man in dark blue overalls and plastic boots, his child standing next to him on top of the riverboat. I smile, thinking he got a kick out of scaring me with that noise. I could have slipped and fallen between the ship and the pier. Better keep walking.

Chalet Suisse is a few meters away. I increase my pace and open the wooden door. The smell of alcohol and smoke assaults my senses. Sitting at the bar I imagine the rot of grease, garbage, brackish water, huge cranes and boats from around the world mingled with male sweat of labor: My harbor. I'm standing on ancient soil. Remember? Dad used to work here. I did too. Right there, each Tuesday, I'd watch the Holland America Line depart for New York.

"One sherry please." I ask.

Old stinking Rotterdam! In the hospital they cut my umbilical cord severing me from my German mother. But today this place feels vibrant, alive with lots of large boats pushing toward a wayward Northern Sea. For a moment there is no hate in my Rotterdam, no hate for my mother, hate for myself as a child of a Mof. There is no German enemy in this moment.

Trudie and I decide not to stay at the Chalet. It is not who we are. We do not feel in place at this elegant Swiss bar. We stroll back to our bicycles and notice a docked boat with Indonesian Wayang Kulit designs. Is it true? Indonesian food in the Rotterdam harbor? Ah! Selamat Makan. Harbors taste good. I am a child again.

BIRTH OF A CROSS CULTURAL CHILD
1949

I HAVE LIVED MY LIFE in reverse. I was born an adult who became a child. My death will surely be a resurrection.

Rotterdam was my place of birth. We are Dutch people and speak Dutch not Deutsch. Deutsch is a language that belongs to our then—and for some maybe still—less favorable neighbors to the East, those German folks.

A September Virgo, I was destined to be a harvest child, to connect to the earth. My horoscope says so. I feel it in my bones. I carry that yearning in my heart—to go into the earth, embrace it and live from its core, my core.

Leaves with red, yellow, and brown cover the ground. Patches of varied shades of blue appear to have been lifted from the palette of Vincent van Gogh and dominate the grim skies. Relentless rains sharpen the outlines of tall brown tree trunks that line the streets. Chestnut leaves adhere to the soggy dark soil and migrate to the thick soles of my shoes. In the coming winter months in the absence of the sun, Holland will morph into dark shades one finds in Rembrandt's Night Watch.

We lived in the center of Rotterdam far below sea level in houses built on huge wooden pillars hammered deep into the wet ground.

A dike and lock system keep the sea, the river Maas, and other rivers in their place. If it weren't for the dikes, dams, seawalls, locks, and windmills pumping out the water half of my country would be little more than a salty fishing pond. Centuries of money focused trade had browned that filthy Maas. What would it look like with a nature focused approach?

All along the west side, Holland is entirely wet too, bordered by that wild rough grubby water of a tricky North Sea.

Inside our apartment of two bedrooms and an attic, the family gathers around the square dining table draped with a Dutch carpet to sip coffee and share German Kuchen.

"In the name of the Father and Son …" I make the sign of the cross taking in my dad's big bony hands and his observant blue eyes. I close mine. "Our Father who is in heaven …" Dad starts. We, the rest of the family are supposed to chime in but he speaks fast.

Dressed in a dark suit and tie, his presence dominates our family ritual. Eat with your mouth closed, eat all that's on your plate—don't you know about the poor? His directives leave no room for misinterpretation or, G*d forbid, feedback by any of us.

I bite my nails. "Stop that," he says.

I put my thumb in my mouth.

"Oh, you don't like this? Here are some more Brussels sprouts…" Ma dumps another helping on my plate. Smiling, she gives a large piece of meat to my dad and a smaller one to me and herself.

"*Salz, Pfeffer*," salt, pepper, Pa imitates Ma's German *Pfeffer*.

"With you Germans everything is a command," he says.

Giving orders contradicted the five-foot brown haired and sensitive woman's physical stature. She who prepared a delicious meal from near to nothing and who kept an impeccable house where Dad's house shoes awaited him after his long walk home from work.

"My baby," as he lovingly called her; others would refer to her as a German *Mof*.

Hör auf she'd respond to him and laugh. "Stop it, Marinus."

"The pork tasted good, Christa." Dad sat down in his chair, took his jacket off, filled his pipe, and read his Catholic newspaper. Ma and I clean the table and do the dishes. Coals glow in the black stove in the living room, the only room heated. It is winter, and darkness comes early.

In the summer, the Dutch like to go to the sea and although Ma was afraid of water, the family did go to Zandvoort a lot. My non-swimming parents sat up straight on their small towels in the sand.

"Inge don't go too far, *nicht weiter* than your knees," Ma yells.

"Yeah right, I know how to swim." I keep on running.

On the beach stands a large wooden sign with the words posted in bold red, "Gevaar," or DANGER depicting a swimmer in an undercurrent and what to do in such a case. Many adults and children drown here.

In an embarrassingly cheap bathing suit, showing my yet undeveloped breasts and nipples, I step into the fierce North Sea's waves, jumping over its brown spew. They lift me up and after setting me back down I step forward moving deeper, deeper, and deeper. "Over there is where I go."

My toes barely touch the ground as my body rises with each wave. I tilt my head back to keep my nose and mouth above the salty water.

"No fun without the crest," I mumble out loud.

I swim back toward the shore a little until I reach the noisy waves that rudely slap against my face. It hurts. And there he is, the surprise, a huge one, hidden right behind another, kind of sneaky not coming straight at me like the others, calculated and sly with unforgiving strength. I feel excitement and alarm. The wall of water roars, pounding my body with its sheer weight covering my face with a mass of foam. Its water mass forces me under.

The current is pulling my body, sweeping me sideways. I cannot see anything.

I fight back in a panic struggling to right my feet and legs on the ground, and then the red letters "*gevaar*" flash like a reader board in my brain.

"Don't struggle, don't fight against it," people often warn.

I let go, surrendering to the current's force. My feet graze the sea's floor and I try to stand up. I gasp for air and am sucked back helplessly propelled parallel to the shoreline.

Don't fight it, I tell myself.

Just when I am ready to give my last breath to the salt, current and water, the North Sea lets me go like a cat who has tired of playing with a mouse.

Jesus … it seemed like an eternity.

I try to stand but fallback gagging into the filthy water. Willing each muscle to move I crawl on hands and knees onto the beach. Still coughing and disoriented, I cry. Disoriented, with eyes on fire from the salt, I look around, but my parents are gone. How far has the water taken me? Are they looking for me?

I walk the shore into the opposite direction where the water first yanked me and spot my folks. They haven't even missed me.

"Ma, I am hungry," I say.

That "letting go" during that fight with the sea current would make its appearance again when I had to let go for the sake of my sanity at the age of thirty-four.

I had nothing to lean on, or a place I could hang my hat when things got tough, as happens in life for all of us. My sense of identity faded away, strained under the responsibility I carried within the family for my siblings and more, the parental neglect, the unspoken grief and anger of my parents and the prejudice of the people of Rotterdam. This eventually, at eighteen, began to fester into frequent thoughts of suicide.

Wartime demanded frugality and Ma hoarded sugar, flour, toilet paper and rice. She bought me shoes with white *spekzolen* (bacon soles.) that would never need repair.

With those shoes, blonde hair straight as carrot sticks and somewhat untamed, I could easily be mistaken for a boy. Meanwhile an unconscious inner strength began to awaken. I jumped barbed wires, avoided the cracks in the sidewalk, oblivious to my whereabouts. Instead, my thoughts absorbed the sounds and smells around me. My soles squeaked as they touched the ground. Buses and trams thundered next to my thoughts through the narrow city streets. I'm a dreamer, a child of a *Mof*.

My dad tells me repeatedly: "Inge, if everyone jumps off the bridge into the Maas River, it doesn't mean you have to. So what if all of your friends are allowed to stay late… I want you home early." His directives, I think, attempted to avoid a repeat of what happened in Germany with boys and girls from the age of ten. They became the Hitler *Jugend*, the brain-washed masses.

In this harbor city, we have a couple of parks which we call woods. The Kralinger Wood is one of them; weird guys hung out there. At thirteen years of age, I rode my bike through those woods on my way to school, and my fear drove me to pedal like hell.

I'm in the moment. Halfway through in the distance, I make out a tall figure standing to the right of the narrow and long red-paved bicycle path stretched out before me. I rest my feet low on the paddles and slow down. *Verdomme*, nobody is around, it's just him and me! I panic. He stands motionless in a grassy clearing just off the side of the bike path. I'm too afraid to turn around. I get closer and pedal even faster, my heart is pounding.

I am horrified.

I look up and he is looking in my direction. Faster, closer, faster, faster. What does he want? He looks down at himself, this tall guy dressed in a long beige raincoat.

He turns towards me, his trousers open and pummels his penis so I can see it. My heart throbs in my throat. The blood pulses in my temples and I look away down to the ground, holding my breath as my bike swerves to the left of the path. I turn my head sideways, so I can see from the corner of my eye that he's not coming after me. *Kloodzak*, weirdo—couldn't he go to the red-light district in Amsterdam and pummel his dick there?

And then in contrast my thoughts take me back to the center of Rotterdam, right after that terrible World War, where a sense of normalcy seemed to have returned. Tall women walk on sidewalks arm in arm, dark shoes, grey and black clothes, thick stockings. They lean forward into the wind. Men on their knees with rubber hammers repair streets surrounding us. Rotterdam is on the move, rebuilding from when food was scarce—people eating tulip bulbs during the occupation of the Nazi regime. People now keep little vegetable gardens in special sections of town. Ma had always loved flowers and in tandem with her new country's tradition, she biked to the weekly market and bought twenty carnations for a guilder.

—ⱿⱿ—

Watching the North Sea flow into the Rotterdam harbor for the first seventeen years of my life instilled in me a love for the stink of polluted water, and diesel. Pilot boats pulled enormous ships into the Rotterdam port. I would come to embrace this scene and energy in every port around the world.

Rotterdam's streets were paved with black cobblestones slick from daily rain showers, locally referred to as *kinder hoofdjes* (children's heads.) Noisy buses and trams packed with soggy human bodies rumbled nonstop through the streets. Between seven and eight o'clock in the morning hundreds of bicycles moved through the city headed for school or work no matter how hard it rained, snowed, or stormed. Thirty wet students, a classroom filled with soaked clothes and damp leather satchels created a recognizable whiff of humans in damp clothing. The wet Dutch sea climate and a cultural dissonance would nudge me out of the country.

Alone as a child, at the age of eleven, twelve and thirteen, I often biked to the harbor. There I'd walk the sidewalk close to the water, feeling at home, especially when in view of the Zadkine monument, a tall and muscular male iron sculpture. A gaping hole appears where his heart should have been. His strong arms stretch upward with hands folded backward as he screams to the heavens. The statue emanates despair. It captured my loss of identity, a black hole, which like a sunken ship I had to haul up to piece my life back together again. Later, the clay statues of my own artwork had hands pleading the heavens also, sometimes with even more than two arms and hands.

Zadkine, a Russian artist, embodied the collective emotion in the statue known as "Jan Gat," Jan with the hole called by the people of Rotterdam. *"Jan met de handjes"* he became called as well. This referred to his huge upward titled hands.

Zadkine's chest reminded us of the German blasts that had ripped out the heart of Rotterdam. Despite Hitler's hypocrite promise not to attack its civilian population, the German bombs decimated the center of Rotterdam. People burned to death trapped in the fires that consumed the city and its crushed buildings and homes.

But the people of Rotterdam are resilient and known for being direct. Predominantly a working class, they stuck together … I wanted to stick together like them. Instead, at four years old, maybe even younger, and far into my teens, I moved around as in a dream, yet mindful of the prejudice of wounded people. In third grade I began counting the lines between the pavements, the trees, the light poles 1, 2, 3, 4 while turning the pedals of my bike. Later we had a car, and I moved my feet in tandem with the light poles. It rains a lot in Holland and alone in a bedroom the raindrops merge, they splash against our window. I watch them for hours. This weekend I'll go to the harbor I think, I want to see the boats and smell that stinky Maas, I want to feel the rumble of movement, sailors, cranes, ships. It wakes me up; I feel alive and Dutch. I may be a street child but I'm not a *Mof*.

In old Rotterdam near the River Rotte stands St. Laurens Protestant Church, which dates to medieval times with its World War II bombed out steeple.

"We don't go in there, we're Catholic," says Pa.

The weekly market was held right under the elevated railroad tracks. New and used goods were sold while trains thundered overhead on the rails. Dad found an antique self portrait of Rembrandt there that someone had painted on wood.

Dad liked the harbor too; I could sense his happiness. The city's energy grounded us both. I intuited that Dad felt the same after having been in Germany for five years. This marketplace helped both my parents for a moment to forget their post-traumatic life after the war.

'Give me a daalder, not a guilder, not for five, no for a total of ten—Chiquita bananas from Guatemala, ok, for that little woman there with the red coat," a merchant yells. He stands in the rear of an open truck filled with bananas straight from the harbor. A shipper from Scheveningen wears a long plastic apron and tall boots, blood from fish guts stick to his apron. He yells, "Two guilders a pound, now or never," holding up some greasy smoked eels.

Nearby some bystanders hold salty herrings by the tails above their open mouth; heads lean backwards as the salty herrings slides down their throats. Here's a quarter. Dad picks one of the herrings by the tail holding it between thumb and index finger, steeps it in chopped onions, and he throws back his head. The fish disappears into his mouth. "Not too salty, it's a good year," he smiles and buys a few more to take home for Ma.

Vegetable and fruit merchant's voices compete with the fish vendors "*Alles moet weg,* everything got to go."

Ma hurries from one to the other fruit stands smiling that she scores a deal. The vendors know her by her German accent and like her. Merchants at markets treat her nicely, yet in the shops she remains a *Mof.*

While Ma checks out vegetables for the week, I hang on to Dad who will indulge us children in Belgian Cote d'Or chocolate offered at a corner stand. No questions asked, my brother, sister and I prefer to stay with Dad, always! He's the candy guy!

I passed the tall bronze statue of my humanistic Catholic friend Desiderius Erasmus (1469-1536) on my way down through the Hoogstraat. I learned that he could hold two opposites in his mind, much to the discomfort of Martin Luther and many others of his time.

He stands directly in front of the Erasmus University, eternally reading his book and yearning for freedom and reason. His statue was originally from stone. It was the first statue of that caliber the Dutch had in the 15th century and was placed in Rotterdam's busiest *Grote markt*.

I read one of his books once, surprised that not much had changed in five centuries. I wished I'd learned about him as a child. I might have been better able to reconcile being Dutch and German. Like Erasmus I might have adopted a more neutral stance. Erasmus reconciled the powers of church and society as a theologian. Or maybe I could have reasoned myself out of society's hate and anger toward Christa, my German mother who did not speak Dutch after the war. Ma was not welcomed in bombed out and pillaged Rotterdam. Ma was a *Mof*.

A *Mof*, means a "muff," or one of those fur warmers you stick your hands into during the wintertime to keep them warm. *Mof* was already in use before World War I. Germans were *Moffen* and Dutch people were *Kaaskoppen* or "Cheese heads." After all, our cheeses made in Rotterdam, Gouda, Alkmaar and Edam, are internationally famous. Only the word *Mof* turned ugly during World War II.

Ma tried to please everyone.

"Go home to your country" the neighbors tyrannically yelled. I felt weak inside when people spewed their hate, but like Ma I never responded to them. In stores people ignored us as customers. Rotterdammers were angry and deeply hurt, grieving over lost family, and recovering from years of hardship, hunger, and financial ruin.

"You lived in Germany Ma; did you not know that they gassed all those Jews?"

This question festered within me, deepened by Dutch citizens' hatred toward the Germans, as well as frequent school trips to war monuments. It made me feel guilty for being the child of a nation who had committed these horrific atrocities. I cried for all those Jews. Then there was my sister Gisela, who had died a year before my birth. Why did my folks have to give her such a German name? Now I couldn't talk to anyone about her.

I was an outcast in school where teachers and parents of friends referred to me as a child of a *Mof*. What was I, a *Mof* or a Dutch Cheesehead? How could the Dutch be so mean? What had turned the Germans into Nazis?

In the fifth grade I took my first foreign language class, which was French. A few years later I would add English and German classes.

I'll be good in German, I think. "Pa, let's speak German at home."

He looks at me sternly and then turns to Mom, "There will be no German spoken in this house."

I wait until Pa is out of the kitchen. "Ma, why doesn't Pa let us?"

Ma addresses me by my German name, "Ingelein, I think Dutch is a pig's language," referencing the snorting sounds a pig makes. We giggle and make gagging sounds and laugh harder.

I've never been sure what my first language was. No doubt Ma spoke German the first few years and Pa of course Dutch and the last one stuck. Ma never learned to write in Dutch but spoke it with a heavy German accent. She despised the sound of the Dutch language. *Verdammt noch mal*, the only German curse words she intermingled with her German Dutch when she was upset. We copied her German accent and often teased her.

Those Dutch Cheese heads did not realize that Ma had also suffered loss because of the war, that Ma had lost her own mother and other family members. As a forced member of the *Hiltler Jugend* in Wanne Eickel, she lived in fear and had experienced the horrific *Kristallnacht,* their destruction of the synagogues, demolition of shops owned by Jewish people, and execution of those who did not join the SS and were betrayed by other Germans. On the other hand, Dad, one of twelve children born to a family in Amsterdam, was fortunate to have attended a Catholic high school shortly before the war, although he had to borrow his oldest brother's shoes and pants to wear.

While German soldiers battled the war abroad, Germany needed other men to keep the war factories going. After the Germans took over the city hall of Rotterdam in Holland, it wasn't hard to get the names of men to work in German factories. Consequently, Pa and his brothers were sent off to Germany and one of them to France. Dad answered the summons after the second notice, so that he could choose his work location and maybe end up in the same town as his brother. If he would have ignored the Germans, they would have hauled him off and in that case, he could have been deported in the trains to camps in Germany or elsewhere.

"Don't come back home with one of those German women," his mother had admonished when he left. Of course, he did. Upon my parents returning to Holland, they would live in Dad's mothers' house. Devout Catholics, Ma soon became pregnant. However, born with the cord around her neck, Gisela, died several days later in Rotterdam. With the announcement of her death my dad collapsed. No one attended the funeral. After all Gisela was the child of a *Mof* which merited no sympathy.

Dad's mother could not reconcile Ma being a *Mof*. One morning around ten o'clock, the time when people in Holland gather to drink coffee, Ma invited her to come upstairs to our borrowed living quarters. She slowly climbed the wooden stairs to our little place right under the roof and sat down looking at Ma as she handed her the cup of coffee. Shaking her head, she lamented, "I just don't get why he married a *Mof*."

Ma cleaned, washed the clothes by hand and shopped for the entire family all while taking care of Dad. But neither family nor neighbors would acknowledge her humanity.

My folks had suffered so much, seen the bottom of life. Why didn't Pa go to America when he had been invited? Maybe it was because Ma was afraid to go. Instead, they struggled together in that raw city of Rotterdam. Dad worked long hard hours, and we missed him.

Rotten *Mof*, they yelled whenever my mother and I would go out in the street. She lowered her head looking at the pavement as she hurried our pace pulling me along by the hand.

IN LOVE DURING THE WAR

1940−1948

We lift ourselves above others be it a family member,
colleague, friend, culture, a political opinion, a dress
code, a religion and so on. It creates war within us, our
families, and countries. I'm trained well. Dad did not
like group think after the war. I look the part with
my blonde hair and blue eyes. The Nazi dream
of a white and pure race.

Stampeded by the Dutch daily hate of the Germans I
try to find myself. Where do I place my heart, with the
Germans or with the Dutch? I want to understand how it
is possible to fall in love with the enemy during the war.
What makes a person join the Hitler Jugend, build gas
chambers, salute Heil Hitler, Heil Hitler?

Fear of my father's anger expressed at times through
slapping my brother and occasionally me and not talking
to Mom for days created a sense of shame in me. Mom
rejected by the Dutch sank into depression. To love my
mom's family creates a cultural loyalty conflict. My
essence seeks a way out. I feel worthless. The flame of
love and truth guides me. So, it was also for my parents
during the war.

THE NAZIS TOOK OVER ROTTERDAM'S City Hall in
1940. There they found archives of all citizens, which they
used for deportations. Every employed man was required to regis-
ter. Marinus, my dad, just eighteen years old along with his friends,
his brothers, and thousands of Dutchmen, received orders by mail
to depart for work in Germany. The men and their families were
terrified.

"Rinus, you better respond to this. Karel, next door, didn't
answer his calls for deportation and those Nazis hauled him off in
a truck yesterday. No one knows where he is. If you go voluntarily,
you might be able to work it out for you and your brother, Wil, to
end up in the same town," Marinus' mother pleaded.

Both mother and son sat at the dining table in the middle of the
room, their bodies slumped forward, elbows on the woolen carpet

that draped the table. Marinus' mother, my grandmother, or Oma, usually talkative and upbeat, sipped her black tea and warmed her hands around the cup. Together they stared into the distance. Long silences punctuated their conversation. There was no way out.

Marinus sat in his chair; his face serious under blonde curly hair neatly combed back. His mother studied him, her face a mixture of pride and concern. He had just finished high school, spoke quite a bit of German, English and French. She had had a different future for him in mind, for all her boys.

"Mam," he stood up and put the chair back and placed his hand on his mother's shoulder.

"I'll go to City Hall. Hans might still work there. Maybe he can arrange for us to be together and not so far from the Dutch border."

Hans did still work at the archives. Marinus prepared to take off and gathered one set of clothes, an old long dark winter coat, and some English books from school. He needed to report to work the next day in Germany.

"Don't you dare come back with one of those short German girls, Rien." His mother teased again, making light of his departure.

"Never."

They ended up in service in a dirty and black polluted area, cities saturated with steel, iron and coal emissions. The Germans placed Marinus in one of Europe's largest Nazi-supporting steel industries. He was assigned to Gelsenkirchen, a four-hour train trip from Rotterdam, and the same town where his brother Wil had arrived earlier.

People called this densely populated area *Ruhr Pott. Ruhr*— after the river Ruhr and "*Pott*" since one could not escape the coal dust and fumes. At night you'd spit or sneeze up black phlegm. If the clothes you wore that day were white, they had turned pitch black by the end of the day. It would still be like that eighteen years later, when I moved to the same area to figure out if I wanted to be German or Dutch at heart.

Marinus's younger brother, Albert, found work with a Dutch construction company which had aligned itself with the Nazis. It wasn't long before he along with many others would ride the rail-cars to work for the Germans in Dortmund, also part of the *Ruhr Pott*. In short order Albert was relocated again, packed in train wagons headed for Berlin, the capital of Germany.

"I can't sleep Wil," whispered Marinus. "What's happening with Albert? G*d forbid, he joined the German Nazis! We must find a way to warn Albert. From Berlin he might be drafted to go to Russia with the Germans. That will be the end of him".

Both brothers, like all their siblings, were very tall, and their feet hung over their beds in the small dark room while uncertainty grew in their minds. Their room in the house belonged to a woman whose son fought abroad. She fed my dad and uncle well, hoping someone would do the same for her child. The two brothers could not sleep. Close by, a church bell rang, one, two, three o'clock.

"Are you out of your mind, Albert knows what he is doing. He'd never join them," Wil uttered after a while. "Besides, you are not talking about the next town. The capital is far from here, we are not allowed to leave this area."

"Berlin, that's where the big battles will be with the Allied forces; It's too dangerous to go there, Marinus. They'll shoot us. You never know who will be on those trains."

The following Sunday morning while it was still dark, the two brothers, Marinus and Wil jumped on the train enroute from the north to deep into Germany, its capital, Berlin. Under the noise of the steam engine and scrutiny of many German people traveling, they retreated in silence.

Once in Berlin they were happy to learn that Albert's name was among a list of Dutch people who had been sent to Finland. The Germans had enlisted him to sew uniforms there. The two brothers prepared to take the night train back and rested on a bench in the busy railway station. Exhausted the next morning, they dutifully reported to work.

At the United Steelworks or *Vereinigte Stahlwerke A.G.*, the main artery for Germany's arsenal supply and storage, thousands of workers labored to keep the bombs in ready supply. Black smoke spewed from the inferno of the smelters. Despite the city's dark atmosphere, Marinus, multilingual and 6.5 feet tall, became enamored with a brunette barely five feet tall.

"This is not right. I'll bring her danger. Romance is not allowed. This office is full of Nazi's." Marinus wrestled with his conscience, recalling his mother's words. "Don't you come home with one of those short German girls."

"She's beautiful, gentle. She's available. Those high heels. I love the way she wears her long hair with those three curls in front. She is kind, too. She often offers to share her lunch with others."

Marinus was feeling lucky.

"I'll never marry a German." Christa repeated to herself. And soon mutual eye contact lingered longer than usual. She seemed fragile, smiling under hazel eyes both beautiful and sad.

"Let me carry that heavy typewriter," he offered.

In return, Christa offered to mend clothes and holes in Marinus' worn knitted socks.

"Jan, give me your socks for Christa to mend; mine are so far gone that they are more hole than sock. I don't want her to know," he negotiated with a Dutch country man.

With the little money he had saved Marinus offered her a ticket for the movies in Gelsenkirchen.

"*Warum kommen Sie nicht zu uns nach Hause?*" Christa invited him, addressing him in the polite "*Sie*" form, to come and visit her at home.

"*Ja,* I'd like to meet your family, your dad and sisters."

She lived five miles from Gelsenkirchen in Wanne-Eickel. Her dad Isidor was a short fellow with bowed legs. He leaned forward peering at Marinus, the foreigner.

With curious yet smiling eyes behind glasses he spoke "*Willkommen.*" Like Christa, he was barely 5 feet tall. His somewhat bald head stretched to look up at Marinus. Isidor remained standing. He walked around in the small room that had a bed, a couch and served as a kitchen.

"How many eggs do you want? Two or three?" Christa began to prepare food.

"How many eggs?" He hadn't seen any for months. Then he remembered Isidor kept chickens. Isidor's chicken farm, in the middle of town, had been in the newspaper. He felt at home.

Marinus and Christa had fallen in love. Had people in the office noticed? If so, it made them both traitors. In 1940, falling in love with the enemy in Germany carried a high penalty, and in Germany the Dutch were the enemy. Vice-versa in Holland, the Germans were the enemy. The young couple risked being imprisoned or worse, executed.

Lonely, surrounded by fear and suffering, love became their ally. She needs me, he thought, she just lost her mother.

At night Marinus, on the way to his beloved in Wanne-Eikel, would pick his way around deep craters dropped by the British RAF. He left Gelsenkirchen at dark. Alert for the SS, he walked the hour and a half route late at night and back before morning.

A figure in the distance emerged, but it was only a couple meeting for a late-night walk. Marinus breathed easier once he could see that the man did not wear a uniform. Moving with long quick strides Marinus shivered in the cold.

Foreigners were not allowed to leave the city where they were stationed. He was always required to wear identification. Despite the risks Marinus made it safely each time, thinking of Christa and the food they had, eggs.

Marinus and Christa worked for the large company, he as an electrician and she attended the reception and accounting area of the steel works. Many of the employees were Nazis, which made for an atmosphere of fear and suspicion.

On weekends Christa met with her aunt Trude from Koblenz, a town south of Wanne Eickel, to exchange food. She would bring eggs and her aunt brought wine, which they would exchange for vegetables and bread. Christmas was coming soon.

"We'd like to get engaged," Christa told her aunt on Christmas day in 1942.

Trude looked excited and concerned. "It's dangerous, you'll be a traitor. Maybe I should talk with Herr Schiller who lives above us. He can help us, give us some advice, even though he's with the NPSD. He's trustworthy."

Herr Schiller opposed the idea of the engagement. Now secrecy was imperative. The family got busy.

My Aunt Trude melted a gold statue of the Virgin Mary to have a ring made for Marinus. Christa would wear her mother's wedding ring. After their clandestine Christmas engagement, it was back to work at her desk located at the main entrance.

"Go there behind the telephone panel," Christa ordered her Jewish friend in panic.

She had spotted one of the employees, a known Nazi, coming toward the entrance.

"*Mahlzeit*," he greeted her, tipping his hat he walked by and didn't notice the man hiding behind the panel.

"Julius, Marinus, and I found two people dead last night, shot alongside the road. You must leave this area, stop coming back here. They will not employ you. This place is full of Nazi's and they don't want Jews."

But that night she found a man dead in the gutter of the road, his face smacked against the sidewalk and his eyes open and staring. He was not alone, nearby lay another colleague. She stood paralyzed unable to look away, covering her mouth to stifle a scream and the urge to vomit. Only yesterday they had talked. Why didn't he leave like she had told him? Who did this? A distinct rumbling sounded from the sky interrupting her thoughts. Loud sirens spurred her to run for shelter.

Knowing the shortest way to bomb shelters near the factory meant life or death. Christa and Marinus, together with German and foreign workers spent a great deal of time in foul smelling shelters after the Allied Forces began bombing Germany's northern industrial areas.

"*Der Zuckerturm*" (sugar tower) was one such shelter situated in the center of the steel works. It was an unusually tall pillar bomb structure that wobbled when bombed.

"Germans only!" people screamed while cramming into the doorway. A group of foreign workers began to form, pushing toward the door, holding their breath and immobilized in fear. A man in front had taken charge. Foreigners had to wait. See if there'd be space.

Outside of the steelworks there was an area "*der Zintelberg*," a twenty-meter mountain formed by slag dumped from the steel-smelters. People had carved strutted corridors into the mountain as bunkers for protection. When the bombings increased in frequency, many Germans were too frightened to leave the bunkers anymore and stayed in them continuously. It became a smelly place of human sweat and urine stench. The foreign workers were not allowed. Later, when the bombing became continuous, they were allowed in if there was still space.

"*Keine Russen. Hau ab! Verdammt noch mal. Rauss.*" Russians were never allowed to enter any shelter or bunker. The shelters were reserved for Germans only.

Once, after having endured a long night in the shelter listening to bombs explode nearby, Christa's family and Marinus left the shelter.

"*Mein Haus is still standing Gott sei Dank!*" exclaimed Isidor, Christa's dad.

He ran as fast as his legs could carry him through the smoke, heat and dust. A small group followed, excited that their building still stood. Breathless, they crept closer and closer. Suddenly, Isidor froze throwing his arms in the air. Only one wall of the house stood tall against the dark smoky sky. Behind it lay a huge pile of rubble from their collapsed four-story apartment building.

In shock and still trembling everyone began to dig into the rubble of the house in the *Moltkestrasse* of Wanne-Eickel. Hungry as they were, the knowledge of two dressed chickens ready to be cooked, and which they left just before they fled, fired them up.

"*Da sind sie*—We have them!" "There are my dresses and that red suitcase! Can you pull them out Marinus?"

The clearing took days and only a few belongings could be salvaged. The hard work made Marinus hungry, causing Christa's family great astonishment how much a Dutchman of his size could eat. They shared the little they had, and their love deepened as they clung together united by fear. Bombs fell incessantly day and night. Marinus began contemplating his escape with Christa.

—m—

"Christa, can you find us a bicycle somewhere? We cannot tell anyone about our escape. I'll have to visit the Gestapo."

A generous friend provided the young couple with the brandnew bike which would transport them from northern Germany toward the southern German Hessen area where it was believed the American Army, on their way to Berlin, would soon arrive. Christa's family also lived there. It was a calculated risk to leave farther away from the Dutch border, while moving deeper into Germany.

"We will be safe there. I speak English."

Increasingly the word came that the Germans were being defeated in Russia. Some of the German soldiers would even defect during that cold winter.

Prohibited from leaving the city of Gelsenkirchen, Marinus updated his permit to live in the area. The *Aufenthaltsgenehmigung* allowed him entrance to the area where he worked only. Not beyond. Die *Gruene Polizei*, the Gestapo in Gelsenkirchen dictated all travel.

The officer sat behind his desk straight backed and authoritative in his green Waffen-SS uniform, his shiny black boots stretched out in front of him. "*Die Schweine——was wollen die jezt schon wieder.*" Those pigs--what do they want now? He despised the foreigners who had come to work in his country.

Thus, Marinus' entrance received no greeting or acknowledgement. "*Aschloch,* what does he want, that foreigner. Where is his respect, his Heil Hitler? Why isn't he working?" He continued his concentration on the papers spread out across his metal desk.

"*Heil Hitler,*" Marinus sarcastically thought with equal disgust. He approached the SS officers' desk who continued to ignore his presence.

"*Entschuldigung,* it's too dangerous here with the bombings. I'd like to go to a farming area nearby, where the bombs are less. *Bitte,* grant me the exit permit so I can be safe and leave this town."

The tension mounted as the officer dragged deeply from his cigarette then returned it to the ashtray. He resumed his focus on the papers in front of him, his face noticeably irritated. The rhythm of the officer's breaths increased. Discord filled the room mingled with cigarette smoke. What would be the breaking point? What could he do to me? I must stick this out. I'll be killed here either way, if not by him than through the bombs. Dad thought. Marinus' heart raced, his blood rushing to his head. Sweat trickled down his back. He was a nothing. Damned Germans. My life is in his hands. Dictators! Bureaucrats!

"I will return immediately and report to you when the bombings become less," Marinus pleaded. The officer gave no hint of acknowledgment.

Suddenly he shoved his chair back, Marinus bones absorbed the jolt. The officer stood up, reached across his desk, and jerked the passport out of Marinus' hand. Still standing, the Nazi abruptly stamped the permit, hurled it across the desk still wordless. Marinus picked it up from the floor and made his way out. Numb, he increased his pace, almost running with his temporary permit.

"We must get out of here today."

They made their escape away from the rubble and despair on one bike with a back seat for Christa who clutched a red suitcase holding a few belongings away from the rubble and despair. They rode into the dark night. The couple kept to the mountain's back roads, while overhead were frequent reminders of the surrounding dangers.

"*Schnell Christa leg dich hin im Grass, die sind schon über uns.*" Fast, Christa, lie down in the grass; they are flying already over us.

Low flying planes searched for bombing targets, scanning the landscape for signs of movement. Their red suitcase is an easy target. They traveled for days, often sleeping with farmers on the way. They were not alone.

"You sleep there with the women. You, long one, over there with the men," the farmer pointed to a stable.

"Christa, I don't trust it," her Dutch lover whispered. Let's meet at midnight under that tree over there near the road and get away."

Christa couldn't sleep lying on the ground next to a strange German woman. In a nearby building Marinus, kept apart from the others, prepared to bed down on some hay. Both restless, their thoughts reached out to each other.

"It's strange to be separated," he thought. "What's this farmer up to?"

Pretending to relieve himself Marinus waited at the tree along the roadside where their bike was. Christa joined him, stepping out of the shadows.

In Alsfeld, 36 kilometers from their destination, they froze at the appearance of a tall German soldier.

"Too late now, Christa, … He spotted us already."

The soldier commanded the road's crossing in his big boots, green uniform, and helmet. And he carried a pistol in his holster.

"*Hallt!*" he screamed, gesturing angrily with his red stop sign marching toward Marinus and Christa.

"*Ausweiss bitte,*" he yelled. A group of defecting German troops stood behind him.

"*Koenen Sie mir den Weg nach Fulda zeigen*"? Can you tell me how to get to Fulda? Christa interrupted his thinking. Lightheaded with fear Marinus stood tall, gripping the bike's handlebars allowing Christa to do the talking. Marinus Dutch accent along with an expired permit, pertaining to another area, would be a dead giveaway. Christa's ease in the German language convinced the soldier, and they were told to go. Silent, Marinus peddled faster, his body weak from fear.

Christa broke the silence. "*Wir sind ja fast da*, one more mountain to pass." The small German farm village of Ulmbach lay ahead. They would be there before dark.

—ᴟ—

Upon their arrival Aunt Mathilde ran out of the house. She embraced Christa and immediately pulled Marinus by the arm.

"Go to the cellar, Marinus, there's food there. I'm still hiding and feeding some defected Germans on the farm. Stay there with them until we come for you!"

German soldiers came back from Russia, limbs, and toes frozen from the harsh winter months they had not been prepared for.

After some shooting, American tanks and infantry arrived just as expected. The German soldiers surrendered, all but one out of the groups hiding in Mathilda's cellar. At Marinus' urging, she hung out a white flag welcoming the US military. Christa's family opened their farmhouse to the American soldiers.

"Come upstairs," Mathilda yelled into the cellar. "We need a translator."

"Any Germans here?"

"We still have an Italian in the cellar. He wants to surrender."

Dad negotiated the surrender of Italian born Silvio Krobath into American custody. He was a truck driver according to his *Soldbuch*, a booklet comprising his personal information, including his dental profile. The booklet also noted that he possessed a pistol, a gas mask, a package to disinfect his skin, as well as a stamp of a gas chamber test.

"Get on that truck over there." The American soldier pointed to a truck loaded with several other Germans they had captured.

Thus, the American Army division, tanks, and all, rolled into the small village of Ulmbach on their way to Berlin. The village consisted of a few small farms surrounded with grazing sheep on pastures of rolling mountains.

The people of Ulmbach were simple folks, living close to the earth. Women, dressed in black with their hair covered, worked the fields. Hand-built chapels scattered alongside the roads expressed their Catholic beliefs. In the center of the community stood a brick bread house, a domelike oven heated with wood. The women gathered and baked their bread here. Calm existed at this juncture in the middle of the war. But the arrival of the Americans, French, and soldiers defecting from Russia would change calm into a different danger.

"Van Zanten, tomorrow you direct all men to appear at the village square near the bread house." an American officer ordered Marinus. US officers divided the men in their custody into Germans, French, and Russians.

"You, van Zanten, you're the only Dutchman; you go with the French."

One of the Americans handed Marinus a rifle. He looked at it carefully, held it loose, not knowing what to do with it. It was the first time in his life to hold a gun. The prospect of having to use it gripped his body with memories of dead bodies in Gelsenkirchen and those sprawled along the road on their journey to Ulmbach and made his body feel light and weak again.

"All of you get a good night's sleep! Tomorrow, it's up to Berlin to fight for its liberation."

Marinus glanced at the French soldiers. Then his eyes focused on the grass blanketing the open area where he'd be sleeping that night. He had no coat, one pair of socks with holes, and worn-out shoes. Not exactly a soldier's outfit, but Marinus gathered courage. His length gave him a confident and strong appearance. And rifle in hand, not timid, he walked to the French officer.

"*Pardon monsieur, est-il possible de dormir avec la famille de ma fiancée dans la village?* Can I sleep with the family of my fiancé?" asked Marinus in his best high school French.

The Frenchman, much shorter than him, and not impressed, snapped back: "*Non, ce n'est pas possible vous rester ici.*"

Under cover of the dark evening Marinus stopped an American jeep and asked the officer the same question.

"As long as there are no American soldiers needing space to sleep at your fiancé's house, you can sleep with your family." It was an emotional reunion. Christa wept. She had watched the round-up at the bread house and thought she'd never see her Dutchman again. The family fed him, and it was back to the cellar. With the arrival of the Americans the end of the war was in sight. Marinus didn't join the French or any of the other soldiers. He remained in Ulmbach with his love and her family. The US army departed.

Marinus would remain loyal to the Americans for the rest of his life. As for the French, he retained an interest in their language only, often inserting French vernacular when speaking to his Dutch children.

"*Pas de quoi.* (Never mind, or the friendly version, you're welcome) was his favorite term. As a teenager I'd beg him to take me to Paris, but he never did. When I was eighteen, I went alone.

At the end of the war, the people of Ulmbach invited him to become their mayor, which he politely declined. He had a different plan for his and Christa's future.

By May 1945, with more than sixty million people killed the war was over. Foreign workers and those who survived found their way back home. Gates of concentration camps in Germany and in other countries opened. A time of freedom and healing began. But not for all.

Christa and Marinus returned to Wanne-Eickel, northern Germany, intending to cross the border into the Netherlands, but Christa was not allowed to enter. Not a surprise.

"What was her role in the *Hitler Jugend*?

"Nothing." How could she prove that? they asked.

"I'm not crossing alone. I'll find work with the British until we get your papers." Marinus told Christa. He looked for work with the British Army in Essen, the same area he had fled during the bombings. The Royal Traffic Office at the Essen train station offered a job clearing rubble.

Marinus' connection with the British Army would foster close friendships and work relationships in England. After the war, many English, Americans, and of course Germans would visit our house. As a kid I noticed that the Americans had a different way of being than the English. Americans were more relaxed and open. Germans stood their own. Attracted by their sense of freedom I aligned with the Americans, but not before I had reconciled my own identity as a temporary German resident. Should I align with my father's or my mother's country? Should I go to America? Wasn't that where Dad had dreamed of going after the war?

But this was all before I was born. My parents had to find a way to cross the border into Holland. The administration in Osterode had the authorization for the clearance.

Marinus and Christa stayed with family in Herzberg, where Christa gathered wild nuts from the woods. A friend processed the nuts to make a bit of cooking oil for them. In the meantime, Marinus walked the eleven kilometers to the bombed-out town of Osterode where he negotiated with a Dutch officer to get Christa's papers.

"I'm sure he will help us get your papers. He's Dutch after all. He'll understand!"

"*Wat moet je hier nog verrader*?" What are you still doing here traitor?

"No, I'm not a Nazi. I worked here for five years, after deportation from Rotterdam. I found a German girl here and we want to get married. I didn't want to leave her behind."

"Get the hell out of here, *donder op*," the officer yelled.

Disconcerted and confused he walked home as thick thunder-clouds rumbled in the distance. This visit with family in Herzberg appeared more bitter than sweet.

"I'm going back to Fulda. I need to work and earn a living."

They took the challenging train ride back to connect with the Americans in the south of Germany. Most trains from Herzberg were routed through the newly created Russian zone, which divided Germany in two parts. The two changed trains often to escape the Russians, finally arriving in Fulda.

While working for the American Grave registration, Marinus became deathly ill with peritonitis, an internal rupture in the abdominal area caused by infection. Christa visited him in the hospital bringing him food. "Here, eat this, I sold cigarette butts for these."

Marinus health continued to decline. He weighed ninety pounds, and no longer spoke. *"Oh mein Gott,* he's dying." Marinus' condition was alarming. Screaming, Christa ran past all the nuns and nurses.

"Hilfe , hilfe!" She rushed toward the surgery room, flung open the doors, and in a panic pulled a doctor to the bed of her fiancé. Immediately, doctors performed an exploratory surgery.

"He's Catholic, isn't he? Let's get *Herr Pastor."*

Despite having survived the war, he now received the last rites. Christa's father began making funeral arrangements and she returned home to a wreath hanging on the door. However, Marinus had not died yet! The next day Catholic nuns, Ursuline sisters and nurses who operated the St. Elizabeth hospital in Fulda gave Christa a prayer for his recovery. For the remainder of her life Christa would recite this prayer before she went to sleep.

Gebet zu Maria, Hilfe der Christen.
Prayer to Mary, Helper of Christians

Jungfrau Mutter Gottes mein,
Virgin Mother of G*d,

Lass mich ganz Dein eigen sein!
Allow me to be totally yours!

Dein im Leben und im Tod;
Yours during Life and into Death.

Dein in Unglueck, Angst und Not;
Yours in Failure, Fear and Need.

Dein in Kreuz und bittrem Leid;
Yours in the Cross and in bitter suffering.

Dein fuer Zeit und Ewigkeit.
Yours, in all Time and Eternity.

Jungfrau, Mutter Gottes mein,
My Virgin Mother of G*d,

Lass mich ganz Dein eigen sein!
Allow me to be totally yours!

Mutter! auf Dich, hoff und bau ich!
Mother! My hope is in you, and I build on you!

Mutter! zu Dir ruf und seufz ich!
Mother! To you, I call and plea!

Mutter! Du Guetigste steh mir bei!
You with your Goodness support me!

Mutter! Du Maechtigste Schutz mir verleih!
Mother! Your Power protects me!

Oh Mutter: so komm hilf streiten mir!
Oh, Mother: come and help me fight!

Oh Mutter: so komm hilf leiden mir!
Oh, Mother: come and help me suffer!

Oh Mutter: so komm und bleib bei mir!
Oh, Mother: come and remain with me!

Du kannst mir ja helfen, oh Maechtigste!
You can help me Oh Mighty!

Du willst mir ja helfen, Oh Guetigste!
You want to help me You good One!

Du musst mir nun helfen, oh Treueste!
You must help me Oh faithful One!

Du willst mir auch helfen, Barherzigste!
You want to help me My Merciful One!

Oh Mutter der Gnade! der Christen Hort!
Oh, Mother of Grace! of the Christians!

Du Zufluecht der Suender! des Heiles Pfort!
You whose gates sinners flee to!

Du Hoffung der Erde! des Himmels Zier!
You, Hope of the earth and Heavens Décor!

Du Trost der Betruebten, Ihr Schutzpanier
You, comforter and Protector of sad ones.

Wer hat je umsonst Deine Hilfe angefleht?
Who has asked for Your Help without reply?

Wann has Du vergessen ein kindlich Gebet?
Did you ever forget a child's prayer?

Drumm ruf ich beharrlich im Kreuz und im Leid,
I call in need and in suffering,

"Maria hilft immer!—Sie hilft jederzeit."
Maria helps always and in all time.

Ich ruf' voll Vertrauen in Leiden und Tod:
I call on You in trust, suffering and death,

"Maria hilft immer in jeglicher Not!"
Maria helps always in every need.

So glaub' ich und lebe ich und sterbe darauf:
Therefore, I believe, I live and die on it.

"Maria hilft mir in den Himmel hinauf!"
Maria helps me into Heaven!

—A prayer of surrender to the mother of G*d.

Marinus' illness had come at a time of bad water, little food, lack of shelter and unsanitary living conditions, which ignited epidemic illnesses across Europe during the war's final days. In the Netherlands, famine was pervasive. Families ate tulip bulbs just to stay alive. In Rotterdam Marinus' father's legs were swollen with edema from the lack of food. Toos, his youngest sister, walked on shoes made from pieces of wood tied to her feet. Risking possible death, she begged for bread from a German soldier camp in the center of Rotterdam. Walking miles in those "wooden shoes," the family held their breath fearing for her safety, Toos returned with some bread.

Along with a group of children, Toos and her younger brother Leo, were sent to the southern part of Holland, just below the Rhine River. This area of Holland was mostly Catholic and farming country. In exchange for work Toos and Leo received food and after gaining some weight and strength returned home after a few weeks. In early 1945, driven mad by the stress of deported children, no work and hunger, Marinus' father, my paternal grandfather, jumped out of the rooftop window.

Marinus was fighting his own battle for life and without Christa's love and devotion, he might have died. The news of his father's death did not reach him until they were allowed entry into the Netherlands. He didn't know it on a conscious level, yet I imagine he could have intuited the abyss his father faced. As Marinus' health improved so did his appetite. "Christa, please locate some rhubarb. Someone told me it could be good for me."

He ate it raw daily, the natural antibiotic in the rhubarb strengthened him. Marinus soon inquired about working for the Americans. Within a couple of weeks after his hospital release, he went to work.

My parents married on July 13, 1946, in the town hall of Fulda, Germany. A year and a half later, November 16, 1947, they knelt together there in front of the sacred bones of Saint Boniface, an English missionary of the 6th century, and exchanged their spiritual vows.

Saint Boniface, renowned for his efforts in Europe, signified the union of the new couple of geographically close worlds, yet so disparate culturally.

Again, they traveled north, this time much closer to the Dutch border. Marinus found a job with the British army in Essen and again worked the Grave Registration. In retrospect I have wondered, Dad is that why you played those strange and frightening games when I was a kid? I bet that those dead energies had to go somewhere. So, you often played dead. Did you know it frightened the heck out of me and Mam?

With the help of the American FBI in Frankfurt, who could mediate with the Dutch government, the couple received papers from the Dutch Embassy. Christa, now stateless, and Marinus a Dutch citizen, both cleared; they crossed the border into Holland.

Once in Rotterdam his mother was unrecognizable after that long winter of starvation. When Marinus inquired after his father, his mom gave him the horrifying news. The pressure of the Catholic Church in those days to stay together and to procreate took its toll on his parents. Their marriage was contentious with twelve children, no income, and hunger during the war. Four sons had been deported by the Nazis to Germany, Finland, and France.

Marinus' father, my paternal *Opa*, had been a dark-eyed proud man with ancestral ties to Spain. He had fought in Aceh in Sumatra, Indonesia during the WWI. After Indonesia he worked as a mounted policeman in Amsterdam, one of the toughest Dutch cities. World War II took its toll, and he withdrew from his family. Isolating himself and affected by the hunger winter he had leapt to his death. My parents, upon returning from the war, would live in that upper room as part of their living quarters and not have money to go elsewhere.

I hated my grandfather for doing that. I wondered how he had felt, making that decision. How could anyone do that? Marinus, Christa, and I lived in that room upstairs. Its walls kept a secret. Maybe that's why I remember not being happy. I too became depressed early on.

I never knew him, my grandfather, but I would often sit in his big chair in front of the window he had looked through. I was told he played the mandolin and often sang songs. The photographs portray him as a handsome and gentle soul.

After years of despair, war, and uncertainty my father didn't know how to grieve. Dad internalized his emotions. He had to process the loss of his dad, followed by the death of his first child, my sister Gisela after birth, compounded by the rejection and anger of him and his German wife by the people in Rotterdam. His stress and anger mounted. Twenty years would go by before he spoke of his father's death. Our family consciously or subconsciously internalized his outburst of anger. The years of not speaking with his mother and siblings about the suicide of his father, not knowing how it happened, lingered as a quiet shame moved from one generation to the next.

The result of people wounded by war becomes a generational wound. In Christian religion referenced as the Sin of the Fathers (and/or Mothers) moving through seven generations. However, what would we, the next generation have known about our grandfather, his traits, his sayings, his love, his being if the dogmatic rules of the Catholic church had not shoved all that into silence. A silence that condemned those who suicided.

My mother directed her grief and displacement from her country of birth to herself and became depressed. Today, we recognize this as post-traumatic stress disorder. There were no words or understanding of this disorder then.

My father's life relived his own parenthood. His responsibilities as a father would reach further than he could ever imagine then. After his illness, he never expected to live beyond forty.

My father had become a dad in bombed out Rotterdam living on the same floor, in the very room his own father isolated himself during the war. Where else could my parents have gone, without a job, money, or a house? They turned to family.

As an adult, I contemplated the rejection that existed in the marriage of my grandparents. I thought about the years of not speaking about the suicide, or for that matter not speaking about my grandfather much at all. I witnessed how my dad pondered the bad marriage of his parents because of the Catholic no divorce rule. It occupied him till his final days.

I, too, wondered about rejection in life, not only rejection of others but also self-condemnation, unresolved trauma, and grief.

Was it true that this wound and its shame is generational? The whisper of a quiet downward spiral?

I hung up a picture of my grandfather thinking maybe it could heal some of that rejection. I can tell people about him and release the anger I had for killing himself. I learned about his job with the mounted police in Amsterdam, where he kept demonstrators in check. Before Amsterdam he served in Aceh as a *Huzaar* in the East Indies, the country where I would find myself living in Borneo for a while.

I look at his picture, and in my mind's eye I see him sitting in that big chair, astride his horse, playing the mandolin, smoking a cigar. I see his face in my dad and my uncles.

Something inside of me has always yearned for a man like *Opa*; I looked for him in every man I dated. Maybe I internalized my father's unspoken longing for him along with his grieving anger. However, neither do I forget that glitter of hope and dad's positive outlook, possibly sparked by the suicide of his father.

In Rotterdam, a port of entry for many, two young people reconciled opposing cultures, religious values, political views, and family background to begin a new life. They started their own family and hoped for better. The war was over. Each day Marinus walked home from work instead of taking the tram.

"*Komm Baby*, let's go for a walk, and get a Dutch herring," he'd tell Mom.

He'd ask for a salty fresh one while she, my mom, pointed to a sour pickled one.

OMA'S HOUSE

1949–1953

Opa and Oma van Zanten

To know an old city, you must live in an old house. One
built on wooden heipalen studded piles that reach deep
into the soil. Walking up the long stairwell you hear the
old wood crack under your feet. You sense the secrets
absorbed in the walls. You haul coals to heat one room.
In the WC, a waft of sewer surrounds you. No shower or
bathtub is in sight. This opens the ancient, the history of
a people inside of you.

I needed to remember my beginnings, that sense of
Rotterdam Dutch. Rebuild my sanity and identity.
Together with my cousins, some of whom lived on the
fifth floor in Rotterdam West, I set out to learn more

about Oma, Opa van Zanten and their children. The mystical family at which interaction my cross-cultural experience began.

Old houses on the *Mathenesserweg* of the city of Rotterdam had big white numbers painted on their roofs and walls. Bomber pilots during WWII avoided these civilian areas. Families covered their windows and dimmed their inside lights. The chaos after the end of the war ignited the muscle of the Rotterdam people. They stomped forward into the future. Rubble and broken hearts did not allow time for pause. Their wounds caused by the Nazi war machine oozed unnoticed.

Trams thundered through our shopping street. They transported people to the inner city. I felt the house tremble a bit. A tiny room with two small roof windows on the fifth floor of Oma's house became our space. My Oma, a clairvoyant, laid cards. When the future showed dark, she sadly put the stack away. Opa spent time in deep depression in these quarters during the war. The hunger winter at the end of the war caused Opa's edema. His body swelled from the scarcity of food. He slept under newspapers. We lived in the quarters under the roof he later jumped from and died. These family roots, the inner-city heart destroyed by the *Blitz Krieg* fire, our family now coming together, all persuaded my mom and dad to reject an offer. An invite to move to America by their US army friend Davis. They had worked for him in Germany. Ma was scared to go.

"Out of the way—it is the *kolenboer*," someone yells from downstairs. A man with a black face and cloth on his head stomps up our stairs. Bent over, he carries a jute bag on his back. He is out of breath. Ma opens a door in the hallway. Loudly he deposits the coals on the floor of that closet. A cloud of black dust fills the area. He goes down and hauls up another one. Enough coal to heat both Oma's and our *kachel*.

Our little bedroom held a metal double bed. We shared a kitchen with a table. A small metal tub on top of it bathed the babies. Dad crafted our first furniture from empty fruit crates rounded up in the Rotterdam harbor. There was no shower let alone a bathtub. A white-painted square metal sink stuck next to the stairwell under the roof window. It supplied cold water.

The Roman Catholic Saint Nicolas Church rang its bells to call for Mass. The Catholic patriarchal power structure permeated the van Zanten family. It dictated childbirth, marriage, chosen friends and life choices. Some cousins stated "*Opa* suffered from religious schizophrenia after he returned from serving as a soldier in Aceh on the island of Sumatra." Opa served as a *Huzaar*, a soldier during WWI in that Dutch East Indies colony.

I hesitated to relate it to his Catholic dogmatic belief, though religion can become an escape of trauma. Diagnostics in psychology then had not integrated post-traumatic stress disorder. Even today, the trauma experienced by soldiers returning from war atrocities is complex. WWI violence in Aceh, Indonesia, and his occupation with the police in often brutal Amsterdam may have mounted his anxiety. Later Nazi Germans sent off four of his sons into forced labor to unknown destinations throughout Europe. Enough to give up hope. A hunger winter followed. Nazis had blocked transportation of food to West Coast cities like Rotterdam and Amsterdam. His two youngest are sent off to the south of Holland to survive on food from farmers in exchange for work. It is more than enough to turn a gentle soul into psychosis. Thousands, living in the city, died of hunger.

All van Zanten's children survived the war and returned home. Numb they received the news about their dad. I think: "Holy Mary pray for us; Saint Joseph and Guardian Angel protect us."

A row of tall, elegant houses much like cracker boxes surrounded our house. From our busy street, a straight, dark stairway led to the fourth floor to my grandmother. Bicycles, groceries, baby carriers, cooking petroleum and garbage had to be hauled up and down the stairs.

My heart beats funny going up the stairs. When I cough a few times, it beats normal again. Out of breath Ma and I arrive at the entrance of Oma's living quarters. Ma carries the bags with rationed groceries. I look up and see the wooden coat rack. Oma's hats. My Oma is a hatmaker. She likes big hats like those worn by Dutch Queens, Wilhelmina and Juliana. "Hallo ich habe Roggebrot gefunden" she says in German while standing in Oma's hallway. She found some bread, dark bread. Ma seams tense upon arrival.

The bell rings. I am scared when Oma pulls a rope upstairs that reaches all the way down to the street door. The house door opens so everyone and his dog can enter the door downstairs. I peek down into the dark stairwell, but do not recognize who's down there. A tall figure walks up the stairs. Finally, when he's very close, just behind the stained-glass door of the third floor, I recognize him. It is Uncle Wil and not some bad person. He makes me laugh. I'm going to hide in my cave.

I spend much time sitting in my cave right under that white metal sink next to the stairs coming up from Oma's floor. I can see everyone coming and going up and down the stairs—not many come. I wait here for my dad to come home. He is late. He walks home from work instead of taking the tram to save ten cents.

It was at two years old while sitting under the sink that I began to become a mother. From my vantage point, I noticed everything. I also became a dreamer. I connected to my parents' life force and their needs, their feelings of unsolved grief, isolation, and depression. Their emotional needs mingled with the angry German-hating Rotterdam population. My own feelings slowly spiraled inward. Shame about who I am sets in. I would have to pay a high price for that later in life when tragedy struck, and I didn't have a wall of my own to lean on.

In my mid-thirties I began the big task of unlocking these feelings, bringing them up from that deep chamber. "Who am I?" I asked myself. I faced my fears and the forces of anger, isolation, depression, which had mingled with those of my folks, the family, and those of the people in Rotterdam. It created the essence of my destiny. I began to see a larger world, its various cultures and people. The cells in my body still hold these stories, the ugly spirits and trauma of a generation after war. Ma apologized to me. "I did not eat well during my pregnancy with you Inge. I often gave priority to save money for a better future."

It is cold under the sink. I hear the wind and rain splash against the roof and window. Ma washes clothes. She does not have enough soap. It is scarce. I see her wash all people's clothes, ours, Oma's clothes, and those of Oma's two children Tante Toos and Oom Leo, who live downstairs. Ma washes them by hand. I see Ma often upset and confused when it comes to Oma.

Oma was a wide hipped heavy-set woman. Fierce blue eyes express either happiness or anger. Birthing twelve children, her body looked like that of Queen Wilhelmina. The long hallway from the living room to the kitchen she walked even paced and calm. From the kitchen, the aroma of soup cooked all day on a *petroleumstel,* with its wick and oil. The kitchen had a small table, a ceramic blue and white coffee grinder on the wall. A big ceramic pot held salt. The sink's cleaning rag smelled on account of lack of soap. Slowly meat, butter and bread had become available again.

Oma and all van Zanten's had flair and dignity. We had royal aspirations. The family had a saying they lived by "to stand tall as if we had a guilder on our forehead when even with only a nickel in our pocket. Marinus, your shoes need repair. You need to stay home from school today."

Dad makes Ma buy the most unusual hats, I think they are funny and the green one looks like a flowerpot. German people wear hats too, they are different from Dutch hats and have feathers stuck in them. Dad wears a hat also. It makes him look like a detective.

The artistic Friesian and French heritage from Oma's side permeated the living room. The decorated ceilings, the small French cupboard, two Asian blue vases all had style. She spent most of her time in the large front room with the two big windows. A mirror installed on the outside of each window helped us to see people walking in the streets. Oma could spot who rang the bell.

I like to sit in the big chair. Opa's chair. I can check the little mirror and see people outside, but I can also see the whole living room, Oma and two plants. The piano next to me sounds happy and loud.

The black piano, pulled up to the fourth floor with a rope and moved through those windows, now stood against the wall in the living room. *Oom* Wil, my dad, *Oom* Leo, *Oom* Jan and maybe *tante* Toos played piano. Behind a wallpapered door, Oma stored a big stack of *Klavarskribo* sheet music. It guided the grownups through fabulous self-taught music. Oma had no problem with noise when her grandchildren hammered away on the piano. In this room *Opa* used to play the mandolin. "*We zijn huzaren, we zijn huzaren, rood wit en blauw,*" my dad sings, a Dutch Aceh march *Opa* sang with his children too.

Freshly brewed tea in an aluminum pot smelled strong. A metal tea light powered by a battery kept it warm. French style carved flower ornaments adorned the corners of the high ceilings. My great grandfather had lived here also. "He helped create the old gable of the bank on the Coolsingel in Rotterdam." Oma proudly shared. The arts, be it drawing, music or woodcarving had a natural space in the home. Family visited around Oma's dining table. I could hear them laugh and talk when I listened from inside my cave upstairs. I hoped they'd come and visit us also; they did not.

On birthdays we'd all gather in Oma's living room. Then she'd say to another adult "Hold yourself by your word, little children have big ears." They stopped talking then about something interesting. During these family gatherings Oma's grown children conducted shows with singing and presentations for the family and offspring. These family acts by six-foot tall men with rolled up trousers as a joke, surrounded them with laughter. The van Zanten's have a flair for performance and humor. Oma thrived with her family around. But when she did not feel good, she would say, "You must have something for your pickled sins."

The kitchen door is shut. Oma is out or her *humeur;* she then probably talked about someone behind those doors or didn't want to see us. Other times she'd disappear to one of her older children in Rotterdam and we didn't know whether she was upset or not. Rumor has it that there was no lack of gossip.

Mom doesn't like her because of her moods and because Oma is upset that her son married a Mof. I love my Oma, she listens. I think I'm her favorite. On Sunday after church, she gives the

adults a chocolate while kids get a candy. Oma gives me a choco-
late. She and I go to the slightly dark middle room with that tall
wide brown closet with many drawers.

"I used those drawers for the kids to sleep in when they were
small," she says. Even though Oma birthed twelve children, I
don't really think she did not have enough money to buy them a
bed and instead put them in the wooden drawers. Yet something
inside of me thinks she could have put babies in them at times.
In one of those drawers, she keeps a little metal box. "That's your
Uncle Wil's long black braid of hair from when he was young."
She and Uncle Wil are close.

A Catholic cross with Jesus nailed on it hangs in her bedroom.
I usually see the cross first, then her bed. I walk past her bed to the
two large windows in that quiet bedroom. I kneel and stare way
down into the inner court with all its yards and white numbers
from the war. I'm often lost in thought—dreaming. It's the quiet,
being alone, that makes me dream. My parents and the family suc-
cumbed from fear, anger and losses. I even crawled in my Oma's
bed once. It had been my initiative—but a feeling of I should not
have done so surrounded it.

Ma became pregnant and Pa started his fatherhood in this house
together with his brothers and sisters. Their first child, Gisela, died
two days after birth.

Gisela was perfect but died a few days after birth because she
fought the birth cord around her neck for too long. Dad collapsed
when she died. I think Gisela did not have a chance from the time
of conception. We lived in a bombed-out city without a heart.
Death surrounded us.

Gisela tried hard to live, but those mortal energies prevented it.
She had a perfect body, my Dad said, but she couldn't breathe with

that cord around her neck. I looked up the meaning of her name and found it to be an ancient German name meaning "pledge." In Wikipedia, under her name, it says: "It was a practice in the early Middle Ages for rival factions to offer a person, often a child, to each other as a pledge of peace." Had a similar pledge surrounded Gisela's death? Had she become the bridge to a little more peace within the family—some compassion?

I came along fast afterwards. How could I have been a child in all this confusion? They needed a parent. I became one. Well, not exactly. Somewhere in those first four years I began to be a mother to my mom. The relationship between dad and me was different, more as his favorite peer and even that is not the right word.

Ma and Pa did not have children for four years after me. "What's happening Marinus? Why is Christa not pregnant?" an in-law questioned. The Catholic faith dictated procreation. Soon Henk, my brother arrived. Forceps used by an inexperienced young doctor at that Franciscus Gasthuis Hospital damaged his brain. The arrival of Henk dug my "Mother wound" deeper.

I like to be a mother. It makes me feel big and secure. I am a mother to my mother, to my brother and my sister.

Today, if I don't watch it, I'll be a mother to you. It's a hook I must guard against like a dragon. It robs one from having equal relationships.

—〜〜—

Stateless for five years after arrival in Holland, Ma was lonely, depressed and a stranger in a new land. At times while grocery shopping, people would yell, "Go home to your country *Mof.*" I do not recall playing with my young cousins living on the same floor. Visits to *Tante* Corrie Huygen became out of the ordinary. She welcomed my German Ma and even had a little play kitchen set ready for me to play with. We visited *Tante* Corrie. She did not visit us at home, nor did I have toys.

Dad worked long hours six days a week. I think Dad worked so hard because his colleagues knew he had married a *Mof*. His boss did not like *Mofs* so he worked doubly hard to maintain his position. "Van Zanten, it is better you do not come to the office party with your German wife," his boss told him.

Dad could not celebrate my birth at work by passing out cigars and *beschuit met muisjes,* as is a Dutch custom. He had a child of a *Mof.* I can imagine the humiliation and emotional confusion Ma felt lying in Saint Franciscus Gasthuis Catholic run hospital with a perfectly healthy baby. She had only Dad, not her own mother or any family, no celebrations, or congratulations. Most of the family, their neighbors and the entire city of Rotterdam rejected my parents. In contrast, a few beds away, Mia, my cousin was born a couple of days earlier surrounded by family and other visitors.

Yet, better times peaked around the corner. Ma spoke a few more Dutch words. We moved to our own apartment in Overschie, a suburb of Rotterdam. The following years I was always outside. A fever for adventure, excitement and freedom rallied me out of a lonely "mother world." I remained the child of a *Mof,* yet subconsciously my search for freedom began its flow.

LIFE IN OVERSCHIE

1953–1962

"I prefer playing with boys. I find them less mean than the girls. Jose, she bit me in the nose last week and that did it. From now on, I join the boys on their bikes or across from the house in the field playing soccer. The games boys play are more adventurous anyway. They are not mean, although Bert kicks me sometimes real hard during soccer. I just can't hurt others I feel their pain. Boys like me because I am gutsy like them."

D AD CONTINUED TO WORK MANY hours to pay for our two-bedroom apartment. We'd go to bed, depending on age either at 8 or 8:30 at night. On the mantel above the coal stove that kept the small living room warm stood a large statue of Jesus with his red Sacred Heart. Before going to bed, all three of us had to get on our knees in front of that statue near the stove and say "The Our Father," followed by the protection plea to the Virgin Mary, her husband St. Joseph and the Archangel St. Michael.

My younger sister Ilse and I slept in the attic, which we entered by climbing a ladder connected to a square hole in the hallway ceiling. The attic had Dad's tools on one side.

I began sleeping in the attic around seven or eight years old and later my sister joined me sleeping in a double bed across of me. Henk slept downstairs on account of his epilepsy, but at times he too came upstairs because he felt left out. We'd all ended up in the double bed and draw pictures on each other's back.

"I am scared when lights are out. I can only look through that one open tile in the roof through which I can see the grey blue sky during the day. Now, at night the attic is pitch dark. Why don't we have a little lamp? What if I have to go to the bathroom? What happened to that huge spider above my bed yesterday? I'm afraid to get out of bed and in the dark find that hole in the floor and step out onto the ladder. Then the thunders are there, and that strong Northwestern Sea-wind blows and splashes its rain and wind smack against the tiles of my roof. It's cold. Thank G*d for the German featherbeds. I see shadows in the attic and strange lights coming from the open tile in the roof that make them move. The thunders even make the attic rumble.

Yesterday, Ma hung the laundry up in the attic because it rained outside. She was up there, and Pa and I were downstairs. Pa was being funny and took the ladder away and sang with a laugh "Ma can't get down anymore."

Ma, often in thought, didn't hear it and suddenly Ma stepped out of the hole up in the ceiling and fell on her back. She lay there for a while; I was so scared. She was angry at Pa. "leave me alone." She just laid there. She was OK.

Pa thinks scary things are funny. He likes to call me in a very angry voice and then when I get there, he'll give me a piece of licorice.

"Inge, come here immediately."

"What did I do now?"

"Here's some pocket money." He offered me five cents for licorice.

He also likes to play dead, and Ma and I think it is funny for a while, but if he doesn't wake up for a long time, Ma and I get scared.

"Inge *opstaan*," my Pa calls from downstairs in the morning. "Get up".

I try hard. I want to, but I am not in charge of my body. I see myself lying there in my bed with the heavy feather-filled cover tucked around me, unable to move my legs or hands. Slowly I connect as I watch my hands and fingers for a while until I have command over them. I do the same with my legs and my toes. Oh, it's light outside, I can see the sky beaming through the small tile opening, I'm happy. I am ready to go and hit the street again, feel the fresh air, to see that enormous sky. I pick up John and together, hand in hand we walk along the rotten fish—smelling Schie-canal, counting the dead fish floating in it, to the St. Maria Elementary School. We cross the water over a pull up bridge.

I dream many times of that bridge. In my dreams a tall dark man stands on the bridge and is waiting to grab me.

John and I pass St. Peter's Church. It has a kind Chaplain who sometimes comes to our house with water from Lourdes, France, to heal my brother Henk. I want some too. The priest passionately kneels next to him and gently holds Henk's head while his body goes blue and crooked. He pours the Lourdes water over Henk's head.

Henk was born four years after me. Dr. Bender, our family doctor had decided on a home delivery. Yet far into the birthing, Ma was rushed to the hospital where Henk was delivered with forceps by an inexperienced doctor. He damaged Henk's brains. Henk grew up with epilepsy and the right side of his body had paralyzed muscles which slightly improved over the years.

Yesterday Henk turned blue while I had him on my little bike. He collapsed on the ground. When he has a seizure his body goes real strange sideways and his hands and feet go strange, too. People came running from everywhere and they didn't listen to me.

"Leave him alone he'll come back to life," I scream. "He'll be all right."

Like I'm a nobody and stupid, they shoved me aside while they pounded his back like mad to make him breathe again. He was out of it all right. Yet soon Henk gave out this groaning that seems to come from deep inside of him. I had been waiting for that one to come—it meant he's coming back. All stand in silence as if not only Henk, but also all around him come back, too. It's over, he lies still like a mouse, slowly opening his eyes—who are all these people looking at him? I shove everyone aside and offer Henk my hand, "Get up Henk. We are going home."

Every Sunday I go to church. I often went on Saturday evening at seven as well, Pa told me so, for the services of the Monstrance (a receptacle in which the consecrated Host is exposed for adorations) … I like to sit in the front pew close to the big blue statue of Mary with her baby Jesus in her arms. I like the silence. It feels peaceful here. It's quiet and safe and it smells good, too. I like that smell of innocence, I mean incense. Too bad Mariette wouldn't go with me today. It makes me happy to show her this place. It's kind of my home; it belongs to me. Oh, and see there on the altar they bring some more incense and take the golden cloth cover off the shiny golden Monstrance. The white Host inside the Monstrance, behind the glass, that's Jesus. I don't want to think about that, because on Sundays, they give me the Host and I always think that I am chewing Jesus, so I chew softly—and carefully mix it with my spit, not biting down, just enough so I can swallow. The boys from my school are on the altar and loudly ring the bells. Lights go on. Strong smoke surrounds the Monstrance. It keeps hanging around.

I breathe in a lot of it. Suddenly, a dark thing, a mouse, scurries across the altar.

Everywhere are brightly burning candles. For long periods I squint my eyes looking at them, creating beautiful figures.

SCHOOLDAYS

"You stand there in the hall and think about where you were yesterday afternoon."

Mind you, I couldn't have been older than eight. Yes, for days on end he'd made me stand there in that hallway just because Ma had kept me home one afternoon. It was against Dutch law to keep your child at home.

The Headmaster of our elementary school, Mr. Bohré, obviously hated all Germans and me, an offspring, too. The stigma of being part German followed me throughout my childhood. While in elementary school, teachers either really liked me or hated me. Those who hated me because I was part *Mof* mistreated me in every way possible.

I cannot remember having a nice teacher except my first and fifth grade teacher. Mr. de Klerk, in my fifth grade, always spanked the boys hard with a long stick. Thank G*d I wasn't a boy. Another teacher Mr. Dijkstra at our Catholic school was mean also and we had to open our hand so he could hit us with a ruler. He also pulled kids ears to get their attention. He came close to me because I was doodling on everything, dreaming of things I could be doing. Regardless of professional conduct or pangs of conscience, the hate of many around me popped out. Despise oozed from their inner wounds of war. Mr. Bohré rather brought me down than assisted me in any form to move forward.

And again, I felt guilty for being part German. In fact, when questioned about my own mother, I was puzzled by the atrocities committed by Germans against the Jews. How could humans change to become monsters creating gas chambers and labor camps?

My parents' emotional absence, Dad's authoritarian behavior, and Henk's epileptic attacks, as well as being a "mother" had drained all my energy by the time I entered high school. Our anti-German headmaster tried to convince my parents I was not high school material and advised I should go to a homemaker's school instead, you know, where you learn to cook and sew. They wisely chose not to follow his advice.

When I behaved as a child or tried to be the child I was during daily time spent in the streets, I did dangerous things. I hung around with those kids who were on the edge. I needed thrills. All I knew were the anxious feelings from my brother's eleven-a-day epilepsy attacks, my mother's depression and many a day soaked in parents not speaking to each other. They were overloaded with making it after the war and dealing with Henk and the unspoken hidden emotion of grief from the huge losses they individually carried.

"Ma, why don't you be good with Dad again," I begged her in the kitchen. She was angry and wouldn't be good with him.

Then I'd go to Dad. "Pa why don't you speak with Ma again; it's already three days."

Sometimes they would make up when I asked them to and the same night Ma would be upset, she had given in and the whole darned thing started over for another few days of the silent treatment.

One week Pa got so mad and wanting to be funny he took her by the arms and put her outside on our balcony off the kitchen. He locked the door.

I feel how mad Ma is because she can't yell for embarrassing herself with the neighbors. Dad is laughing, yet I don't think it is funny at all. It feels just like when he takes me by the hand and puts me in our small bathroom when I talk back to him. Dad says I am a hysteric. I hate standing there in that bathroom for so long just like Ma on that balcony. Dad says Ma is hysteric also and compares her with my quiet Aunt Hilde who is in an asylum in Noordwijkerhout because of the war and all she had to witness, and experienced including being engaged to Egon Mayer, a Jewish man.

Sometimes when we have our own opinions and he gets angry, Pa threatens to bring Ma and me there too, that scares me. People there are strange and behave crazy. They smoke fast and wobble back and forth on their chairs. They even scream. Ma confronts Pa about that one "I never say anything negative about your father's suicide." That was the end of it. He never called us hysteric anymore.

Hi, Ma," I yell coming home from school. Ma's doing the laundry and I help her squeeze it through the wringer. Ma has lots of laundry because Henk's not dry yet due to the epilepsy attacks. With each one he wets himself.

Leaning forward I push the handle with both of my hands while the water splashes into a big sink and my dress gets soaking wet. I help her hang it on the clothes lines off the balcony and sure enough our neighbor steps out into her garden below our balcony. She looks up and yells: "Why don't you go home to your own country, dirty Mof?"

She never yells while my Dad is at home, always during the day. She's nice to my little brother and Dad, but not to Ma. I call that woman "Ma Butt." Dad says she doesn't come out of our class of people.

I like to play outside till I have to go to bed at eight. I made a new friend, and she took me home and her dad asks about what kind of work my Pa does. I tell him my Pa sells grinding wheels from England and that my Ma is from Germany. He answers,"Oh so your Ma is a Mof." Then he tells me about what the Moffen did in Holland, while his voice changes. I can feel his anger. I tell him,"I need to go home now."

I was too young to carry or defend myself against the collective hate that existed in Holland after the war. Naturally this weight of anger all around us, combined with the isolation from her family and culture, pushed down Mam's and my sense of identity. It contributed to my challenges with unworthiness later as well.

I like the kids from the halfway house. I feel sorry for them that they don't have a family. One of them is from Germany and I take her German magazines and sometimes German food from home—Ma doesn't like me to hang out with her, because she is older and too experienced. My new German friend told me that one of her friends would escape from the halfway house and hitchhike somewhere. I was very curious, and we joined her to the freeway that week to see how a car stopped and they took off. I too want to take risks. I like to see how fast I can go, running, biking, playing soccer, you know up till when you don't think anymore and go really fast."

The bell rings at our upstairs, second floor apartment. A dirty man makes his way upstairs and begs for food and a drink. Ma's a little scared. Ma walks to the kitchen to fetch him a glass of milk.

She tells me, "Stand there at the door so he will not come into our apartment."

Different people come and go through our street … There is the milkman delivering our milk every day, then there is the man with his bicycle and cart to deliver bread, and weekly "*de schille-boer*" the "peels farmer" yells loudly to alert us to his presence. His cart for compost he pushes with the attached bicycle. People save their potato, vegetable, and apple peels for him. Every Friday the "*Mosselman*" comes through as well. He yells too and sells fish, especially "*scholletjes*," a flat small flounder that's our favorite but expensive. Ma buys fish each week at the market, straight from the harbor. Everyone knows Ma because she has such a thick German accent.

In Overschie there is an Indonesian woman, one who knew, because of her culture and color, about discrimination. Her Asian culture began to mix with my already complex cultural German-Dutch lack of identity. I see her while taking care of Henk and Ilse. At eight years old I walk Ilse around in the baby wagon while Henk wobbles next to me. "You are like a little mother; the Asian woman would say.

Mom befriends her. Call me Aunt Enny, she says to me in a soft-spoken gentle voice. I feel special when I visit her.

A FOSTER MOM FROM THE DUTCH EAST INDIES

1956–2008

Enny Rooseboom and
Ingeborg van Zanten Hayes

E NNY WAS ALWAYS COLD IN Holland and missed her father, the Javanese food, the tropical climate, her *Indië*. She had
nightmares about her dad and suffered severe headaches throughout her life. I knew her dad had been in a Japanese concentration
camp. Her mom, a quiet and traditionally dressed Javanese woman, would soon follow her to the Netherlands.

Enny belonged to a line of Dutch aristocrats from her father's
side. He, a Rooseboom and related to a former military governor,

fathered her, an only child, with a Chinese woman while married to his Javanese wife. His wife raised her as her own and Enny had a marvelous happy childhood.

Enny was born in Tandjong Pura, Mid Batavia of the Dutch East Indies. Later that name Batavia was changed into Java, the largest island in Indonesia. *Indië,* also called Dutch East Indies was the former name of what now is Indonesia. In Holland we'd refer to the Dutch East Indies as Indië. The Dutch began their colonization in 1621.

Chinese Indonesians were discriminated against in Indië. That discrimination followed her into Holland. "Poop Chinese," is what many called her. She'd be singled out because of her color. Teenagers snatched her purse in busy shopping centers several times.

Enny arrived exhausted in our cold and small "country of frogs" after a month-long trip on the military transport ship the "Kata Baru." At twenty-four years old in 1946, she had to leave her mother behind for a new country where she'd marry a Dutch Marine. The Dutch colonizers were thrown out of Indie. Enny's father was Dutch. Some Dutch who wanted to stay because of marrying an Indonesian woman or other reason could do so but would lose their land and possessions. Enny's father had died in a Japanese concentration camp on Java. She left Java after meeting Aad her future husband.

Her Dutch middle class in-laws living in the centuries old city of Delft would be against the cross-cultural relationship. "She's too aristocratic and doesn't fit with us."

The lonely sea trip packed with people leaving the East Indies was extra slow because of the mines in the sea. On the way through the Suez Channel, all passengers received new and warmer clothing for Holland. Enny, because of her teaching background, was expected to take care of the many children aboard. Upon arrival of the ship in Rotterdam all people were sent by busses to different parts of the country. Enny ended up living next door to us in Overschie.

At eight years old I was lonely like her. She manifested wisdom, patience and an elegance of body and soul that those born in Dutch East Indies typically possess.

Ma and I visited her. They each must have felt as outsiders in Holland; Enny, besides being a different color was Chinese Indonesian, thus different from the other Indonesian people living in the Netherlands and Ma considered a German *Mof.*

I walked her dog Tjoepie and bought that strange dried-up fish for her cats.

Ma doesn't like animals inside the house. Tante En's house smells different, a little bit stinky from the Trassi, that Indonesian shrimp paste she uses to cook food. Ma says she makes the best Soto Ayam-soup in the world.

"How about getting me some stockfish for the cats, *Meis?*"
I loved when she'd call me *Meis,* it was nickname for "sweet girl."
"Can I take Tjoepie along?"
"You're like a little mother with that carriage with Henk and Ilse in it, *Meis.*" She praised me often. Sometimes, I did something wrong and she'd warn me with that Indonesian stop word: " *Adoe,* leave it alone, *Ingeping,*"

Aunt Enny, would become my foster mom—my *ibu Angkat*— as they nowadays would say in the new Indonesian language. She spoke with a soft voice to me with that Dutch-Indonesian accent *Indo*'s had. She became another one of the many divine helpers in my life.

Mom and Dad became close friends with them. Often Enny and her husband, Aad, had parties where people would sit on the ground and tell jokes.

"Let's burn some incense, a lot of people will come tonight." Many of their friends were Jewish, some were even divorced. That was a big deal in my strict Catholic family. We didn't know anyone who was divorced.

Uncle Aad and Aunt Enny went on vacation to faraway places like the North Pole and New Zealand. They even went to Australia. They'd go on vacation alone, each by themselves, sometimes. Ma thought that was unacceptable in a good marriage. Pa and Ma did everything together, including the shopping on Saturdays and all vacations as well. I didn't mind Enny and Aad sometimes went separately.

The Dutch East Indies was a large Dutch colony and many colonists left in 1946 after World War II and the Japanese occupation. The country gained independence from Holland and in 1948 the name of the Dutch East Indies changed into the Republic of Indonesia with Soekarno as their new president. Their motto became *Bhinneka Tunggal Ika* (Diverse yet unified.) People had to choose between Dutch or Indonesian citizenship after 1954. If they chose Dutch they were forced to leave for Holland where many of them, well educated, found work in The Hague, the seat of the Dutch government. If former colonial landowners chose to stay in Indonesia they'd lose entitlement to their land.

The now forbidden Dutch language became *Bahasa Indonesia*, which would unite all the different dialects spoken throughout the largest archipelago. *Bahasa*, a grammatically easy to learn language, has singing soft and sharp tones that correspond well with Indonesia's Gamelan traditional music, dance, and puppet storytelling.

Their schools, modeled after the Dutch, became open to all citizens, rich and poor, instead of the privileged upper class during the Dutch colonization.

In 1979, while living in Indonesia with my family, I'd be embarrassed to find out that local people in Jakarta during colonized time would fall on their knees when a Dutch official would drive by in the main street. I wondered how my own grandfather as a soldier in World War I, had done on the large island of Sumatra fighting in the Muslim city of Aceh, a longtime problem area.

—⚬—

Enny's dad, born in Friesland, a province in the Netherlands, died on Java during World War II in a concentration camp run by the Japanese occupants who had invaded the Dutch East Indies. Her dad had owned a tea plantation on mid Java and married a Javanese woman there. Plantation owners who decided to leave for the Netherlands lost all their belongings to the new government of Indonesia. Her dad had passed away and her mom too lost the plantation. In Holland *tante* En belonged to an organization for children from old plantation owners.

My Indonesian Aunt En and I began a soul friendship that proved to last a lifetime. She became my foster mom. Our visits became a repeated ritual where through her sensitivity my feelings opened. I'd walk to her place; I knew it was time for a visit. "*Dag lieve Meis, kom binnen,*" she welcomed me inside her home. Both she and I knew it was time, time for a visit.

Like a faucet you open, tears began to roll. I didn't know why I was crying just that I had to. Enny didn't push for answers; she just encouraged me to cry and said that it was all right.

Balanced after the tears, our "real visit" began. "*Laat maar gaan Ing*," let it go, she'd say. She understood. My feelings had become too big and with her I didn't need words. I had none. I was incapable of translating my feelings into words. Not many at home had time to speak with me much less realize the emotions I carried. Meeting with Aunt Enny in this manner became a habit. She did not help me with many words, her calm and gentle presence became enough.

After a few years she moved from Overschie to Delft, an old Dutch town with notable history. She lived in a large typical Dutch house with small rooms and an inner court, in a narrow street. Exiting her short street were many canals.

People like painter Vermeer and Willem van Oranje had lived in Delft. Willem was shot in the 15th century. The "New" Church overlooking the main square harbored floors consisting of tombs containing Dutch royalty. Though called new, that church was many centuries old.

"Here Ing, a guilder, some money so you can climb the tower of the New Church. Come back when you're done to say goodbye and eat some food."

At ten years old it was an adventure for me to ride my bike from home to Delft and pay her a visit. The eight-mile trip was on a secondary road with on one side the freeway and on the other side of me were green meadows with cows.

"Let's go to the Indonesian "*Toko*", Indonesian take home food store, and get food and fresh *Sambal Batek*." There she'd make sure I'd visit with the cook, an old woman who'd be busy in the kitchen.

I smelled that typical stinky *Trassi* smell again. "Be sure to shake her hand and say goodbye when we leave the *Toko*." Older people from Indonesia seemed to be treated as more important than the younger ones I learned.

"This is crazy. You can't keep ducks and birds here all the time. There are shelters." Aad, her husband, would say. "We have paid enough to the animal hospital." Enny, a wildlife activist, co-founded the committee for protection of threatened animals and often spoke on the radio. Besides her cats and dog Tjoepie, she cared for wounded ducks and birds. All walked freely around the living room. There, Aad, her husband, let Tjoepie lick his face or ears and sit in his lap.

"Inge, Tjoepies and all dogs' mouths are much cleaner than yours," he'd say when I looked all grossed out.

The interior of her house saluted the origin of her dad with a huge traditional Friesian clock, its sides draped with two sea mermaids. With a deep tone the clock announced each half hour. A picture of a Rabbi, bought from a college student in Israel, stood out as an icon. Her house felt different with batik drapes, pictures of her Dutch dad and Indonesian mom and that Indonesian smell. A birthday calendar overflowing with names hung in her bathroom. In that same bathroom, next to the toilet stood a green *botol* (bottle with water) a culturally different way of cleaning. I found most Indonesians in Holland had a *botol* too, and while I lived in Indonesia later on, I'd be caught in bathrooms with *botols* and no toilet paper as was the custom.

Tante Enny became a positive force for me. Her empathy unlocked the cropped-up feelings of my life at home. There all attention went to my brother who had epilepsy and was physically challenged. The marriage of Mom and Dad was often full of tension.

"Let me feed the cats first, I'll make you some tea." Cats and dogs, the Indonesian smell and Enny's calm and sweetness surrounded me. She became a role model for me.

Then one day my Mom and Dad withdrew and broke off the friendship. I was still young, a teenager, and was devastated. They were upset as well. "Why are they angry, Ing?" she'd ask. "What happened?"

I just didn't know. "Why Mom? Why aren't you friends anymore?" I asked.

I'm upset with Aad for treating his wife wrong and tired of all the animals she brings along."

But maybe, it happened because Dad suddenly got up and kissed Enny in the living room. She had come to visit. Ma got some coffee and cookies in the kitchen and in an upwelling of inappropriate passion, while I sat there witnessing it, Pa got up and gave her a big kiss on the mouth. That's all that happened.

Determined I took my bike and peddled the well-known road to Delft. "Please Aunt Enny let us stay friends."

We did for the rest of my life.

At fifty-six while living in Texas I received a phone call from Aunt Enny's French and German language teacher. Enny had passed away three months after my own Mom had died. A closet had fallen over her and crushed my tender foster mom at the age of eighty-six in Delft, the Netherlands. I was in shock.

Her husband died some years before. He had prepared all paperwork for Enny including their will with assistance by their long-time accountant. Enny had started battling depression. She had received home visits from a social worker and medicine to help her, up until her death.

"I'm so glad about your letters, Ing, I read them over and over again. Please forgive me for not writing. I just can't."

During that time Enny had met a young Indo, who was familiar with plantation owners living in Holland. They befriended each other. Together they had begun changing her finances. At those times she was always worried about not having enough money and preoccupied with the lists of distribution of her assets he asked her to make.

It became a daily occupation, almost like a job. The long-trusted accountant was set aside and she entitled the young friend to be her executor.

—⚮—

The police in Delft ruled her death an accident. From Texas I contacted them and expressed my suspicion. Had she fallen pray at the end of her life? While most of her estate would go to charity organizations as she had wished, and the executor led the funeral with respect, he soon went on vacation to Australia. Was there integrity or was she taken advantage of?

While she had mentioned years before that she and Aad had left me a little something in their will it was omitted in the later one. The large multi-story house was sold by the executor. I don't know if anyone received insight into the will. Not being her *legal* foster child, I didn't.

Aunt Enny, I long for you and can almost see your compassionate eyes, hear your soft voice pronouncing my name "Ing, sit down," continued with the gesture of putting a soft pillow behind my back. I miss your familiar surroundings, the Indonesian smell, your home and cooking. I miss the ringing of the Friesian clock and the drawing of the rabbi reading the Talmud.

I still have a few pictures, and then some things I brought from Indonesia myself. Yet I go to stores like World Market and seek out the Indonesian made merchandise to bring a little bit of you home.

Ik noem u Moeder	**I call you Mother**
Dank je wel lieve pleegmoeder.	*Thank you, dear foster mom.*
Dat was u al vanaf mijn	*That's who you were*
vierde jaar—in Overschie.	*from my fourth year in Overschie.*
Dank je wel voor je fijngevoeligheid.	*Thank you for your sensitivity,*
Voor alles wat je me geleerd hebt	*for all you taught me*
in de laatste 53 jaar.	*during fifty three years.*
U was er voor me,	*You were there for me,*
Uw ziel zo groot	*your soul open*
voor mensen, voor dieren,	*for people, animals*
voor planten, voor vrienden,	*for plants, friends*
en voor Uw pleegkind.	*and for me your foster child.*
Ik hoefde niets uit te leggen,	*No need to explain,*
U nam mijn verdriet weg.	*you took my sadness away.*
Eendjes en vogels huisden bij U	*Ducks and birds found a home with you,*
honden en katten van ver.	*dogs and cats from afar.*

Geen wonder dat ook ik

lieflijk werd omringd met uw

oneindige oerkracht.

Nu een stukje ook van mij,

Uw Indië, mijn Indonesië op
*   Borneo.*

Ook ik maak nu mensen bewust

van de jungles die verdwijnen.

Uw rustig tempo, nu ook van mij.

Uw volledige aanwezigheid,

is nu soms ook van mij.

Uw dieren,

hopelijk ook mijn dieren.

Uw, ja sorry, uw Sambal Badjak

nu ook mijn sambal.

Uw openheid, uw elegantie

nu ook een beetje van mij.

Uw uitgesprokenheiden

bovenal Uw trouw.

Nooit, ondanks alles, heeft U mij

nooit vergeten.

Er was blijheid en gastvrijheid.

Zelfs van zover tot in Texas.

Not a miracle that I too

became surrounded with your

primal strength.

Your Indië, my

Indonesia too with life on
*   Borneo.*

I too bring awareness

of disappearing jungles.

Your calm pace, also a little
*   mine now.*

Your full presence,

sometimes mine too.

Your animals,

I hope will become mine too.

Your Sambal Badjak, sorry,

now mine as well.

Your openness, your elegance

now a bit mine too.

Your directness,

above all your loyalty.

Through all, you never

forgot me.

There was happiness and welcome.

It extended as far as Texas.

Samen vakantie op Vlieland en

Weer was je er voor mij en

de kinderen.

Tante En op de fiets nog wel

Ja in een tent.

Na al die jaren met u als voorbeeld

Het Wereld Natuurfonds,

de verre reizen van U met Oom Aad

Uw lessen in Heeuwbreeuws, Duits,

Frans en Tai Chi.

Uw gesprekken op de radio en

Hard werk met the T.N.O.

Door Uw levenskeuzes uw lieve stem

en volledige aanwezigheid,

werd ik groter in mijn zijn als vrouw.

Ik ben dankbaar en trots Uw
    pleeg te zijn

voor altijd.

Nu is het aan mij

Uw oerkracht door te geven.

Ik kijk in uw ogen op foto's

en zie de diepte van uw ziel.

Uw tederheid voor alles dat leeft.

Together on vacation to Vlieland,

again, you were there for me

and the children.

Tante En on a bike...

Yes, in a tent.

I received years of your example

activist for The World Wildlife
    Fund,

the travel of you and Oom Aad,

lessons in Hebrew, German,

French and Tai Chi.

Your talks on the radio and

work with T.N.O's international
    faculty.

Your choices, your sweet voice,

your presence

enhanced me as a woman.

I feel grateful to be your foster

Always.

It is up to me now to

share your primal force and spirit.

I observe your eyes in pictures

and see the depth of your soul.

Your tenderness for all that lives.

U raakt mijn hart.	*You touch my heart.*
Ik hou van U.	*I love you.*

Uw Meis, Ingeping en Uw pleeg.

Tante En never wanted to go back and visit her country.

"Let's go together. Together we can handle it. We can also go to Kalimantan, where I lost John." "No, Ing, I want to keep the memories."

It became clear to me that such a return would open a wound in her too large. It would destroy the good memories of her childhood. We explored other places we might go to together, Thailand and Vietnam. It was not destined to happen.

> *I also don't want to live in my place of birth, the Netherlands anymore, too much pain to hold, although I consider Delft, and later Roosendaal where my mom and dad lived sacred places. As for Indonesia, I lost John, miscarried there while living in Kalimantan with Toby. If that wasn't enough my friend Ursula got brutally murdered in Bontang, the place we lived first. Yet, for now I just want to think about Enny's gift she gave me, being her emotional daughter. This heritage, and her Asian roots, shifted my longing and personality.*

Enny's love for animals, connection to the international faculty at the TNO, Netherlands Organization for applied scientific research, her leadership with the World Wildlife Fund, and her emotional presence engraved a deep desire to grow up and be like her. I would seek relationships including romantic ones with people of her color. I admired her weekly practice of Tai Chi. All her life she learned languages such as Hebrew, German, and French. Of course, she was fluent in English.

Later my life included living in Indonesia, her country of origin, and the country my grandfather served as a soldier in World War I. In America, I too chose to work at a university doing international work and spoke some on the radio. While I have instilled a love for animals in my children, something I so missed in my childhood at home, I have yet to become the activist she was in the World Wildlife Fund.

"It would make me very happy, Ing, if you'd become a member of the WWF. Have you done so already?" she encouraged me to contribute to the small area left as habitat for orangutans in Borneo. After my family and I lived there we learned that loggers destroyed their jungle habitat.

Aunt Enny often spoke against negligence of the Catholic Church during World War II when they didn't speak out against what happened in Germany.

She supported my walk with the Native Americans and learning their medicine. Long phone calls from Texas to Delft kept up her walk with my life: "I believe in that Ing, *vertel*, tell me all."

Like a parent she empathized with my life. Though as a child I physically grew up with my own folks, Enny with her loving presence sustained my emotional wellbeing. This balance was badly needed. There simply isn't enough time, focus and love from parents to go around when there is a challenged child in the family. Henk's challenges had spilled over into my life. Dealing with his epilepsy while I watched over him, evoked regular adrenaline rushes. These emotional charges, now a part of my life, later had to be matched. I looked for the edge, for adventures that brought me into that same current of life.

SKATING ON THIN ICE

"**M**A, HENK IS TURNING BLUE again." I yelled for her as his four-year-old body collapsed in the living room, while his face turned dark blue. It is quiet around him. His legs covered with dry fish scale skin pull up a bit. Ma rushes into the living room and kneels besides him. Henk is gone. His body now wretched in a cramp curved sideways. His hands and its fingers changed as if deformed; stretched to unnatural forms. I panic. On the inside I want to scream for this to stop. Instead, I sat there calmly next to him and Mam, waiting. I waited for the puddle of pee that always accompanied his *grand mal*. I longed for the sound of his big sigh that grasped for air when he came to again. What did I do wrong? Was I too loud? What excited him to bring this one on? He's back. Ma started the cleanup for the third time that day. Henk doesn't know what happened. Bewildered his questioning eyes looked around as if he just entered a new world. Then he looked at us, rolled over and got up. He calmly started to play.

"Ma I'm going outside to skate" I yelled. In my own way I too grasped for air, as I flung my skates over my shoulder and ran down the stairs to be outside.

I wrestled with the wind as the sharp and humid cold air cut against my face. I bowed my head to escape it. To balance I spread my arms sideways. Thus, I moved forward, one foot in front of the other, on my wooden skates. I tuned in to the sound the sharp steel blades underneath my skates. It was a clean, dull-sounding long scrape amidst the silence, a pitch that skaters recognize the world over. My thoughts wandered from the damp icy environment to

Henk at home and then again to the joy of skating. The images followed a sudden plunge into feelings of loneliness. That notion of standing alone was my friend.

At nine years old, I received the Dutch winters by testing the ice with friends on canals and ponds around Overschie. Rarely would the ice be strong enough that they closed the schools for a day of fun. On the ice, a sign read *Gevaarlijk ijs,* letters in red put there by the local government. Yesterday, a group of friends, most of them boys, threw big stones on the ice to see if they'd fall through. The *kwakkel* winters, keeping Holland around the freezing point are at times not cold enough to put sufficient ice on the canals.

"Who's going first?" Nervous, five of us hesitated. Some laughed out loud to hide fear.

"Een, twee drie." Wim stepped out on the ice first, a few steps along the side while softly jumping up and down.

"*Wie gaat er naar de overkant*? Hans, one of the older gutsy boys from the white village where the low-income people live volunteered to walk across. Hans' dad once came to the school and had a fist fight with Mr. de Klerk. the 5th grade teacher. Mr. de Klerk had hit his son because he talked too much in class, so his dad came for revenge.

"Hey, what about those spots with water on top?"

He made some skating moves with his old shoes and walked across. One watery spot interrupted his smooth show off as one foot went through the ice creating a hole. *Kut* another hole.

"Thanks a lot *Kloodzak*, like there aren't enough of those. Dickhead."

"John, I'm skating. It's an old sign they put out."

I parked myself in the frozen grass on the edge of the canal and put on my old-fashioned wooden skates. You know, those short ones, not the Friesian *doorlopers*, long distance ones, with a curl at the front. No, they were used on canals between towns in the northern Friesian part of Holland. Those required an exceptionally cold winter. For that people put out Dutch flags, made hot chocolate and the competition began. Newspapers and the radio followed each day of skaters en route to eleven Dutch towns, all connected by canals.

"How long will I be able to stay on them this time?" I acknowledged the anticipated nuisance of my shoes sliding sideways off the wood. The wooden platform of the skates had a sharp steel blade underneath to skate on. A leather strap in the front fastened my feet and a thin rope in the back, tied across my ankle, fastened my shoes. I either pulled the straps too tight so it would hurt my feet or every kilometer or so repositioned because my darned shoes had slipped halfway off the wooden skates. Yet, that is what my folks could afford and what most kids used.

"*Wakken,*" people yelled in front of me pointing out the holes while skating. Each winter newspapers told horror stories of kids who drowned in those holes on the ice. They had slipped beneath the ice surface. Adults would risk their lives to help children and often drowned themselves.

"Watch out for *wakken,* Inge." My parents warned often, creating a deep fear. I noticed they mostly occurred on the edge of the canal, so I skated in the middle.

There were quite a few of us, even some adults, and knowing them as my neighbors gave me a sense of security on the thin ice. Straight ahead in the distance I saw the bridge and two church towers. To the left stood the Protestant church one with a hen on its steeple, and on the right a Catholic one with on top a cross. The water underneath the ice I skated on flowed into a larger canal, which connected Rotterdam and the city of Delft. In the old days, when free of ice, horses on the road along the canal pulled boats all the way to Delft. There were quite a few windmills in the area since four rivers crossed here. Loading and unloading from boats was easy. The century-old mills took care of water overflow, while others were used for carpentry. Most of them milled wheat for the preparation of *jenever*, Dutch gin.

"*Uitkijken.*" Someone yelled, frustrated with my lack of concentration and manner of skating as if I were alone on the ice. Awake now, I looked around and compared my skating with others around me, I'm doing well. Many kids had a parent with them.

I wished my dad would be with me on the ice. I never understood why he never joined in with any of my activities. Maybe his experience during the war made him more cautious with his body. He told many stories of his dad and him going on the ice as a kid. Maybe he is tired, I reasoned. He worked hard. He wasn't home much. He liked to stay with mom. And of course, there was Henk, with his eleven times a day attacks to be looked after.

My thoughts didn't last long. Skating pulled me into the moment; it swept me up in the fun and excitement with the many on the ice. In front of me a man and his wife, with crossed arms elegantly skated in tandem.

"They love each other," I thought while my eyes followed them for a long time. There is Rita's mom and her friend. They have professional skates." I wanted some too. It was a beautiful scene much like Dutch postcards or paintings by Hendrick Havercamp of winter scenes 400 years ago.

Craaaaaack! … My thoughts and rhythmic motions, alternating legs smoothly sliding my skates backward, were interrupted by a sudden loud cracking of the ice beneath my feet. I immediately connected in my mind what had happened.

"Damn, they put the watermill on."

People began screaming in panic.

"Get off," people yelled as they quickly moved to the sides of the canal. Mixed feelings of fear, excitement and daring increased inside of me as my breath became shallow and my eyes focused on my surroundings, especially the ice. I noticed air forming beneath the ice, but continued skating. It fit my style to stretch my boundaries and feel the adrenalin rush I knew well from home, from the multiple epilepsy attacks that unannounced would transport my brother's consciousness to another planet and altered my comfort zone. I became gutsy, testing, a risk taker. Unaware, I played with a power that created adventures in areas others didn't dare to go. Yet as a young child these forces were undirected, wild and dangerous.

The ice began to look milky; cracks formed like a huge spider web. Clear spots showed that the water under the ice disappeared. The city had pumped the water from underneath the ice over the dike into the river located above.

Despite inner fear, I and one or two others continued skating, waiting, stretching for that last moment, curious how this would unfold exactly. Most others quickly skated toward the sides and jumped off the dangerous ice. Then I felt an inner warning as if I could hear my Dad yelling at me. "Inge, get off it."

I sped up and veered off to the side, jumped upward on my skates with a half-round twist of my body. It landed me on my butt in the frozen grass at the edge of the canal. Out of breath, my heart pounding loud inside, I observed in awe how the ice loosened from the sides and in the middle of the canal created huge sheets that came upward while simultaneously the ice collapsed into a void.

"Jesus, I just skated there."

Among the onlookers I noticed John, a school friend, a few meters away from me.

"Hey John, did you bring any cigarettes?" I hollered.

"*Ja*, I took a Pall Mall from my dad."

We hid behind a shed in a spot where my Ma could not see us from across the street. John shared some puffs. I didn't inhale, but John did. I walked home with my skates over my shoulder and a contented look dreaming about tomorrow.

After school my friends, mostly boys, all on our skates, made a chain across the delicate ice on a large pond next to the school. We took turns on who would have to be at the end of that chain, the spot where you'd go the fastest, there, where your arm and hand would be pulled to the point of pain while circling around with incredible speed until you couldn't hold on any longer. I loved that spot at the end, staying upright on my skates with all my might, feeling the air around me and totally in the thrill of the moment.

One day though we had to use several ladders to get one of us out of the water on the ice. An adult crawled over two ladders he had extended on top of the ice toward the boy who earlier messed around a water hole with sticks, poking the thin layer of ice around it. Unexpectedly he fell though. After some splashing around he now hung with his legs in the hole immersed in the cold water. He attempted to hold on to the slippery sides of ice around him with his arms. A few of us stood speechless on the frozen grass along the ice. I bit my nails and feared the worst, focusing on the boy's head and hoped it would not disappear into the water. Eventually the boy and the man crawled on the ladders and safely reached the shore. Relieved, the onlookers hurried home. *Ma shouldn't know about this; she was scared of all Dutch waters and couldn't swim. She was German and didn't grow up with the sea and canals around. No, she'd not let me go again if I'd tell her.*

My mood had changed. I trembled inside for that boy in the water. Wondered what his Ma would say when he arrived home. How could I possibly tell what happened? I decided not to. I rang the bell and walked up the concrete stairs to our apartment. Ma stood behind the gas stove in the kitchen.

"Inge," she sighed and shook her head. "Where have you been so long?"

I walked right past her without addressing her question. "Hoy Henk."

Henk scooted himself forward on the floor. He could move himself lying on his back. He pushed with both legs and bent his head backward. In the family he and I were close. He gave me a curious and understanding look that said, you're in trouble but you had fun, right?

"How did your feet get wet?" Ma yells.

"What?" Busy I moved right along to the living room, the only spot besides the kitchen stove with heat in the house. Taking off my sweaters and socks, I made my way to the coal stove. I got as close as I possibly could stand it with my frozen hands and toes. I knew when tingling sets in they'd soon recover to normal.

"Jesus, thawing my toes hurts."

During dinner I did not say a word and later helped out a lot until I had to go to bed in the attic. Dad was late and tired. He sat down to read the newspaper.

Each following day the ice showed larger puddles. The incident with the watermill had announced the thawing of the ice. I noticed ducks standing on the ice their feet wet. Winter backed out and warmer weather announced itself for other thrills and excitements.

—⁓—

I received my first very own bike, an adult one, when I was twelve and thereafter, I refused to stay close to home. Before that I borrowed Ma's. I was on the move. The Rotterdam harbor, its old houses, an inlet where a man sat on a bucket playing accordion music became my domain. In an old majestic building was the Museum of Anthropology. Dad took me there once and while I became impatient with him standing forever at some of the exhibits, the subject matter grabbed me.

"Dad, can I have 10 cents for the museum?" And off I went on my bike and took the long trip to the harbor. I was hooked. It didn't occur to me then that I was often alone taking long trips in areas that were not safe for a twelve-year-old girl. These trips inspired my sense of adventure that eventually grew to all corners of the earth once I'd met my husband. A deep longing had occurred.

"Don't go with any strangers; don't walk too close to the water." Ma put the fear in me.

On weekends I'd visit my grandmother downtown. I biked straight through that big harbor city of Rotterdam. Halfway I had to decide. Go the long way or take a shortcut through a remote industrial area. The shortcut always won. It gave me an "edge" of dissidence and was in line with my increased risk taking. I encountered weird guys who hung out under the dark tunnels I had to bike through—at least in my imagination they would always be there. So, I peddled like mad; clear of all thinking, totally in the moment, just looking down at my pedals. One day a car had planted itself smack on the *fietspad*. A dreamer, I drove straight into it.

—⁓—

Young guys noticed me and my white hair.

"Hey *meid*, pale face did you fall in the bleach?"

"Don't look so mad," they'd often say. *Always that paleface stuff— am I really looking that mad? I ignored them.*

"Ma, I need some nice shoes and a bra."

That evening Pa gave me money. I knew we didn't have a lot of money and they trusted me to buy the right thing the first time. I biked to the other side of Rotterdam, where many shops and things were reasonably priced. It was a hard decision to buy those on my own and I checked many stores, especially for a pair of Italian leather shoes. "You did well," my parents said. Yet those shoes were too elegant for the person I really was and the places I'd go.

I thought about guys. Not those that yelled at me. I didn't like them, but Wim, who goes to the baker's school. I like him, he's peaceful. So, one night I caught him coming home, and he handed me a roll of bread he baked. We visited sitting on the side of the walkway. I asked, "Wim do you want to go with me, *wil je met me gaan*?" Thus, we declared our friendship, but Wim didn't join me swimming, I had other friends for that.

I loved swimming in the river with my friends. A fatal water-borne illness called "van Weil" caused by rat urine in the water was prevalent, but that did not stop me or the adults I'd go with. I felt freedom while swimming. None of my dad's discipline had rubbed off on me. Feeling alone, something inside of me always pushed the boundary. I couldn't stop myself.

I can still smell and feel the stinking bilged water of the river-boats and the heavy tar on the wooden buoys guiding the boats under the huge bridge in New-Overschie. I climbed the buoys and dove off into the murky water. At school I'd brag that I jumped off the bridge into the water, which wasn't true; I jumped off the buoys which felt like jumping off that pull-bridge. I knew that busy bridge from above and below. The icon of a bridge in my life didn't set well. The bridges of my youth were not sturdy at all. I drove across this high built pull-bridge on my new bike.

"Louise, let go of your feet," I yelled to my friend who peddled while I sat behind her on my new bike.

"*Meid*, let go—I just showed you how to do it." Then Louise just for a moment did let go of the steering bars, took her feet off the peddles and we were almost freewheeling going down that bridge slope. Louise was not as gutsy; her Mom didn't know that we were so far from home.

Again, I reminded her, "let go of your hands, put them in the air".

Louise wouldn't and I finally had to lean forward and yank them loose from the handlebars. We laughed and laughed, frightened like hell, going 30 km an hour down the bridge when finally, our restlessness and laughter made the front wheel twist right. We smacked down onto the road.

"Are you all right? I checked out her knees and mine. Then we discovered her arm injury, Louise had a big bloody scrape the size of a flat mandarin at the top of her arm. It was bleeding, but we were content that the wound was not deep. We walked the long way home. I had to avoid her Ma for a while.

A short time later, the poorly constructed huge pull bridge collapsed into the water below. Luckily, I was not on the bridge or underneath it when that happened. No one was hurt and the city rebuilt the bridge—it wasn't a hang-bridge anymore. It was a good image of what would come into my life. And though the bridges of my youth weren't sturdy, they were many and I messed with them. Eventually I married an engineer who dreamed of building bridges, the "Indian" in him he said. Together we'd bridge connections with cultures and consciousness across the world. I didn't know then about that passage in my life, and I continued my wandering and flirting with bridges and tunnels in my youth.

Another bridge, a very old and larger one over the Maas River in the center of Rotterdam, was wobbly and shook when big trucks or trams rolled over it. One day a loaded milk truck failed to stop when the bridge was open to allow a riverboat to pass. The truck slammed on its brakes and stopped, hanging off the edge where the bridge lifted apart. The bottles crashed onto the street, now flooded with white puddles of milk and broken glass.

After that, I looked through its cracks and saw the dark water of the Maas River flowing below. Shivering, I walked across that bridge, first watching that no trams or trucks were near to make my crossing wobbly. The bridge keeper sat in his tiny house and watched the boats down below. I always imagined the bridge opened while I was on it. *I walk fast keeping an eye on the man in the little house with its tiny balcony overlooking the Maas. My heart pounds and I hold my breath. What should I do when the bridge suddenly opens? What can I hang on to?* Until I reached the black cobblestones on the other side, my breathing did not become normal again.

I don't think I was being a child even when I was one. By risk-taking I was getting rid of those weird energies of being a mother and handling all the epileptic anxiety at home; Henk breaking out with a deep sigh, falling to the ground, turning blue. While playing outside away from it all I felt free and able to breathe deeply. Yet there was no escape from the anxiety, not at home or in the illusion of freedom outside. Without realizing it I became addicted to thrills, wanting to feel the edge, the fear, the curiosity, a Bluebeard woman in the making. I mean the Bluebeard from the fairy tales of Grimm who warned women not to look behind a certain door. Yes, floating in the illusion of freedom while playing outside in the fresh air, the frequent turning blue of my brother, had penetrated who I was and unfurled a risky yet spiritual path. Unknown to me then, Henk's physical challenges and simple I.Q. would add to my life's character and level of empathy. He became the true shapeshifter of my life. The extent of this I'd only realize at the time of his much too early death.

PRAY FOR THIS BABY TO DIE
MY BROTHER HENK

"P RAY FOR THIS BABY'S DEATH," doctors advised on May 17, 1954. "He has no chance and will grow up to be severely handicapped." An inexperienced young doctor had delivered Henk with forceps and smashed his brain. Initially Ma began Henk's birth at home, as usually happened during that time. But seeing the complexity Dr. Bender, our doctor, changed his mind and rushed Ma to the hospital.

Henk surprised them though. At two years old, and four years younger than I, he scooted himself on his back through the house. This scooting caused a wound at the back of his skull. Dr. Bender cut it open, and sewed it shut with me looking. No hair grew on that spot as big as a quarter for the rest of his life. I don't think Dr. Bender belonged to the best of doctors. Who in his right mind would consider a home delivery after the former child died; then the insensitivity of cutting Henk's head with me present?

All decisions in our family began to center on Henk. He needed physical therapy. He had daily epilepsy attacks. Ma arranged for schooling and swimming for children handicapped like him. I admired Ma, being a foreigner, a German at that, to arrange all that with the school and the state. She had to go way out of her comfort zone. She, a *Mof* to many, found these places across the big city of Rotterdam.

Pa had a hard time dealing with Henk's short comings. He longed to have a son next to him. He even told him so. He couldn't connect with Henk as fathers and sons do. Maybe, all of us aimed too high for Henk. None of us realized the mental and physical effort it took him to walk, write, play and live. In fact, all decisions were done by Pa, Ma or me and didn't receive Henk's input at all.

His frequent seizures and taking care of him during the day, especially outside, forced me to take charge of him. I walked him around in a baby carriage and later walked our sister Ilse as well. At four Henk became my companion when we played outside all day. Later he attended the Mytyl School, a school for physically challenged children. Each day a big taxi picked up the children at their homes and brought them back again.

At this school Henk appeared to be one of the best physically. He walked with a limp, dragged his right leg. His right arm, less strong than his left one, appeared somewhat hanging. He learned to write with his left hand though he naturally tried to do things with his weaker right side. His school, non-denominational, had a happy atmosphere.

Henk communicated with his teachers, had rapport, and made friends, especially with those he could mean something to through helping them, because they were physically more challenged than he was. He helped those in a wheelchair. He experienced a sense of freedom there. He found a different relationship with adults from what he knew at home. At home, our dad did not communicate in dialogue style, so what we knew about Henk was limited. Henk took up fencing in school and created clay sculptures. He helped the teachers with the other children. He gained self-confidence. I felt proud of him.

Henk had a simple vision, a farm with animals. He had a relaxed pace in harmony with nature. He too had that connection with the earth and followed in his German grandfather's footsteps. No words were needed for either one of them. Both loved the land and its animals, especially Asta the shepherd dog. Clearly, Henk identified with Ma's German heritage. He looked like his German cousins and wanted to be like them. Regular vacations to be with his grandfather in Fulda, as well as his cousins in Ulmbach where he led the cows into the fields enhanced his German anchor. Our family however, challenged by the recovery after WWII, now lived in the harbor town of Rotterdam. A vision of farming didn't fit.

Henk stretched and stretched to be the son he couldn't possibly be. His interest was not technical like that of our dad. And after elementary school choices became harder for physically challenged people. He learned to read and write, some math, but at home the distance between him and dad grew. He'd receive the emotional support from either mom or me.

After elementary school the Dutch educational system had a void for people like him. He ended up attending a lower-level technical school. He learned to become a carpenter, distant from his own desires. There, kids, none of them physically challenged with teachers not equipped to handle those students, pestered him for his funny walk, his genetic skin disorder, his epilepsy and more. Upon completion he received a special award for his endurance. But the emotional damage was done.

As a carpenter, he couldn't handle a competitive society. People began to take advantage of him. He searched for love. He set out for a carpenter's job in Schiedam. Henk decided to live on his own. This attempt to live alone would be the first of many. Dad and others helped him to get the furniture and move. Shortly thereafter fear overcame him. A sort of paranoia set in. Then he'd move back home. Over and over again this happened, while at times his paranoia deepened.

In Roosendaal, after our parents moved from his beloved Rotterdam to the southern part of the Netherlands he sank into deep depression. He stayed in bed for days. His face, especially the right side, darkened. His right eye drooped under the stress. In fact, he looked a bit scary now, this tall grown often angry man. He had shaved off most of his hair.

With my parents desperate for help Ma spoke to a local priest who worked at the hospital. He agreed to meet with Henk and to our surprise first a friendship then a love affair began between the two. Henk was homosexual.

The relationship with this man, fifteen years older, had various sides: One of deep compassion, one of lovers, and the other of care-taking. I may add the suspicion that Henk was seeking a father figure. His own dad's emphasis on religion maybe heightened his attraction to this priest. Both Henk, and the priest, in their younger years attended carpentry in a technical school neither one of them had chosen. They had that in common.

Henk entered a more festive time living with Leo. He explored cooking and German baking. They traveled abroad for vacations. He developed his artistic side through flower arrangements for the hospital chapel. Mentally he became stronger. It wouldn't last.

Meanwhile my parents, devoted Catholics, confronted the spiritual dilemma of their son in relationship with a priest. The only way to not lose their child, they concurred with the relationship, supporting both. Some of my folks' friends did the same. Quietly they accepted the situation under the guise of caretaking. After five years the relationship ended and again Henk fell into a deep pit.

Quite a few men took advantage of his longing for love, unconditional love, his handicap and immaturity on several levels. It became quite messy. Additionally, it included at some point alcohol and drug experiments.

After the breakup two other attempts to live alone failed. It ended up with his hospitalization in a mental hospital. Dad didn't believe in psychologists. Henk dealt with his life there on his own.

Fortunately, a decision to live in a group home followed. There Henk spent hours in his little room upstairs. The German programs he watched on TV helped his knowledge of German. No, Henk was not dumb, just a simple soul. He took care of the cooking and joyfully arranged the elaborate Christmas and Sinterklaas decorations in this group house.

In May 2004 on his fiftieth birthday, at the side of his dad, Henk collapsed. He was rushed to the hospital in Roosendaal, the Netherlands, and given seven liters of blood. Cancer of the pancreas was the verdict.

"All I want to do is die with mom."

"They have a treatment with spiders in Heidelberg, Germany" were his first few reactions.

Thankful that I could be with him during these first few days, I later flew back to Texas where I lived. One night, sitting with my feet in the water of a lake during sunset, I thought of Henk. A broken spider web came falling out of the sky. It landed on my legs.

Spiders, especially the white ones, have been my friends. They'd wake me at night in my dreams when I left a candle burning. At other times the black ones would appear when I wove a relationship with a person that wasn't good for me. Sometimes they appeared when danger lured.

Not wanting to kill, I caught a black one and put it out of my house.

So, it was with Henk on the day he died. A large black one, this time on the outside of my living room window visited me.

With the Lakota people the spider is not a good sign. But in my case it is, especially those white ones. Some link the spider to being too much in the past or future, rather than the present. That piece of web landing on my leg told me, "It's over, this is a done deal; Henk is going to the other side. The web is broken." Spiders continue to enter my space. I see them jump in my chair. I recall the fact that thousands of spiders are caught in jet streams 30,000 feet above the earth. As a feminine cosmic layer, they travel through space ready to walk different parts of the earth and spin their webs of destiny.

Is the spider truly about living in the past? I remember the photograph of a man next to Henk's bed. I am vaguely reminded of a love relationship Henk had with this man. They had met in a park in Roosendaal. The man had died. "I want to be cremated and my ashes spread in that park," Henk had said.

I ponder the sculpture Henk made in his youth, a heap of white and green glazed clay with hands sticking out everywhere. Very much like a spider and its many legs. Did Henk live in the past too much?

After I return to the US still expecting a miracle after my first visit, I had emailed his doctor pleading for a team approach for not only his body but also his mind. A few days later they had transported Henk to the Academic Hospital in Rotterdam, the city where both of us entered this world. A team of surgeons supported by psychiatric care attempted to remove the cancer.

I decided to fly back to Holland again. Would he make it? Would this be the last time I see him? What could I do to help? Would he let Peter, the Lakota medicine man, doctor him? "Henk there is so much you don't know about me, and I too have many questions for you.

The Intercity train took me straight from the airport to Rotterdam. A Middle Eastern taxi driver brought me to the Erasmus Hospital, at the edge of the harbor. Henk was hooked up to about four bags and other electronics. He seemed alert. His room in the old part of the hospital resembled the hallway of a large ship. Patients walked to showers and bathrooms in the hallway their tubes and bags attached to them. A Korean nurse kindly motioned me to a hospital bed next to Henk. Henk was relieved to see me and momentarily forgot the tubes going down his throat.

I spent the next five nights with my pillow at the wrong side of my bed to have eye contact with Henk. He moaned with pain and large bouts of anger in between. Gasping for air, his death-fearing eyes penetrated while the greatest nurses in the world and I assure him that he isn't going to die right then.

The second night he pulled off two of his hookups and ended up in a puddle of blood, and a little later the contents of another bag as well. "Damn," I think.

Two days after his surgery, early in the morning, I cleaned up in an unhygienic shower and took a walk along the harbor. The docked boats were still present as if they never had moved in thirty years.

Rotterdam, my place of birth, had shocked me. Large posters throughout the city advertised vacations in Turkey with five naked butts in thongs. It appalled me. What happened to my Rotterdam?

Memories of years ago went through my head. Dow Chemical where I began my working career, the Friday evenings with colleagues at Chalet la Suisse in the park, and Christmas parties where I sang "The Yellow Submarine" by the Beatles for a crowd of people. Nevertheless, after five days in Rotterdam I fell back in love with that culture of "harbor attitude workers" poking in each other's business and caring, deeply caring.

"Where have you been so long?" Henk pleaded. "I missed you." If I went to the restroom in the hall, he missed me. I was his security blanket and in those five days Henk and I came full circle. We held hands, I stroked his arms, his face, and we talked intimately. Attempting to deal with the no-hope verdict, he exploded in anger: "I haven't had that good a life you know". "Don't you dare do euthanasia on me." "You have no idea about that Joor, that nurse at the group home. In your face he's very nice, but he is so mean." On and on Henk spouted like an erupting volcano. Yet through it all I began to recognize the story, the story of his life, Henk's gift to us.

Henk rejected the invitation that Peter, the medicine man and my friend of many years, could heal him. "You with your Shaman stuff," Henk yelled. Quietly I took Peter's picture I had sent him from the bulletin board across from his bed. I surrendered and remembered Peter's words: "You must console him and let his Spirit decide."

I attempted to breathe away my own needs and longing. I focused on Henk's Spirit and the choices he had to make. He is the courageous one, the Hero. He taught us about compassion, the courage to be a homosexual, and the courage to speak his truth, even though it was in anger.

I don't think any of us can fathom the effort and strength of spirit it took to overcome and live with his physical challenges. Not only that but the psoriasis, a family inheritance, and the epilepsy changed people around him forever.

Years of dealing with the religious and societal norms put upon his orientation had left deep wounds. Naturally, other priests did not agree with his relationship with the hospital priest. The already small circle of people around him and the priest became smaller.

I had observed the communication between Henk and Dad, each making efforts to find and express love for each other. It didn't happen, despite Dad's unending love and care, forgiving Henk's anger. Both were unable to understand each other and come to that peaceful space of soul connection. Dad deeply loved him. He did everything possible to care for Henk. But in Henk's early years, when times hit hard at work for our dad, Pa's frustration was often directed at Henk, sometimes hitting him. Maybe, these encounters created distrust and much fear that resulted in the avoidance of intimacy. And coming full circle in Henk's adult life, his own anger and outbursts couldn't fix or overcome the distance. Henk and Dad were irretrievably different in their character and life goals.

For five years after his mental break down, Henk had lived in assisted living. Guided during the day by a team of nurses, social workers, and others. Four men on medication lived together in a condo. Henk had a very small bedroom with two tropical birds in a cage and a TV. He spent most of his time in that upper room, smoking one cigarette after the other as if the nicotine could heal him or this situation of living in a group home.

San, a male nurse, had taken the authority to recommend regulation of Henk's medication. He had the power! Even though Henk hadn't seen a psychiatrist in five years, San gave Henk more and more medication. Henk accepted the pills in fear of being sent back to Vrederust, the psychiatric hospital. Someway San communicated, probably with the family physician, that increased medication was necessary. Never mind their side effects and with no psychiatric oversight.

Why was Henk's fear of authority never addressed in a way other than through increased medication? Why was his only joy, raising birds, restricted to not more than two? He could have enjoyed a large birdcage in the common area, where all patients shared them, helping the community spirit. Instead, he retreated to his bedroom for long periods of time. What influenced Joor to restricting a small joy like that for a patient?

Why wasn't there guidance or care about the constant pain Henk complained about? Weekly phone calls by Henk to Doctor Loot were either rejected or dampened by this family physician. Henk received medicine for ulcers without any additional research in a whole year. "Put a pillow in your back," said Joor upon Henk's sharing his pain.

While in the Academic Hospital in Rotterdam, the psychiatrist there changed his medications for the surgery. His doctor deleted medications he took because of redundancy. Side effects of those deleted were epilepsy, liver conditions and a whole lot more. Not a very smart medicine for a former epilepsy patient, I thought. Henk being on less medication now, was able to communicate normally and I became close to Henk. He didn't withdraw, in fact I found him a better communicator than many other people I knew. Here at the highest stress level any person on this earth faces, Henk handled it well and courageously—even with less medication.

I looked at the red thread of his life. Had we conditioned Henk to be mentally dependent? Had all of us around him kept him from being as fully human as possible with all his potential? Did our care and seeing ourselves as more competent and smarter because he was physically challenged and had epilepsy deprive him of his potential?

I noticed my own arrogance over the years, almost like part of me was better, more intelligent, not on the same level as Henk. I had become his mother on many levels. The price was a great distance between us as a family. Unable to reach one another's heart, our communications were from the head. We talked about Henk, what was best for him. We talked without Henk's input. How had all this happened? We talked at Henk but never with Henk. Never exploring or supporting his dreams.

Again, he wanted to live on his own, to stay in Rotterdam after his surgery. We simply listened and didn't see a possibility to realize that. It hadn't worked for so many times and years. Then there was his longing for a partner, especially after his relationship with Leo the priest had ended. We were tired, tired of all the previous attempts that didn't work out. In our family Henk was accepted as being different, explosive, and finally residing at a safe place in the community home. His parents now in their eighties were exhausted.

No, we never celebrated Henk, however, his illness awakened a dawning in me. How dare I put myself above any human being, be they physically or mentally challenged? How hard is it to connect heart to heart? Why had it taken this for me to reach the true Henk again, to hear him, to think with him, to touch him, to enjoy him, and to see how handsome he is?

In spite of this, as time drew nearer and Henk needed to leave the hospital in Rotterdam, we-his family, decided for him that he cannot go back to assisted living. Henk agreed that he would not physically be safe there. He needed Hospice care.

"I want to stay in Rotterdam, I completely bloom here," he said. "People accept me here the way I am." He reflected on the Rotterdam culture and his experience with the nurses in the hospital, some of them openly gay like him. We foresaw the end of his life, and the difficulty it would create for Dad, who didn't drive freeways anymore, to be with him at the end. As always, we talked him into choosing our idea—Hospice in Roosendaal. "It *is* the best decision Henk." Yet, while time was running out, I hoped that Henk got a chance to do exactly as he wanted, just for one time in a big way: He the courageous one.

Henk's dying at fifty and witnessing his pain pushed me to a different level of consciousness. A higher sensitivity and level of empathy emerged. I painfully realized that putting someone outside the group has tremendous consequences. I pondered the cancer, the courage it demanded. Once "cancer" is pronounced, hardly anyone thinks positively anymore. How hard it is to get people to think about a future for Henk, a good future. Doctors gave up with this kind of cancer.

I did believe in the power of thought. Henk faced a struggle not only with his own thoughts for survival, but he also had to deal with the negative thoughts of those surrounding him.

While in hospice care, visitors do the only thing they can do in their helplessness—they fed him more and more. Henk ate and ate.

"Do whatever you want to do," they said to him. So, he ate, french-fries, the Dutch *krokets* he loved and paid for them dearly with pain the next day. What is it in a person that they always must feed someone who is sick? Surely there are other ways to give.

"*Heb je even, heb je even tijd voor mij?*" "Do you have some time for me?" were the words of Henk's favorite song. The idea of offering someone your time doesn't fit the economic strife in present society.

These days I try to find balance. Will I forget his redemptive lessons: "Do you have a moment; do you have some time for me?" Will I forget that too? Henk is dying after a very tough life—without that much happiness.

"I learned a lot from you," I told him. He looked at me with surprise.

Henk's life was troubled and challenging. Yet he did experience love. He received love from Leo, the priest. He received love from our mother, endlessly dealing with the epilepsy, the laundry it caused, the emotional bonding she gave him. He received love from my dad, trying to help him get jobs and as an adult trying various ways to help him live on his own. They had endless patience with Henk's anger. Their love lasted a lifetime. All loved Henk on their own terms and in their own way. His challenges became our gift.

The gifts Henk's life showered upon our character are endless. The level of compassion living in a family with such gaping trauma wounds instills closeness that fosters several generations. These values became engrained in my sister as well. It would take years to become aware and own the gifts she and I received through Henk's challenges and through our mother being a *Mof.* First, we needed to accept the negligence we experienced growing up. To cope as a child, Ilse became invisible.

SISTER ILSE

I F YOU KNOW THE SILENCE that a thick layer of snow brings to the world, you basically have an idea about the presence of my sister Ilse, the invisible one. Six years younger than I, she hid from visitors. She'd play in a corner, often cutting paper. She liked to hide things too. That was during the day—nights were a different story.

Ilse had stomach problems. She wailed night after night as I lay next to her. Sometimes, I could not take that wailing anymore. I wished it would stop. And I thanked G*d when she would finally vomit and go to sleep. I noticed Ilse would vomit after she had been with certain relatives. Ma cried about Ilse being thin as a stick.

> I am envious of Ilse; she is beautiful, and she knows how to play. Ilse has friends and they all have nice parents. Her friend's parents made a huge carpet together—they had a good marriage. Another friend's mother makes tea when they came home from school. Ma makes French fries on Fridays and huge German pies which we eat in one setting.

We were allowed to bring a friend to eat dinner on Fridays. All other times we played outside. On Wednesday afternoons Ma ordered me to watch eight kids who ended up in our tiny living room to watch a one-hour children's television show. We were the first to have a black and white TV on our street.

Ilse sleeping in the attic made me mad. With fear in her voice, she begged from up there each night, "Is Inge coming to bed already?" She'd keep it up until Ma sent me to bed, just to get it over with, no matter the six years of age difference.

As a teenager, in contrast to me, Ilse could get angry. She'd run after me and kick. She'd get angry with Ma too. "Witch," she yelled rushing down the stairs of the apartment. Ma followed her and yelled in German "*Komm hier Freundchen.*" She threw a shoe after Ilse.

One day, Ilse fell out of the attic as well. She played there around the laundry hanging from lines. She had forgotten about the hole in the floor and fell hard on her arm. It hurt so bad that she got to sleep downstairs that night. The next day, because she cried all night, Ma took her to the hospital. "Your arm is broken," said the doctor.

Those early years, Ilse and I never created a real friendship. Maybe the age difference had to do with it. I had to lie down with her to take her naps. It would cut into my playing outside time. I behaved as a "Ma" to both her and Henk. Such patterns were hard to shake, especially being the oldest one.

Culturally we expressed ourselves differently too. Ilse's heart connected with an aunt from Germany, who took the role of replacing Ma's mother who we never knew. Silently and alone Ilse went her own way.

In our early years her connection with Pa was different. "Why do you try to tell him everything?" she'd tell me. "I just don't go there. Just do what you want."

Ma could not protect us. We all became a victem of society at an age when most of us needed to be able to play and be innocent. Certain people took advantage of our emotionally unmet needs.

Later in life, Ilse bridged her quietness and turned out to be a powerful woman and teacher of the German language. She created a balanced identity as a German teacher, mentor of students, and a closeness with Dad in later years. She also cared for Henk in his last days. Ilse became an advocate for those who couldn't speak for themselves, like people with Alzheimers. As a high school teacher her sensitivity became noticed. She led faculty on a path of understanding and dealing with abuse of and by students. On a personal level both Ilse and I needed to turn our way of living with antenna tuned to what's happening around us and turn it into a way of living from our center of being. Henk's frequent epilepsy attacks had triggered a way of life always on the alert ever shifting to his need. The lack of dialogue with our trauma filled parents did not help either.

"Give that toy to Henk," my parents said. "If he gets upset, he'll turn blue again." Ilse, closer in age with Henk than I, learned to be quiet.

In addition to other family challenges, Ma often had to go into the hospital while we grew up. Henk and Ilse would be put into a home with the nuns. I'd be old enough to go to school alone. At night Dad and I visited Ma. I'd sit on the backseat of his put-put motorcycle. Together we trekked to the hospital in downtown Rotterdam.

Thinking back to the strain of our early years, Ilse's and my generational trauma created an obstacle to true love and intimacy as siblings. It's like two tectonic plates, each with their own history and experience that rub together in a way that never quite fits. I find that hard to accept, as if our true love is hidden deep and muddled. It's a lesson of letting go. It's as if I intuit the potential in this dance. Unconditional love might soften the edges and tear down our defense and fear, replacing it with trust. I'm grateful for my sister Isle, her generosity and love. We shared the same riverbed. Together we progress, and continue healing each in our own way and at our own pace.

THE OLD HOSPITAL

S<small>T. FRANCISCUS GASTHUIS HOSPITAL, AGED</small> and dark with its connected chapel and convent, had moved. The new hospital had white tiled hallways, high ceilings and that strange repulsive "clean" smell. It grossed me out to see all these ill people hooked on bottles and other strange gadgets. We visited the hospital often and large buildings like that make me feel wild and lost to this day. Dad and I spent a great deal of time in that space visiting Ma in one of those ten to twenty beds along each side of the long wardrooms. Ma had staph infections of her breasts. Each day a doctor opened the wounds to drain without anesthesia. Ilse and Henk in the meantime stayed at a Catholic home where nuns took care of them.

Every day thirty to forty visitors gathered at the large entrance-way of the hospital blocked with powerful cattle gates waiting to visit loved ones for forty-five minutes—and never a minute longer. Ma enjoyed telling us stories of patients who challenged or talked back to the nuns or the doctors.

A bell rang. Droves of people obeyed on the dot and departed.

The hospital improved over the years. I remember visiting Ma's bed next to a double glass window. A room now held only six patients.

After our visit, she would stand by that window, wave, and watch me perform cartwheels on the busy sidewalk below. I did as many as I could to make Ma happy and smile. Sometimes I walked funny just to make her laugh.

Glad she'd return home after a few weeks, I helped with chores, took care of my brother Henk and took him to physical therapy.

Pa worked hard to bring us forward after the war. Desire for success caught Pa and he did not realize how much we missed him at home. The office did give him a Volkswagen to drive, and he did not have to work every Saturday anymore.

Pa sold grinding wheels to cut diamonds and little drills for dentists as well. When he made a big sale, he would come home with *Marios,* a big box of expensive cakes from a first-class bakery. At the end of the year, Pa's company gave him a bonus. We all received new clothes and shoes. These celebrations I carried forward as an adult. I continued to look for opportunities to celebrate small successes or cultural parties integrating other countries.

HOLIDAYS

W E CELEBRATED CHRISTMAS THE GERMAN way with a plate under the tree on *Heiligen Abend* (Holy Night) for each of us, loaded with candy, chocolate and fruit. On *Heilgen Abend*, we placed the tree inside the house but not one day earlier. "It's bad luck," Ma said.

On December 5, Holland celebrates Sinterklaas—Saint Nicolas, a Catholic bishop known for his kindness to children. That night a loud banging came at our front door followed by a dark-gloved hand throwing candy into the living room. Anxiously, we waited until one of us would dare to go to the door to see if "*Zwarte Piet*," one of St. Nicolas's helpers, was still there. If not, we would peek outside and to our amazement, there was a sack full of gifts.

Most of our gifts were practical gifts like underwear, socks and special Sinterklaas candy.

Ma didn't believe in toys. Therefore, Henk had a small bear and a Lego set, and Ilse and I had one doll each. We shared a doll bed, one storybook and a small red woodshop set Dad made. My doll was big and hard, not suitable to sleep with. Besides, I didn't need one, "I was a mother."

Once a year we went to Germany on vacation in the Volkswagen. Three kids, two adults and our baggage all crammed in that little bug. Once we crossed the border into Germany, Ma didn't remember a word of Dutch and spoke only German. She changed. Dad would find the nearest town and make a stop at a bakery to buy German hard rolls and a butcher shop to buy *Fleisch-wurst*, a sort of German bologna. We were all ready to embrace Germany, the land where everything was better than in Holland, especially the hard rolls and that *Wurscht*.

Pa never complained of migraine headaches in Germany and Ma's family was very nice to us. In fact, all Germans in my world were much nicer than most of the Dutch people I knew in Rotterdam. Our big Aunt Trude was always laughing so loud that she got all of us laughing too. She never held back anything. With our overweight happy aunt, we hiked into the mountains and sang German folk songs she remembered. Konrad, her husband, threw in many jokes. Once he told Pa he wished the Americans had joined the Germans in attacking Russia during the war. The World would be a different place, he said.

Ma's families were great cooks and served coffee and huge cakes almost every afternoon. They asked if us kids wanted more. In Holland kids were to be seen and not heard. With Ma kicking at us under the table to say no, Henk said, "*Ja bitte.*" Yes, please!

My parents had married after the war was over in the St. Bonifacius Cathedral in Fulda, located in the southeastern Hessen province of Germany. *Opa* Isidor, my grandfather, lived in Fulda. Opa was the seventh child of thirteen and was a man of the land.

His father, a shepherd, herded 500 sheep through the mountains each day. His mom, Christine, was a faith healer of skin diseases and horses. My great grandparents used to live in Ulmbach, a small village, about 50 miles from Fulda, surrounded by hills and fields with vegetables where women in black dresses worked the fields. My great-grandparents together built a mount. I think they created it to worship. It's still there. *Opa* rented land to raise chickens, pigs and vegetables. *Opa* seldom spoke. His smiling eyes sparkled with peace, and a twinkle of mischief.

I felt freedom on his piece of land. I climbed his apple and cherry trees and ate carrots straight from the earth. I was free. I felt the air and connected with the earth. I felt in harmony with it all. I am proud of *Opa,* he owned so little yet so much. He did not buy into wealth and endless commerce. No, *Opa* remained of the land and so will I.

Ma was a little embarrassed about her dad. *Opa* had built two small sheds with tin roofs on his rented land, located beyond a scrap metal city yard. One shed was built for the chickens to lay their eggs and one for him and his second wife Hilda. I observed everything, the dirt floors, the twinkle in his eyes looking at his wife. He and I never communicated much, yet I adored his simplicity, his land, his animals, his connection with all that. It expressed to me a glimpse of trust and peace.

Opa's shed had a dirt floor, was smoky, dark, and smelled earthy and of chickens. Hay sacks were placed in a self-made bed for sleeping. Another mysterious smaller shed, we could not go inside, never. This place had a small chimney and smoke would sometimes waft from the tin roof. I knew that smoke meant *Opa* was preparing to kill some fat geese, well fed all year for the occasion of our annual visit. Afterwards we had to pluck them. They were still warm.

While with *Opa,* we would hike into the woods. We'd gather black berries near the border with East Germany, where the Russian and East German soldiers were. People sometimes got lost in the woods ending up on the wrong side of the border. They never came back. Every year we gathered the tiny black berries for hours until our buckets were filled. *I'm scared—are there soldiers anywhere? Is that bucket still not full? Is everybody accounted for? Are we still together and, is no one wandering off? Are we still on the German side? Is that bucket still not full? I want to go home to Opa's house where the East Germans cannot get us.*

Back in Overschie where we'd moved in that rainy Holland, life continued to get better over the years. Ma and Pa became good friends with the neighbors. Ma made wine, which we kept in the living room in a large green bottle full of alcohol wrapped in blankets with a strange-looking chemical gadget bubbling all day. The odor filled our small apartment. Our neighbors were very interested, and I remember they were anxious to test the wine. Pa would go down to let one of the apartment dwellers test if the wine was ready. And of course, they always said yes. Then they'd all come up, fill their bottles, and go down again. There was so much laughter. People in the four apartments became like one happy family. Ma worked hard making the wine, cooking plums in a large kettle and constantly tending the brew. I don't know how to make wine. The sulfur they put in wine today affects my heart. During our summer vacations to *Opa's* chicken farm, I saw he made wine too with the same type of bottles.

STEPPING INTO FREEDOM

Ingeborg and Toby with Christa and Patrick

A SEARCH FOR FREEDOM THUNDERS through my life. It awakened when I was six years old and slept in a dark place, an attic storage area adapted to a bedroom.

Without a choice to sleep elsewhere, disconnected from my life force, my legs step up the ladder standing in the hallway. Numb and in fear of the dark, much like a ghost I step through the square hole in the ceiling. From the time I slept in that attic an inner screaming for freedom emerged.

Waking up the next morning, very alert and in tempo, my legs feel for the top step of the ladder. I rush down to the kitchen where the gas stove burners have warmed the space. I eat two slices of white bread with some chocolate sprinkles on top, and still chewing, run down the steps of the apartment. Outside I inhale the cool air deeply, the streets, my world, and my domain.

With that spark of freedom, I race with other kids on a two-wheel toy around the block of apartments. In Overschie, a suburb of Rotterdam, my play mates are boys, they are my companions. I experience them as being less mean. They are adventurous. Their spirit matches mine.

Inside the house, at home my role was a mother, and at school my confinement was the adverse shame of being a child of a German "*Mof.*"

As a teenager the restless feelings of captivity increased. That I had to get up early, that I never could sleep in, and received criticism about my choice of radio stations, those of free thinkers, did not help. Dad was absent a lot. Ma dealt with my brother being physically challenged, and lots of hand-washed laundry due to his incontinence.

Not all was bad, no, not at all. My folks enjoyed making wine and often our big Aunt Trude and funny Uncle Konrad from Germany visited and truly cheered the house. Still, the teasing and jokes about my appearance by my parents, which my siblings copied, and the tension of epilepsy had reached saturation. How could I get out?

My journey for cultural identity focused my attention first on Germany, Ma's country. I never had plans of restricting myself to Rotterdam, my place of birth, or for that matter, to the Netherlands. I fantasized about going to Africa, and for sure I'd make it to the States.

"I'll bring you to school, it's raining too hard." Dad drove me to school in the Volkswagen, the company car. "Here's a *dubbeltje*, ten cents for licorice when you get out." Happy that I didn't have to walk through the rain, I got ready to hop out of the car. My clothes would not be wet and smelly like the rest of my classmates.

That morning, I hesitated. I gathered my courage and turned to Dad sitting next to me.

"Dad, I want to go to Africa, to all those missionary places. I guess I will become a nun."

I do not recall his response exactly, just that he didn't want to hear about it with upset overtones. I was eleven maybe twelve and in sixth grade then.

"Well, Pa, then I'll marry a black man instead." I had begun reading books about slave trade through imperialism and sympathized with the black people, especially those in the US. Frustrated with Dad for not taking me seriously, the thought that I could do it anyway did not occur to me.

In years to come anything that restricted, contained, or controlled my curiosity or adventurous spirit on any level made me want to shake loose. Freedom had shown its beacon.

So, I did escape. At twenty-six years old, I made it to New York. It was my legal entry point with my newly acquired green card. Toby had picked me up from the airport and naturally I wanted to see the Statue of Liberty. It was a cloudy day when I stepped on the touring vessel to see the famous site. Standing on a boat warmed by Toby's arms, my American husband, we came close to the Statue of Liberty. Leaning forward over the rail of the boat a deep "Yes" quavered through my body. This icon stretched my grasp for freedom, my sense of destiny and choice as a woman.

Further deepening the meaning of freedom happened throughout our world migrations. In 1981 when I was thirty-two, we found
ourselves living with our two young children in Caracas. A refinery
had to be built. In contrast to the many barrios around Caracas, our
home nestled against the mountains in Las Mercedes, an affluent
historical area. It overlooked the museum district and skyscrapers.
From a black and white marbled balcony, we overlooked the city.
People visiting us never noticed the barrios right next to skyscrapers, as if they didn't exist.

I volunteered at a Catholic elementary school in the old center
of Caracas during the time our own children attended the international school. I navigated the dense traffic to El Paraiso, the old
center. "If you get into an accident, keep on driving home if you
can, until you can call a lawyer." Toby had warned me. Cell phones
were nonexistent then and in Venezuela you had to prove your
innocence as you were guilty and jailed on the spot. Constantly
honking my horn with the rest, there never was a problem.

"Do you have time to go to the barrio tomorrow?" Sister Lucia
asked me. I had wanted to see where the barrio children lived who
attended the private school. "Don't wear any jewelry," she had cautioned me. "You don't want to be killed over it." I left my jewelry
in their convent and dressed in a simple blue dress and flat shoes.
Sr. Lucia and I crossed busy city streets to reach the barrio where
streets turned into dirt trails as we walked higher up.

The steep dirt trail has a narrow ditch along it. Sewage and
murky water from leaky pipes gush the collection from thousands
of dilapidated houses hustled on top of each other. A sour stench
of spoiled waste mingles with the stagnant air of a constant seventy
degrees.

"*Aqui, Aqui*, this *camino*," the six-year-old Gabriella yells. Sister Lucia, dressed in white, follows us.

Walking in the barrio, my curiosity feels cheap and invasive. Here everyone knows each other's business, the good and the bad, the gangs and drug dealers. Drunken men, barefooted, dirty, with bottle in hand slump on the ground and sit out the day. They yell at us. I feel protected in the company of the six-year-old and the nun. They both are regulars to this place.

Gabriella, who lives in the barrio, with her short black hair pulls me by the hand up the mountain. Her blue skirt and white blouse sets her apart and shows that she attends the school in El Paraiso. Those kids wear uniforms and have short hair as a safeguard against lice.

We have come to pick up the statue of the Virgin Mary from Doña Clara and bring her to the next home. The ritual from house to house happens in May. Gabriella's grandmother, who lives at the top of the barrio, had offered to house the Virgin.

Gabriella points at a shack with a metal roof. I look up the tight snaking path. From a distance a sweet singing can be heard... "*Dios te salve María. Llena eres de Gracia.*" The voices come from Doña Clara's house, a teacher in the barrio. "Children gather there to read and write," Sr. Lucia explains.

Out of breath we enter the room made from *paredes de metal—* metal sheets. Ten women cramped inside smile out their *Buenos Dias.* One apologizes, "No water or electricity. We only get it an hour or two." An opening in the wall looks down a mingling of rooftops reaching down to the old town center.

"*Sientese, sientese.*" Sit down. With tea and cookies in front of us, I notice the timeless force manifested in the altar. Flowers and flickering candles adorn the Virgin, a one-foot porcelain statue of a gentle faced woman... *Salve, salve Maria* we sing.

Doña Clara takes the statue of the Virgin Mary from the altar, wraps her in a cloth and puts her in a box. In quiet procession, we shuffle behind her out the door. Out of respect, women cover their hair with a handkerchief. Gabriella, in her plastic shoes, skips ahead. In the distance a heavy woman, dressed in a black skirt, waits in a shanty doorway. Her swollen feet are too big for the flip flops she wears. It's Gabriella's grandmother who offered to house the Virgin next.

Her house has two rooms. The altar—a pink wooden table—in the corner on the dirt floor has red plastic roses on top. Gabriella gestures to come. Sister Lucia and I bend our heads as we step through the doorway into the second room. This room, like a balcony suspends over the mountainside. The stagnant air smells musty. Light enters through the floor panels. The sewer dribbles below.

"Grandma is too heavy for this room. I sleep here and she with the Virgin. This room can fall off with rain and mud slides. I don't want her to die. I'd rather it be me. I tell her not to come here." Sister Lucia and I look at each other. We stare at the child's face as her eyes sparkle.

I feel a unity with Gabriella. At six years old, I too slept in a dark place. I dreamed to escape out of my circumstance. I'd go to the US, my icon of freedom. Gabriella was six—what did she really dream about? Her only light is a few years of education on account of the nuns. With luck it could lift her out of life in the barrio. Her choices are few. Maybe her dreams are humble, maybe to become a teacher, find a safe place for her grandmother, and have electricity. Maybe she'd want a toilet like those in school.

Since education and my basic needs were cared for in my childhood, my dreams began higher up the ladder. It included, as it did in Latin America, the recognition of a feminine strength that exists in this world. In Catholic belief, the religion of my childhood, it translates into the adoration of the Virgin Mary. Buddhists have a female awareness in the statue of Quan Yin and some Native American traditions have Buffalo Calf Woman.

I do not visit long in that barrio of Caracas. Dark clouds had gathered, and rain could make the trail down slippery. Sister Lucia and I hugged the women and Gabriella said *adios* and left.

I thought about Gabriella. Would she survive the frequent mudslides? Did she, like some in Latin America dream about a better life in the US? I cannot sleep that night returning to our villa and laying in our comfortable queen size bed.

It was in Caracas that Toby and I decided to return to the US. Our conscience no longer could justify working for multinationals. "It feels to me like being a prostitute," Toby stated. After living in remote areas of the world we had become intimately aware of community destruction that multinationals induced, not to mention the environmental devastation. We left Venezuela to make a difference in the US.

Shortly after our return in late 1983 Toby suddenly died. The grief and confusion engulfed me. The need for reflection and discipline broke to the surface, especially after the psychiatric hospitalization. Years after Toby's death a road into avoidance of men began to stream through my life like a river gone mad. Did it come from that curse I gave myself and my dad when I threatened: "I will marry a black man then?" These words rolled out quite spontaneously and childlike from the subconscious. To this day, I do not know if that notion was aggression or something that worked itself out for the good of my spirit. Most definitely it triggered, later in life, interest in the psyche—the shadow, from a Jungian perspective.

The fact of the matter was that men I fell for were prestigious, strong, powerful, and often controlling. So much so that one, a Chinese American had raped me at the age of seventeen. The powerful ones that were good reminded me of my dad. Subconsciously I longed to integrate their power, yet instead lost myself in the relationship. I didn't have a "self." Other than a strong emphasis to be honest and think of the poor, and the compassion we all had for Henk, my brother, I really didn't have a clue. The little I sensed of who I was, a child of a *Mof* and a mother, didn't support any balanced relationship.

It was through my studies as a spiritual director that I explored the feminine inroads and experiences. I welcomed the deep friendships and support women gave each other. Together we explored spirituality, art, and Jungian psychology. Quite naturally I organized women's groups and workshops and volunteered as a spiritual director in a small prison with women. I built my own self-confidence through facing my fears and supported and encouraged others on their road to self-confidence.

I learned about trauma bonding, relationships with people that are sometimes dangerous. At a minimum I had *allowed* them to pull me down into being the victim repeatedly.

I had chosen a sequence of relationships with controlling Bluebeards. Those Bluebeards as mentioned in the children's story where he has a secret chamber containing cut off heads of women; where was my strength, my inner strength? The force of standing up for myself had been paralyzed and hidden deeply inside. How did I become conditioned to not speak up and spit when necessary? Was it my culture or maybe my dad who labeled me a hysteric when my emotions bubbled up? Why couldn't I touch my own strength instead of projecting it on other men and sometimes women?

Caretaking, as in the mother role I had to play as a child, always results in judging. It was a role that was familiar and comfortable and created unequal relationships in my adult life.

In my forties, my challenge became walking the line of balance, accepting the human realities and my spiritual ones at the same time, never avoiding, always flowing, and allowing. Pintkola Estees writes that balance makes our lives larger, and imbalance makes our lives smaller.

I know people who are light, light in their presence. They lack my intensity. I longed to become light as a feather in my relationships with others and myself. "You need some discipline," I tell myself. But I don't like that word. I think I confuse the word discipline with control.

A good friend, a priest and spiritual director, emailed me from the Cenacle, a Catholic Retreat Center in Louisiana: "Ingeborg, be where you is, because if you ain't where you is, you is where you ain't. Be who you is, because if you ain't who you is, you is who you ain't; no judgments, no comparisons; delete the need to understand."

This process doesn't happen overnight and between forty and fifty I finally began to raise the adult in me. I learned about focusing on my needs, my emotional needs, and about my boundaries. I am exhausted yet want more. I want to throw all the doors open.

I am breaking the family rule—I spoke up and stated my truth. I began to perceive a sense of self-support, appreciation, and compassion.

"Freedom is coming, oh yes, Freedom is coming Oh Lord." I felt like a virgin again, the one who stands gracefully able to *receive*. I began to see well-balanced men, recognized their gentleness, their kindness, their generosity, their courage and freedom. This time I had no fear of enmeshment. I had come into my own. I felt graced to see a new echo of myself in the world around me.

Freedom, now from a world perspective, called my curiosity again. I visited the East Coast of the US and found the Liberty Bell in Philadelphia. Focused on the bell, not noticing anyone around me, my step hastened with the prospect of seeing a powerful symbol of freedom again. I walked toward the large object but a sunken feeling startled me, much like when I realized the dangers of Gabriella's room in the barrio of Caracas: "A crack, the Liberty Bell has a crack," repeated in my mind. "It actually has a crack."

Frustrated, I brooded about freedom and how our aspirations could be higher from the get-go if that crack—the essentials of healthcare, education, and retirement—was mended and understanding of what immigrants bring to the US was restored. I wanted a solid-sounding bell that rings in true freedom, building global relationships with hearts and minds that radiate liberty for all.

"Go back to your country foreigner!" Some people angrily confront me when I express my love for the Latin Americans living in the US or point to the injustices of treaties broken with Native Americans. I had heard it all before in Holland, my country of birth when I was young, a child of a *Mof.* "Go back home." It doesn't affect me any longer.

In my seventies and a foreigner who lives in the US, freedom narrows the distance between my head and heart. I visualize the creation of building blocks for the next generation, a task to last until I'm in my nineties. I want to contribute to society, share my own connection with that creative feminine force, facilitating arts and ways to reflect. To the extent that I have the security of decent health care and the outlook of a basic income like Social Security, I can pursue my dream of freedom, I envision a human race coming together, a world that chooses to become bigger in mind and heart, sharing in each other's wisdom. My continued participation in the evolution and creativity of freedom can be life changing.

I realize that a moral collective consciousness would narrow the gap between rich and poor in the world, including young people like Gabriela. Those that control the masses through unjust cheap labor will increasingly be held accountable. I believe that in time the rising of consciousness will do away with the dark stand of entitlement, which doesn't come from those who have nothing. Yes, a strengthening of and fusion with a new feminine presence in this world by innovative women AND men can unlock the degradation of the global human family. The infinite feminine icon of freedom carried by the United States of America is pivotal.

PROVIDENCE

1973–1983

"P A, I BOUGHT A TICKET to Aruba." To utter these words takes about all the courage I have.

I couldn't fathom the loss of dreams he had for me and what he felt with my announcement. An unseen force pulled me away from Dad, away from my family, my brother, my mom and sister, as well as my country of birth, the Netherlands. Far away to that icon of freedom. Providence entered my life through the love of a gentle man, Toby from Texas.

A sunny evening in Rotterdam, one that keeps daylight going till ten at night, my dad is reading the newspaper in the garden. His long legs stretch out in front of him under the round table. His arms hold the daily Catholic newspaper. He continues to read. A few steps away, Ma bakes a cake in the kitchen. She probably hears every word I say. I'm nervous; not because of Ma. It's Pa's response that's important. Slowly he looks up. His face is serious.

Our eyes do not meet. I stand a distance away from him. It signifies our relationship. My naïve heart beats strongly. I can't focus on what's going on for Dad at this moment. Our bond never includes dialogue. He is the force, a tall and all-encompassing presence. I am the child, and his approval is golden. Fear and determination overwhelm my body. "He's taking you away from your family and culture." Dad spoke slowly without looking at me. His words float into the void in front of him. I hear them but they don't reach me.

Dad knew the consequence of what was coming into my life with my announcement of the ticket. He had met Toby, my American boss. This trip to Aruba had ramifications far beyond what I could realize. Dad knew, he understood. He had tasted loss on the deepest level… how else could I clarify the letting go of his daughter that day? He lost family when deported from Holland during the war. He lost his Dutch culture for five years when forced to work and live under Hitler's regime. Then he lost his father through suicide, never able to say goodbye. And, as if not enough, he experienced the loss of his first child soon after its birth.

Dad closes the two large sheets of the newspaper. "You purchased the ticket already." He delivered in a calm tone. Our eyes don't meet. Done! I am not to be stopped. He knows that. Slowly, I walk away through the kitchen with a glance at Ma. I leave the loaded air around me.

Certainly, Pa and Ma talked about it further. I never witnessed them dialogue about painful matters openly. I bet, later that night in bed, they talked about it. Ma probably cried. I don't know. We never explored it further. Quietly, as if gazing at a distance they let me do my thing.

Today, I ponder how I'd respond if my oldest daughter tells me she will go to the other side of the world to visit a man who is twenty-five years older. An older man, foreign, had asked me to marry him. Yet, Dad didn't object. Not openly to me anyway. He allowed it to happen. And I moved forward and planned the details of my trip while much in love with Toby, my former boss. He had moved from the Netherlands to Aruba, a Dutch colony, a tropical island in the West Indies.

—ᴍ—

"Allowing it to happen" is one of the gifts my parents gave me at some point. At eighteen I left for Germany to discover my German roots. I wanted to know Am I Dutch like Dad or German like Mom? Still, with an unsolved cultural identity at twenty-four, I now planned to visit this American, born in Texas, on a Dutch West Indies Island of Aruba where he worked.

I had no clue of who I was as a person. My persona lay hidden in a vague but strong inner fire to do something for others in this world. Dad's strong faith may have instilled in me this awareness of the poor among the human race. "Finish your plate, there are many poor in the world who'd love your food," he'd often say. And maybe I also took on Dad's desire to immigrate to America immediately after the war. His love for America and the Americans he worked for during the war in Germany was well understood in our family. Yet, Ma's heightened level of fear derailed that notion to leave for America. After all, she already left her country and culture of birth, Germany, for at that time the unwelcoming Dutch in Holland.

Pa allowed most things to happen except for my alliance with Victor, whom I dated before I met Toby. Or maybe my parents were just plain tired, exhausted by the boundaries I took them to, the edge, with my focus on underdogs, people in need of food in the world like Bangladesh, my interest in the discrimination of blacks, and friendships with people from Asia.

Before meeting Toby, I dated some boys from Germany, Holland, and Indonesia. Their outlook, except those from Indonesia, had a closed view of the world then. I felt different. I didn't realize that having a Ma from Germany and a Pa from Holland had stretched my world. .

"Would you like to travel, live abroad?" I'd ask my friends. When their future didn't show openness to that, I moved on. No, I wasn't an island of being Dutch, or German or Indonesian, French or... thoughts somehow encompassed a bigger world with stronger men. My Catholic upbringing added to that world view. I maneuvered with the world and its people; people I didn't know and who were different from me. Emotionally too, I felt unlike my peers. Others didn't have a brother like Henk with epilepsy and physical challenges. Possibly Henk's birth contributed to me becoming a risk taker. Life around him harbored a gutsy part. "Henk, get up we're going home," I ordered him regularly after his epilepsy sprawled him on the sidewalk where we played.

My spiritual awareness covered a childlike notion of a G*d being like a father, projected on Pa. It included St. Peter's Church I passed on my way to school and the *Ave Maria* we sang during Mass. "Pastor, can you write me a note—I'd like to gather some money for the people in Bangladesh." Then at home: "Holy Mary pray for us, Saint Joseph pray for us, Guardian Angel protect us." We said it daily at home and in the car before trips. That and the Our Father, before breakfast and dinner—we could do it fast and loud. My dad was fast. Ma's spirituality quietly focused on Mary, the mother of G*d, and her prayers had to do with Pa's near death during the war. A German prayer, she prayed daily to Mary, before going to sleep. She'd never talk about it. The note with her prayer, typed in the German language, she kept on a table next to her side of the bed. My spirituality sided with Ma's. This pretty much encompassed my faith. I was Catholic as naturally as my name was van Zanten. I didn't question my faith. It was different from many Protestants who had strong rules about dancing, going out, etc.

While I never realized the complexity of my family of origin for many years to come, Toby matched a breath of life that opened everything. Suddenly I had dialogue. He listened; he took time to explain the answers to my questions. Calmness surrounded us. Giant doors like those behind the moat of a castle had opened. Our connection felt as truth, our meeting like Providence. It was a communion, a sacred Oneness. We experienced a childlike innocence, as if the wind moved our sails and our boat moved away from shore to unknown waters. Never had I felt love, or peace and freedom on this level. I had to go, to follow and join him. He wanted to travel more and so did I.

I met Toby at the Shell construction site of Moerdijk in the Netherlands. I worked hard as an executive secretary and often went out to lunch with my boss Mr. Toby Hayes, the construction director. Call me Toby," he insisted.

"No, Mr. Hayes, it's culturally inappropriate in Holland." But he continued to insist I call him Toby.

At night I drove back and forth to Leidschendam, an hour and a half trip from work, where I dated Victor, an Indonesian man.

In contrast with my Indonesian foster mom, who came from the island of Java, Victor was born on Sumatra. I had rented a room close to where Victor lived, but mostly stayed at his place. Victor had been separated from his wife for a couple of years, but the divorce was not yet final. They battled with lawyers. His mood and fighting stance shadowed our relationship. Victor didn't want me to do anything by myself. Not the shopping or the driving to work. He argued often, followed by not speaking to me. "You are weak like a jellyfish," he'd say when I was vulnerable with him. He was quick to oversee my finances. I generously paid his outstanding bills. I mistook his possessive and controlling stand for love.

His Indonesian family all from Sumatra, embraced me. Victor's family worked, helped, and celebrated together. They loved music and dance. Their culture emanated "we together." We quietly engaged during a vacation in Austria.

The relationship with my parents after they met Victor and learned more about him came to a breaking point. They were unhappy.

"You are living with a man who is not even divorced yet. Leave the house, get out of here. You are not welcome here anymore. I never want to see you again," Dad yelled pointing me to leave the house.

The door of my parent's home shut behind me. Slowly I walked away. I felt alone, kicked around. Angry with Dad and stunned he'd disowned me, I cried and felt lost. What was truly home for me, my Dad took away when he sent me out. Never had I expected or experienced such rejection. I returned to Victor's apartment. Victor became less important. What stood in my mind, day, and night, were my parents and my siblings.

During the day my sadness about the split with my parents became hard to hide during my work and one day I confessed what was going on to Mr. Hayes, my boss.

At night, staying with Victor an inner knowing grew. You'll go crazy with his non-speaking, and his put downs, I told myself. His compassion after a dental surgery I had bordered on irritation. His criticism surpassed that of what I had experienced at home. This could not be love. I wanted out and pondered how to restore the relationship with my parents. From then on, in the evening, I encountered Victor in a somewhat different way.

"You can wash the sheets and laundry by hand in the bath-tub." Victor didn't want to drive me to the Laundromat. It didn't even make me angry; my anger lie buried. However, my think-ing became clearer: Our relationship is based on control. What I had taken for love, his closeness, his following me every step each day prevented me from meeting anyone else without him. It had nothing to do with love. That evening I packed my belongings in a suitcase. Victor didn't allow me the use of the phone to call a taxi. Thus, I walked out with my suitcase to the nearest telephone booth a kilometer away. I called home.

"Dad, I left Victor. Is it possible for you to pick me up?" Insecure, I uttered the words, my first communication with Dad since he threw me out. He arrived within the hour. Thus, I moved back to Rotterdam with my parents, purchased a second-hand Peugeot and did my daily track from Rotterdam to the jobsite in Moerdijk.

Times had calmed again. My boss and I had lunch, discussed work and life in general. Our conversations were broad. This serenity wouldn't last long.

"Inge, I'm getting a divorce," Mr. Hayes told me one day. .

I had walked into his office to hand him some papers. Except for sharing my problems about my misery with my parents our communications had never been that personal. I felt his announce-ment deeply. And contemplated why a nice person like him gets a divorce. Slowly I walked back to my desk. Dazed I opened a drawer, took a piece of paper, and searched for a pen. "I think I will become his wife," I wrote down. Those words spontaneously bubbled up from the intuitive.

His words, this personal sharing of his divorce, changed our relationship. It made for intimate conversations during lunch in days to come. After work we went for walks on top of the nearby Dutch dykes. He shared about his children, Donna and Nancy his daughters and Tenny and Alan his sons, his granddaughter Jennifer. But life went on. At home I reconnected with friends and at work the job situation began to change.

The construction site of the refinery, my workplace, came to completion. Mr. Hayes announced he'd possibly be transferred to Aruba and a small group of us would tie up loose ends of this project. In a few months, I had to look for another job. Sadness about his coming departure wrapped around me. I pondered what I could give him as a token of our friendship at work.

A goldsmith prepared a coin for me as a gift for him. "Please craft one side of the coin in gold with the other side in silver. The metals signify two lives."

The gold side was smooth as I saw Toby, the surface of the other side, mine, silver. "Leave the silver side rough and on the gold side I like to have a star engraved." On my silver side I engraved the word "*vertrouwen*," in English meaning "trust," and the dates of the years we worked together.

One night, after work, we celebrated with a dinner. The restaurant beneath the dike bordered the water where we could see the river. Big boats floated by, and we could see the jobsite in the distance. That night we embraced and even kissed. We touched and I drove home to my folks trembling. What did I do? What did I allow? What about tomorrow when I see him at work again? We had crossed a line. Romance had entered our relationship. The word "*vertrouwen*" which I chose for the coin would become significant. I thought about the piece of paper on which I had intuitively written the words—I think I will become his wife.

There was a peace and calm about him much like the gentle cobbling of a clear river in the mountains. At twenty-four my hands had a constant tremble.

"You need a break," he said.

That break in my mind was from being a Ma to my mother, my brother and sister and seeking love where there was none.

Toby, a civil engineer, moved to his next assignment in Aruba.

"I'll send you a ticket to visit me there."

"No, I'll pay for it myself," I firmly uttered. I didn't want to be obliged in my decision to marry him. A few weeks later, my family had subsequently seen me off at the Schiphol Airport on my first flight ever.

—ɯ—

"Happy is that person, who feels the connection in all that is living, and, because of that, is loving life and people," a translated quote from Albert Schweitzer that was dear to me then. Those German words directed the first step of my life with Toby in Aruba: "*Glücklich ist der Mensch, der den Zusammenhang mit allem Lebendigen fühlt und deshalb das Leben und die Menschen liebt.*"

On the island of Aruba Toby had rented a room for us with Mr. Irasquin who lived on Lloyd Smith Boulevard on the west end of the island. Across from the house stood several two to three-meter cacti between rocks where large lizards jumped around. The clear blue sea stretched out in front of us.

"I panicked today when I swam in the small lagoon across the street. A school of fish, hundreds of them, surrounded me. By the size of them I thought the Dutch herring had migrated with me." Toby laughed about my adventures and encouraged me to learn to snorkel so we could enjoy the underwater scenes on his weekends off.

"We lucked out today, Mr. Irasquin's maid prepared fish soup, head and all."

I walked to the kitchen to prepare our dinner and glanced outside. "*Verdomme*, goats pulled down all the clothing I washed today."

"Bring it in earlier, they come around at nightfall."

Thus, my visit with Toby in Aruba explored a marital relationship. He worked during the day and I cooked, kept laundry and explored foreign peoples, their habitat and Papiamento, their language.

The West side of the island extended twenty miles from the East where Toby worked. During the day I'd connect with fishermen on boats and purchase food on the East side of the island. At night until dark, we explored the North side of the island along the Atlantic Sea, an area without roads and where the sea harbored sharks. We used a Volkswagen for transportation and made certain we'd make it back before dark to find a path to the main road without getting stuck.

Six weeks we spent together, and I returned to the Netherlands to prepare myself to live the rest of my life with this man named Toby. I had made up my mind.

Our committed love and soul connection became a natural love from the heart for both of us. "I love you more," he'd tease when I told him I loved him. "There is more of me to love you ..." After my departure of six weeks in Aruba, he wrote:

"The day of realization of a love great enough to cause such heartache is, also, the birthday of a love great enough to give great happiness to be shared throughout our lives together. A Happy Birthday for both of us." Another card followed.

"A heart full of love alerts the mind to the millions of beautiful creations of G*d. The capacity to love is a precious gift, to be loved is a blessing, but the supreme happiness is to have someone to love who wants you to love them and can return that love.

If we accept that the heart is the source of love, then it is an incorruptible organ—for it cannot be anything but honest—It can only give love. Love cannot be bought; it must be freely given. A happy heart is one that has found another to accept it as it is given. Thank you for making my heart a happy one."

Back in Holland again, each day that I received mail and calls from him became paradise. Also, I found a new job in Amsterdam and worked for an executive of Canon and culturally touched on Japanese culture and protocol.

"Toby, you will not be able to reach me, I have to travel to Germany." Afraid he'd lose me for my career, he asked me to come to Texas where he had moved. Ruth and he had separated their life together when he went to Aruba. He had prepared for her to begin living on her own.

Anxious and realizing this was very real and that indeed I was about to leave my family I prepared my exit. Doubts and with many "what ifs'" I boarded the KLM flight from Amsterdam to Houston. "Toby's words that "marriage is always a risk—you never know what happens" rang in my head. I gathered courage. We began our life in the town of Nederland, Texas. Culture shock—all day TV, not able to work, I often became depressed. Their divorce became final half a year after I arrived in the US.

—∭—

"I'm taking you off the market Inge," he exclaimed in Durant, Oklahoma where we married. "Let's go in that church there." We knelt in the empty church and acknowledged our matrimony in front of G*d. A marriage between someone divorced like him, could not happen without an annulment in the Catholic Church. This rule hovered as a shadow in my mind.

"I do not want to put my family through the additional pain," he said.

His divorce continued to puzzle me. He was such a good man; I questioned him about this.

"I stayed in an unhappy marriage for 25 years," he emphasized. I stayed rather than get out. Yet the thoughts of what would have happened with their divorce, should I have stayed behind and waited, waited for the divorce to become final, didn't leave my conscience for many years. This gloom didn't enhance my link with his children, most of whom looked upon me then as a young chick who'd married an older man in a midlife crisis.

At twenty-four I had no resources to confidently relate to his children. I lacked an inner compass and life experience. The rejection by his children and family, except for Nancy his daughter unsettled me. "He was never unhappy, just not happy," Nancy said recognizing his shift. It must have been hard for them to not only accept the divorce of their parents but on top of that seeing a new person just about their own age.

Soon our assignments across the world would take us away from this focus.

Toby and I lived on continents that included remote habitats. Each culture, new values, language, food and environment meant new integrations. Excited and curious we couldn't wait to get to the next country and his new tasks. Toby's work brought us closer to the earth. We lived in jungles, deserts, and larger cities.

Cultural differences of our own surfaced within our marriage. We shifted to the Dutch habit of taking regular vacations and daily coffee in the evening being present to each other. There were misunderstandings, like when he'd ask, "Are you my mate?" and I, not knowing that English word, understood "maid." Firmly I asserted no, I'm not your maid. Never! Only later did I understand. Someone said: "It's hard to lose a mate isn't it." Mate, mate, mate he meant mate all these years not maid!

In our life together we became as one in thinking, desires, and happiness. We often thought about the same things at the same time. This abundance of love expanded to the children Christa and Patrick. Acknowledging my Dutch culture, he purchased large bouquets of flowers in the beginning years. In Texas he took the time to pick wildflowers and bring them home for Christa, our daughter, carefully adding a poster of their names and variety.

The grandeur of feelings when one falls in love never left us. Later on, I learned that a love so big, maybe symbiotic, couldn't endure and often ends with the death of one of the partners.

In Caracas, Venezuela, in 1981, on one of our assignments the dishonest feelings of working for multinationals increased to a tipping point. The impact of chemical plants and refineries on people and their community troubled us. At night we talked about a new chapter in life, a new existence with a new community, focused on peace to help the world navigate away from nuclear strife. In addition, it had become time to live closer to the children of his first marriage, he said.

An engrained zeal had hold of us. That missionary fervor, impregnated by our forefathers, that leads to no good. Unbalanced, it flared up. In a church at the bottom of Calles de Bella Monte where we lived, I begged G*d to use me in some form. I wanted to be of service. How and what I didn't know. My volunteer work at a school in El Paradiso, a part of Caracas, with children from the barrios, wasn't enough. Neither sufficed Toby's work, though it should have. He provided for our family and had a heart for those who worked for him. Yet, it wasn't enough for both of us in the meaning and values of our life.

We experienced the cultural destruction by multinationals in the countries we had lived: The tobacco industry mowed down land abroad to expand their tobacco production when it had gone awry in the US. Factories dumped dangerous children's clothing in third world countries when a law was passed in the US that materials of children's clothing had to be fire resistant. Toby and I realized that work had to be done in the US.

However, a premonition of our real future and inner conflict showed in a dream shortly before we left Caracas, Venezuela. In that dream the sun *and* the moon shook strongly. It left me frightened and alarmed.

The energy crisis had hit in 1982. We fell on hard times. Toby became unemployed for the first time in his life.

"I'd love to build a big bridge," he'd say searching for jobs. "It's the Indian in me," he'd laugh. I hadn't really absorbed the fact that Toby was part Indian, as told to me by his brother and sister. That would happen later. Right now, he needed a job and some days, not receiving any response to his applications, brought his spirit down.

"Do you realize you are the only one I have in this world?" he said, reaching out with two arms. The age difference of twenty-five years rendered me incapable of responding to him. Quietly, I hugged him. A feeling inside of me, like a mountain, expressed, "Oh but I have so much more to give, so much more, darling."

— ◊ —

After ten years of marriage, the river of love presented an emotion I hadn't encountered before. My longing for my family and homeland overcame me. Texas was beautiful, but I felt lonely, not connected. A hunger of intimacy with life much like a seed ready to burst open lived inside of me. Toby's children, except Nancy, I felt still didn't approve of us. Nancy's unconditional love on the other hand, like that of her dad, gave us much peace and comfort. Yet Toby's unemployment, the lack of family support, and ten years of living abroad now felt hollow. Unemployment made life dark and uncertain. Stress became a factor.

One day I got angry, an outburst. We never became angry in our peaceful marriage, not once. We had no reason for it. I don't know where this came from. It had never happened before in my life, and I don't remember what I said.

"Sit down, sit down." He motioned pulling me to a chair.

"Mom, are you getting a divorce?" Christa worried that evening. Her question unsettled me, she was only seven. After living in remote areas across the world, not exposed to media, I didn't realize that at seven, she knew what divorce was. Then I recalled Mr. Rogers, a TV program for children she had seen.

"No, of course not. I just longed for my country and my dad."

Something commanding had hold of me. "I want to go back to Holland." I needed to go home. Despite the unemployment and living on money of saved stock, we took the trip. I wasn't angry with Toby. It wasn't him. Something had stirred inside of me.

"It isn't you," I told him.

"I know," he said.

Maybe, human instinct guided me, a sixth sense of what was coming.

—⋙—

"I'm having a real hard time. I don't know what's happening in my life," I told the priest at our church upon return from Holland to Texas. He suggested I visit the Cenacle, a Catholic retreat house. It became a place, a new home in Texas, where in stillness I could reflect and figure out the stresses that had entered our life with the unemployment and return to the US.

"There's a job in Libya, I'd be gone for a year," Toby said. And again, we assessed the risk for our family and our values. "It's not good for me and the kids to stay behind here in Texas for that long." Another offer came from the military, but we had become pacifist. However, the money was good, and we needed it. "Does it bring you and Toby closer? How about you as a family?" someone asked me at the Cenacle while I thought it over from my viewpoint. Toby had not filed for unemployment. It had been a year now. A job had opened at the hospital for me.

One day, a break came with a small construction company in San Antonio. Toby took an apartment there to stay and work during the week. On weekends he'd be home in Houston. We put our house on the market and we explored new homes to live in San

Antonio. In Houston, our house didn't sell. A different river gushed through our lives.

We were a close family. We visited Donna, his oldest daughter, and I noticed Toby's love for her in his eyes. One weekend, while preparing a cage for the rabbits our kids kept the darkness of being out of work for one year, the stress of life, our family with two young children, and years of heavy smoking shook the right lower chamber of his heart. He stretched out on the couch holding his chest.

"It's your heart, isn't it?" Soon thereafter I drove him to the only hospital I knew in Houston, Spring Branch Memorial.

"With the aneurism and his tensions, I'm hesitant to do a balloon," the doctor informed us. The actual heart attack happened at the hospital. Toby returned home after several weeks.

If it were possible, it appeared that our love had even deepened. His renewed love for me and the kids felt beyond the love we had when just married. He touched me a lot, expressed his love many times a day, kissed me, joked around. We helped each other out with simple chores around the house and focused on going forth with our dreams and values as a family. At night, I put my ear on his chest to hear his heartbeat. It sounded regular; we both could fall asleep.

"I want another birthday," he joked one day.

"Oh, really which one would it be?" Tired of having his birthday during the December holidays he began his selection. He focused on October and tried several days. "No not that one. How about October 25th," he laughed while drying the dishes.

Mid-October, anxious that his heartbeat didn't feel right I drove him to the hospital to be monitored. At intermediate care, he had dreams. "I just saw you walking on water," he'd wake up laughing. We decorated his room with memories from our happy time in Guatemala. Based on our connection with the Mayans; we intended to retire there one day.

Cared for by a Philippine nurse he recalled a little girl hurt in the Philippines during the war. I sat next to his bed close to him. He cried. Emphasizing the atrocity, he pushes his hand strongly into my side. "A bomb hit. The girl ran toward me as pieces of metal pierced her body."

Shocked I ask him, "Why didn't you share this with us? Why did you carry this all these years?"

"I couldn't tell my family, no one would have understood. They never understood the war part of my life."

I left the hospital that night puzzled. A couple of days later, he was transferred to ICU.

Before entering intensive care, Toby wrote a note expressing his confidence in my love for him during our marriage and he went into details as to why. However, he also mentioned a challenge he had: "… always your insecurities about my relationship with my children and later our own."

This baffled me for years. He owned his role as a father, and I possibly referenced a negative projection of my own relationship with my dad. My love lacked faith in a universe, a part I hadn't built from the time we got together at twenty-four till now at thirty-four years of age.

And it was true. I wished I could have had positive thoughts and faith and guts and pulled him through with words, encouraging words for the healing of his heart. Words of strength: "We can make it, we can go to Trinity and raise horses, why not?" But I didn't have it in me! Not only the sun and the moon shook, but I didn't feel earth beneath me anymore.

This stay in the hospital would be the last one. I slept in a chair not far from Intensive care. Mary, a Guatemalan friend and nun, took care of the children. Tom, a Claretian priest, gave him the last Catholic rites. Sr. Margaret, who I had come to know as a spiritual director at the Cenacle retreat house in Houston, visited us and handed him a cross.

"Do you know what it means to kick the bucket?" Sr. Margaret asked me returning from her visit to him in ICU. I didn't know that expression. Toby had told her he was "going to kick the bucket." I stepped into the ICU to see him again.

"You better take care of this, Ingeborg." He handed me the cross. "Drive to Bold Spring. Go and sit there. Take my cousin with you. Sit there and think," Toby verbalized with effort. I wondered about this assignment. Bold Spring was the cemetery. His mom and dad were buried there. Alone, I did sit there and did think, but nothing came.

His older children all visited the hospital, so did his aunt, brother, and sister. I took Christa and Patrick who were scared to see him in the hospital with the aid of oxygen and other gadgets. Upset they returned home.

A friend shared: "Sometimes people need permission to die."

What is happening here? He's dying? I pondered negative thoughts hour after hour. Selfishly I too thought about what would happen with me and the kids. There was no income, and we had gone through our savings. I had ended my new job at the hospital once Toby got ill. I wanted to be present for him and the children.

"We have to do a kidney dialysis. It's risky, we need your permission," a doctor said to me. Several days Toby tried to pee, it didn't happen. It made me mad; I knew it was crucial. I uttered some sarcastic words. Silence surrounded us. Then we joked some-what, and I somewhere said, "trust me" and that made him angry.

Now his feet are cold, his nose is blue. Did we pass a point of no return? I have to decide about his kidneys? He had suffered so much already. I need to discuss this with his children. It doesn't make sense to do a kidney dialysis at this point.

I found it hard to communicate with his older children. I feared the confrontation and their reaction. I sank deeper and deeper into the darkness. Then before five o'clock, when the doctors needed our answer, things turned for the worse. Nancy, Donna, Alan and Tenny all visited him one last time. "All you are is negative," Tenny mumbles while walking by me to enter ICU. Finally, it's my turn. I stand by his bedside and touch his body through the blankets. Toby's nose and feet are dark blue now. I try to warm his feet; they feel ice cold. I am scared. Scared of his body and what is happening to it. In fear, I'm touching him.

The blanket between our touch separates our bond.

"We have had it beautiful the four of us," he utters. I sense the effort it takes to utter each word. I take over, while numbers on the machine monitoring his heartbeat drop. "Will you come for us when the house is ready? Will you prepare it for us? Will you sing our favorite song then?" "Yea," a groaning yes is his answer.

Slowly, to help him let go of us, I read the 23rd psalm, the first verse of it, over and over again. "I'll make it with the kids. I can do it," I assure him. Then he slips away ... unexpectedly with one more big gasp he comes back, a large tear travels over his face in a final goodbye. His eyes roll back. The moment he passes I hear the welcoming on the other side. It feels as if his whole family there has been waiting. Together I experience joy and light, lots of whiteness. That part of my faith feels true to the core. I believe in the heavens, the afterlife. No doubt there. Toby had passed on to something beautiful. Something I could never give him.

I knew he was dead. Gone forever and removed from this life. The frightening shock machines, which I observed for days on end in front of his bed, would not bring my Toby back. I knew it. A feeling too big to hold overcame me. The deepest scream a human being can hold came close to the breaking point. Instead, I turn around and walk out the doors of ICU towards my friend Tom, the Guatemalan priest. I motion his older kids to go into ICU and silently departed.

I'd have to pay a high price for keeping all those feelings and primal scream inside. In today's culture we have to contain ourselves in times of atrocities. Terrible things happen in the world and as zombies we allow it without reaction. Our skin is thick, distractions abound. I did not shout it out!

At home I took Christa and Patrick to a room. We sat down on the floor. "Your daddy was very very sick, he died today. He now is in heaven." I cried and held them. It was my presence and sadness which they understood. Something terribly bad had happened to their dad. To Christa a deep sadness struck, her essence comprehended. Upset, she realized that her dad had passed two weeks short of her birthday on that October 25h. It was his new birthday all right; he had announced it himself a few weeks earlier. Patrick externalized his grief by screaming.

"I want my Daddy back, I want my Daddy back," for days on end.

I felt guilty and wondered whether I contributed to his death for wanting to go to Holland. What about the stress for an older person to raise two more young children? Or maybe, his body had endured much with the travel, smoking and the responsibility of large projects to be built. Oh, and let's not forget that drive we both harbored, a Christian drive to do something grand in life. This too threw us into the rift of unemployment.

"Toby was ready, he had completed his life," my sister pointed out reflecting on his deep love. "I'm so thankful he was happy these last ten years," his sister and brother-in-law commented. Yet, I cannot help feeling responsible for part of my own humanness.

All I can do is be grateful for such love in my life. He gave me a life that later became my work and way of giving back. As for all his six children, the four of his first marriage and the two with me, his death was a turning point. We continue to grow in love for each other and make it beautiful. No, his death cannot be in vain.

Would I do it over again? Yes, I would. Our souls continue to be connected. In dreams I search for him as if divorced from me. Many a day I recall his remark in Guatemala, "I'd like to come back as an Indian in Guatemala after this life." At other times, "Stick with me girl and you'll go places you never intended to."

Yet, a second time I would wait a bit longer joining him in a relationship. The fact of the matter was that even though he was separated he had not been legally divorced. This waiting could have brought less hardship for my parents and clarity to his first wife and their children. It would have solved an issue in my mind that lingered for years. "What if I would have waited, would they have returned back together again?" We were wrong in entering our romance before the divorce. The truth is I didn't wait. I had not built a trust level in life at that age, nor did Toby want me to wait. We moved forward.

Immediately after his death a deep-seated fear took hold of me. I had no clue how and where to raise the children. The question of who I am and where am I going hovered beneath the surface of my consciousness. It would soon burst through in a dramatic way.

"It's best you and the children go back to Holland," Toby had advised me before he died. I set out to do so.

My children had become fatherless at an early age. Alan, Toby's son, who had to go through the divorce at the age of nine, his children from his first marriage and his grandchildren, all missed out on a deeper relationship with him/us while we lived our life abroad; Though Alan vacationed with us in Guatemala and Indonesia.

Still, I would do it over again. Toby had to live with the absence of my maturity, our age difference. The children and I were cheated out of a life together with Toby.

"We had it beautiful." These were his last words before he died and when I recall the grace of our life and his parting I stand in silence. I rest my case in love.

Our bond continues a bond through the children, our friends and family. I need to ask for forgiveness. Forgiveness for the heartache I caused Toby when I wanted to go back to Holland. It wasn't Holland; it was my dad I needed to go back to. I hadn't seen him in two years. I had no clue about the psychological father/daughter relationship, that inner child, that must end at some point in one's life. These may have been forces that were screaming inside of me once we returned to the States. Or maybe, my strong intuition felt Toby's death coming. Still, I think I broke Toby's heart, at least part of it. I had momentarily broken the trust of our love. I didn't have enough faith to go around for myself let alone for us two and our family. I had put all my faith in him and our life together. The possibility of his death with him being older had never entered my mind.

Toby's death expelled my naiveté. My life hung in the balance with his passing. The might of his absence, the finish of our marriage, and his mortality had crashed down on me. This unexpected ending threw me into a new chapter of my life with the children. A chapter without him, which I hadn't asked for, had struck the core of my being wide open.

No, I want him, Toby, my husband, their dad. My mind refused to go into a concept of the future. My bones were scattered without life. Toby and I had become one and now his bones were pulled away. I felt amputated. There was no wall to lean against, one to catch my breath on. The hinterland was flat like a pancake, flat like Holland and I didn't like the Dutch, those Dutch that had rejected my mom and me too. With no locality, no ground or culture to hang onto my brain floated into the chaos of no-man's land.

"Sing to the mountains" I'd sung, remembering his reception from the other side at his death. Then the Kyrie and other Catholic songs.

"Mom, I see a black box," or "Mom, I see Dad," Patrick would say in those early days. Christa kept quiet. I gave her a journal and began inviting children to the house, so they both might have peers to share with. Patrick wore Toby's work badge to school and at night they both slept in his T-shirts.

Steven, a neighbor friend of Patrick had come over to spend the night with him. Around six o'clock, the following morning, I opened the sliding doors to our back yard. I stepped outside and walked onto the grass. I thought about G*d and about my faith, and how hard it was for me to kneel in front of such a mystery. Soon thereafter, as if a force had weakened my knees, I dropped on my knees onto the grass. The grass seemed different. I got up. There were blue green patches. They still had dew on them. Looking up I could see forms in the clouds: On the left I saw the United States, Central and South America and to the right I saw Europe and Africa. The two were divided by the sea and above it was a huge bird or angel with spread wings bringing the two together. Dark colored clouds moved to the left and became consumed into an orange cloud mass. From the left sprung a light beam, much like a jet stream, that moved all the way across that ocean to Europe.

"Chris, Pat, Steve come and look in the yard." I had hurried into the house and woke up the kids. We stood there in our pajamas, looking where I pointed. All four standing on the small concrete platform checked it out. Huddled with the kids in amazement, energy slashed me to the ground. I stood up and examined my knees and arms, which had no signs of any hurt.

It has been more than fourty years ago, this vision. At the time it may have been dismissed as part of a psychosis. For me it still stands as a spiritual experience of significance for my life. It will take a lifetime to grasp it, possibly till the day of my passing. This vision was part of a transformation of my essence into a new chapter.

Really, there is no need to push for understanding. It is undefinable and for that matter so is the notion of understanding identity

204 · On Foreign Ground

of one's soul. It's easy to simplify and give myself pseudo identity descriptions of mother, father, wife, job, a longing. The true arc of my life here on earth, the spirit of it, will only reveal itself after I pass. It's all about the love and legacy I leave behind for future generations. Providence is not for me to understand. It demands surrender.

LA VIE EST FRAGILE, LE TRAITER AVEC TENDRESSE

H E ARRIVED BY TRAIN FROM Brussels, in his hand a
little plant, a purple violet. On a little card he wrote: "*La
vie est fragile, le traiter avec tendresse.*" Life is fragile, treat it with
tenderness.

Harry, a priest, studied for a sabbatical year at Luminae Vitae,
a Jesuit Institute in Brussels. Introduced through a mutual friend
he came for a weekend to see me and the children in Roosendaal,
the Netherlands. Harry offered his friendship, warning me he'd be
a tough one to be friends with.

The kids and I had just moved from Texas to Holland, and I welcomed his friendship. Our minds challenged each other, especially
while I attended the Pastoral Institute in Antwerp.

"What is Process Theology?" he'd ask me, as if the concept was
totally new to him. And answering we'd delve deeper and deeper
into it.

Whenever I met with Harry there was always so much to think
about later. He'd say something that made me ponder.

"Oh, you are not yet that far," he said one day looking at me with
tears in his eyes. I believe he referred to the movement of his heart,
the ability to see the beauty of another human being that moves
you to tears. We had checked out several small galleries in Brussels
and finished off with a visit in a simple Belgium hamburger joint. I
knew it had to do with that "fragile flower" he gave me and that he
was seeing beauty in me I wasn't ready to see in someone else: him.

I just wished I'd be that far and be as moved as he was by another human being.

It reminded me of Toby, my husband, how weeks before he became ill, I looked at him thinking, "Darling I have so much more to give you." I felt it, just couldn't express, or even give it. I was just not that far.

Harry returned to South Dakota where he lived. Years later I'd move back to Texas with the two children. Our friendship flourished through long telephone conversations in which we shared mostly our work passions. He visited Houston for a few days.

I in turn prepared for a vision quest in the land of the spotted eagles, in the state where Harry lived. The ceremony, *Hanblecha* called by the Lakota Indians, is a four-year spiritual commitment. This was my second year. Fear and anxiety had peaked after a difficult period in my life. I lost weight rapidly. I planned to visit Harry as he helped to connect me with a Dakota man to do the *hanblecha*.

Harry received me gracefully. I stayed at a friend's close to his house. I visited with the Dakota, and I attended an *Inipi* ceremony.

"Please join us Harry, they welcome you, I encouraged him. Maybe you can receive some healing of the Parkinson's,"

To my surprise he accepted. His first spiritual experience with a Dakota Indian. This brought awareness of the discrimination that existed where Harry lived. "I took the bus today and noticed the driver did not stop at a bus stop where an Indian waited to get on."

I returned from South Dakota to Houston.

Harry and the spirits of the land where he lives trigger hope. With a deep longing for healing, like a magnet, I make Harry the focus of my obsession. An obsessive dance much in character of a boa snake began.

Entangled by guilt, fear, and shame I began the mess up of our ten-year friendship. I became afraid that the energy of my obsession could hurt him and his Parkinson disease. I could not stop myself. I entered a bubble of fantasy, a child-level romantic energy. Harry a priest, a forbidden alliance.

Our open communication resolved the dance. I felt I had hurt our friendship. I judged him: You didn't take responsibility for your part, I thought.

The fact of the matter was that I couldn't handle someone loving me, someone deeply caring as he did in our friendship for many years now.

Wisely, he chose not to further focus on my doubts and fantasies. This resulted in a faster release of that draped boa around me. Yet that boa unexpectedly had marked its presence. Tensed by my fantasy world and emotionally like a child I then thought: Could I marry Harry?

Overcome by shame and depression I called on the spotted eagles to help me. I deeply cried and surrendered. I called on the energies of the six directions of the universe.

"I wish I could take part in a cleansing ceremony now and pour my heart out crying, sorry for all these derailments in my life. I know I would be able to surrender there." While in an *inipi* or sweat lodge, I can enter my Heart and get centered. The spirits of the *Tunkas*, the stones, help me as well as the water and the earth and the singing. Yes, the singing. It's the only way I get out of my head and enter the heart.

Every time I thought about Harry, I pleaded with the eagles to cut off my compulsive connection with him.

I have a spiritual friendship with Harry. That big R.C. Roman Catholic encouraged me for years, with all my spiritual questing. He always saw only good in me and called me forth.

"Damn, I long for our peer ship to be centered.

I wish I could raise myself and stay connected with the universe as my life force.

I feel hooked. Is he hooked too? I'm making a mess; I'm destroying, destroying. "I need to stop my thoughts. Put my energy elsewhere. Be still and breathe—you wandered too far from yourself. Come back, there is work to do and much to see," a voice called inside of me.

Harry's disease scared me and reminded me of death, Toby's death and that coming of my parents, Harry's, and my very own. Tonight, before I go to bed I will center deeply and join the spirits of the birds. I want to feel whole and share myself in a balanced way. I wonder whether the big RC is doing all this on purpose. Is he that smart? He doesn't know about the birds—I wish he did, it's so magic.

Peter and Cindy know about the birds. I think my dad knows a little about the birds. When Toby, my husband, died there were birds all over Christa says.

After visiting Harry, I wrote a poem which I sent to him.

Holy Communion

All my relations

G*d's delight

Spirit teachings; Energy fright

Holy Communion; Peaceful Might

Circle of Union; Center of Truth

Crossing of Stillness

Loving Right

Universe yearning

Breathing Light

Forever expanding

Holy Stride

Intimate Calling

Center of Peace

Stop the Teasing

Stop the Fright

I long for the Stillness

Yet also the Might.

Harry writes back:

"Inge, dear Inge:

Please excuse my memory and me. With the onset of age my memory serves me poorly. I mislaid the poem. You are making a believer of me. May I have the next dance?"

I'd overcome the challenges of falling in love with Harry whose emotional presence and unconditional love in my life I couldn't handle. Next, as part of the search for identity I tried to explain the meaning of many snakes in my life. Did they signify a synchronic presence of addiction or obsession? I venture back in thought.

SNAKES

S NAKES SLITHERED THROUGH MY LIFE like signposts for something I didn't understand. "Let's not get up yet," I told my husband early that morning. It was at a time that in El Estor, Izabal, where we lived then, a plague of tiny insects surrounded our village. Outside, we often walked with a handkerchief over our nose and mouth to avoid inhaling them. At night however, they were attracted to the light in the house and even though the windows were closed, their tiny bodies found a way in. A few of them would land in the bed, especially when we had read before going to sleep.

We woke up early that morning. Toby's strong arms wrapped around me. I snuggled even closer. "Please stay, you're always out of here by seven." He left the house at eight that morning. When he arrived at his office blood splashed the areas around his desk. The custodians, while cleaning, had found and killed the deadly venomous snake. Toby's workers had threatened him by putting a deadly snake in his office; it was a *Barbera Amarillo,* Yellow beard.

From El Estor, a remote area in Guatemala, Central America, we often crossed the lake. On the shores across of the lake, strolling along the edged jungle, something beautiful on a stone caught my eye.

"Did someone leave their necklace there"? I just knew that wasn't so and stood there looking at a coral snake.

The presence of snakes continued with Patrick, our son, at the age of sixteen. He began to take care of a corn snake in the school lab.

"Can I buy one Mom," he begged.

"What kind?"

"A baby California king snake. They are harmless and make good house pets."

Pat would lie on the bed and let the king snake crawl on his chest. We named her Sheila. "Hold her Mom, he'd encourage me, offering me the snake." I'd take a deep breath and very quickly held her cold body in my hands. Shivers went down my spine.

Sheila shed her skin every full moon. At the time that Sheila shed I had vivid dreams.

It wasn't long until Sheila got out of her cage. I was stalked in my own house with Sheila crawling around G*d knows where. Uncomfortable, I stayed on high alert. Several days passed and still we had not found her. I put water out in the room where her empty cage was standing.

Two weeks later I found Sheila's flat body on the pavement about fifty yards from our house. Her beautiful black body with yellow stripes had been flattened like a pancake by the wheels of a car. Horrified, I cried. My sadness wrapped around a newborn empathy for the snake and maybe guilt too.

I finally had liberated my mind of the snake in the story of Adam and Eve. I began to have affection for snakes and saw them as G*d's creatures. One of Sheila's skins now shines on a rattle that I made with an Apache Shaman.

After Sheila there was King Arthur, an eight-foot boa constrictor Patrick also purchased from his teacher. He brought him home in a pillowcase. He built a huge cage with two sliding glass doors, as big as a small single bed, for King Arthur and next to it stood a small cage in which he bred King Arthur's food: rats, a lot of them. Dead mice and rats became common items in the fridge and freezer.

Then there was the speckled king snake that squeezed its cage door open. I had a client that day for the healing I do and while she told me her story, she suddenly looked at me in a strange way as if in another reality. She left shortly thereafter, never coming back—while in the corner of the room where my desk stood papers began to move. I scolded myself for having such a mess on my desk yet walked over to the desk where I found the king snake curled up in a corner.

I breathed out fear, inhaled courage and held my breath, picked up the slimy wiggly reptile while I hurried to Patrick's room, dumping the animal in its cage. I put many books on top of it and waited for my son to come home. I learned after a while that king snakes can squeeze out of just about everything.

All the snakes that lived in our home would get very active at night, right when I fell asleep. It bothered me because I'd feel their spirit. I'd get up to check whether they'd still be in their cages and noticed how in comparison with the daytime, when coiled up and asleep, they were very active.

King Arthur too shed his skin usually during full moon and one night he entered my dream. He was mad and, in that state, nabbed my spine. It happened the night that Christa was not feeling well and had asked me to pray for her. I promised her to do some healing prayer. Tired, I went to bed and forgot all about it. King Arthur had not. His spirit entered my dream and thus he bit me for not doing the healing prayer.

King Arthur had my respect. Especially, after I found him one day half out of his cage. He had opened the glass sliding doors with his body. It was then he moved out of the house with Pat to his own home.

King Arthur may have moved to a new home, yet I was left with a ten-foot python in the freezer. The python had been a gift to Patrick. It had been mistreated by former owners and could not be trusted.

This python developed mites. Patrick and two of his friends familiar with snakes assisted him in bathing the python in a special solution. They had underestimated the slickness of his skin after bathing. While the boys were trying to transport the python out of the tub, fear and anger took hold of it and it lashed out at one of them. Its mouth had a hold of his arm while its body began curling around it as well. It took about twenty minutes to loosen his bite and grip. Both boys were OK.

Patrick didn't want other people to get hurt by this python and decided to put it to sleep. It was put into a slow hibernation in his freezer, which is in the workshop. I did a ceremony for that python and sent off its fear and angry spirit to the Creator to be transformed. The python has been in the freezer for years. I'm through with snakes and have bid them farewell, or so I thought.

THE GREAT BOA CONSTRICTOR

THE EIGHT-FOOT SNAKE HUNG WITH its long body draped over a piece of wood in its cage. His forked tongue sensed the air in hunger. A month ago, he had eaten his last rat. Now food determined his next move. My teenage son handpicked one of the live rats and threw it into the cage. He did it careful and quick so the snake would not mistake his hand for the rat. The rat sensed his last hour. It hid in the corner of the cage. Calm and secure, without any noise, the snake in a split second grabbed the rat. He strangled it. Next, he devoured his meal by enlarging his mouth to the size of the rat.

I looked away. Peeking back with feelings of horror, expecting a gruesome scene, I saw not a trace of blood.

Patrick brought home a variety of snakes. This one was a boa constrictor. He built its cage by hand. We could see King Arthur's every move.

I knew I had to wrestle boas. The spirit of an Apache grandmother told me I had to spend time in a cave with a big snake. Somehow, I linked the image of a snake with overcoming addiction. From my Christian religious upbringing, the meaning of snakes became something I had to overcome. Metaphysically, I understood it stood for transformation.

Dreams persuade me to reflect on my life. I notice my obsessive behavior when off balanced. Its trap would be deadly—like the one of the rats. Oblivious I gradually loose myself. Naïve I live a less fulfilling life. At these times, I bury my creative force and my connections with the ancestors. My talents are scattered around me. Like decomposing dead tree branches they lay on the ground. I walk right over them.

Last night I dreamed of fire. It's like when I dream of my grizzly, which wanders in an empty house. My dreams warn me.

"You became a victim of the boa again; what's going to be your prey this time?"

I'm in a world of fantasy. Obsessed, I chase knowledge. Sometimes the obsessions take the form of eating. At other times I over-admire a friend and give that friend more value than myself.

Hyper, I'm wired and driven with energies too much to handle. I become out of balance. My outer world is far more important than who I am as a person.

I thought I knew who I was. Not anymore. Something has a hold of me. What has happened this time? What triggers these unbalances?

In my adolescent years I danced wildly through the universe. The longing for intimacy I expressed through having boyfriend after boyfriend. I searched for that edgy feeling of anxiety, where my addiction lured; the feelings I knew so well from the epileptic seizures of my brother.

I didn't want sex. I longed for intimacy and emotional presence. Somehow it always ended up in sex. My pleasing nature to the other rather than myself had won.

Soon I recognize the absence of emotional presence. I coldly drop them by the wayside.

I wish I could see these kinds of boas approaching. "Get off the edge woman. Get to the center where the life force is waiting," I tell myself.

The earth and the rhythm of nature illuminate me. I sit and breathe deeply, while a hole in my soul surrenders. My thoughts still wild, I feel exhausted. It's cold today and I wrap myself in the blanket. I remember a prayer that I learned at the Cenacle:

Be still and know that I am the Creator

Be still and know that I am

Be still and know

Be still

Be.

I am getting calmer—my dance in life is slowing down meeting the rhythm of the universe. I'm alive and all is well. The rustling of the wind outside calls me. I decide to take a walk.

I compare my obsessions with the death grip of that eight-foot boa Patrick kept as a pet. I wonder if I learned to obsess as a child. To cope with the craziness around me, I became a pro in spacing out, quietly preoccupied with fantasy. And I became a "mother" at a young age, taking care of the emotions of Mom, my brother, and my sister, possibly even carrying some of the grieving anger of Dad. I counted drops of rain on windows, internalized sounds and counted light poles while on a bike or in the car.

As an adult, triggered by an overdose of fear, anger, anxiety, or shame this boa of obsession awakes again, tightens its grip slowly and sneakily, then drapes itself around my body and squeezes the life force out of me. It happens when I down spiral into negative thoughts created by myself or my surroundings—occasionally joined by thoughts of suicide.

Might someone save me from this grip?

THREE

LEARNING FROM THE INDIGENOUS

STANDING EAGLE, AN APACHE MEDICINE MAN

1991

Regularly, friends ask me for prayers for loved ones.
Others request me to send healing energy. Usually, with
great intent, my focus wanders to the area of my heart.
Once my awareness arrives there, I pass unconditional
love energy from the space in my body where my heart
resides. And in the spirit of universal Oneness, I'm
sending it off, much like an outbreath, in the
direction of the person.

However, today I wonder about that. I realize the
magnitude and vastness of the universe, the earth
moving around its axis and the galaxies we form part
of. I feel small, a dot. I question my daily intents and
business. I want to be in a space of stillness of the mind.
Being that magical mysterious speckle in the universe.

I CRAVE TIMES OF INNOCENCE, where I embody who I am.
I long to detach from the head chatter. I want to observe, feel,
hear, taste. To embody the moment. That space where I create, en-
gage, or quietly sit. I recall times where I am lost in play, writing,
painting, playing ball. A childlike purity. My energy dances a path
where it's needed. If I'm sad it trails out to a most natural destiny. Thus, my outflowing happiness, sadness, love, and anger either
block or unblock some invisible energy out there floating in the

cosmos. Like the strokes on Vincent van Gogh's paintings, they too seem to swirl naturally and are placed where needed, forever swirling. This innocent vigor of vulnerability and curiosity zips me into a different world.

It was humid. The air felt sticky in a manner only the Gulf of Mexico water can do to you. It zapped all my energy. The fan ran on high in my bedroom. It had been a long day of work at the university and my kids were on the phone in their rooms as teenagers do. A candle burned on my table among rocks and some sage I had collected. The beat of the drum playing on my tape recorder had put me in a semi-slumber. Suddenly the presence of a grandmother's spirit took my attention. "You will have to spend time with a snake in a cave," she told me. She didn't mean Sheila, the corn snake, my son Patrick had purchased from his teacher at school. No, it would be a larger one than that.

Standing Eagle's grandmother who was a Mexican Indian had a tender presence. She appeared strong. Her presence didn't feel pushy. It felt calm, clear, and caring. I'd have a quiet moment in the house or be at work and clearly feel her peace and see in my mind's eye the spirit of this short, strong, dark-grey-haired older Indian woman, invisible to most. Only once an intuitive colleague mentioned, "I see a shimmer behind you, it looks like an Indian woman, like a ghost."

The grandmother's presence became constant, and I never felt alone anymore. At night after the children had retired to their rooms, I'd prepare to go to bed. It was just the two of us and we had a clear spirit to spirit connection, an exchange of feelings, words, energy, and emotion. It felt like someone standing at shoulder height next to me and talking, always on the left side of me.

One night, however, she suggested that I allow her energy to enter my body. Thoughts of soul possession crept up. I became scared. This kind of closeness, where a spirit enters your body bothered me; had I been meddling with forces that were dangerous? Who could I speak to about this without them thinking I had gone crazy? I panicked.

"Grandmother, I'm just not ready for that, please leave." She'd do so immediately with her spirit disappearing in the void, ready to be there whenever I indicated and welcomed her again.

The following days I pondered channeling her spirit and the risk I'd take. What would happen to me? Would she honor just going so far? Would I become another person? Could I still communicate with her as before? Where would my "I" go? Would I disappear into the void? Yet, my curiosity and courage increased.

"I'd never let you take over my complete body. You can enter half of it," I told her. Again, doubts would take over: "What would happen if she doesn't leave my body once she is in there?"

And so, I'd let her enter halfway just for the heck of it, to see how it would feel. And it felt all right, not scary at all. In fact, I felt more balanced, and she felt closer. My body felt different, especially on the left side. It felt whole, no, complete. I made up my mind though to not go a bit further because where would I end up?

In one of her messages, she showed me a triangle pointing upwards. She encouraged me to fold my hands like that and sleep on my back without a pillow with my hands positioned on my solar plexus, the area just above my navel, hands folded as in prayer with the tips of my thumbs touching upward as in a triangle.

"It's a way to unlock the unconscious," she said.

My legs had to be in a certain position as well, with the soles of my feet touching each other as in a triangle. It was hard to get used to, but I slept that way for a long time. Later I formed a statue from red clay in that mode and had it fired in a kiln at the university.

—⟋⟋⟍—

I met Standing Eagle on a flight from Amsterdam to Houston in 1991.

"If you turn around and look at me, I will be sitting in a certain position," said a low, male voice inside my head.

I was sitting in the front middle row and as I turned my head to the left next row an aisle over, I saw him sitting there. He was skinny with olive brown skin, had a sharp straight nose, his kinky long black hair pulled back in a ponytail. I had noticed him earlier before boarding, not your regular passenger with that hat, color-fully decorated, and soft leather light brown jacket. His clothing was different from the other passengers, and he wore a necklace of white vertebrae, possibly that of a snake. The man gave me a pleasant smile with his hands in the position just as he had communicated to me telepathically.

Later at a stopover of our plane in Hamburg, we stood up and stretched ourselves in the aisle. The plane prepared for the long way across the ocean to the States and new passengers boarded. We introduced ourselves and talked in a normal way. He handed me a paper describing workshops he had just completed in the Netherlands and Germany.

I found out the man was an Apache medicine man. Both of us quickly found commonality of Sufism, Christianity, and earth spir-ituality. I told him about my friend Helga who had A.L.S., a fatal muscle disease. He in turn talked about someone who overcame the disease in California and now was running a marathon. He wrote down the woman's name so Helga could contact her. Then we each settled in our seats again, ready for our plane to take off across the Atlantic.

I was on my way back to Houston from a visit in the Netherlands because my mom had a terrible bike accident. Hit by a truck, she basically lost the use of her left arm and had been on life support for several days. I was tired from the emotions and attending to Mom while sleeping in the hospital. Yes, I was ready to be home in Texas knowing that my mom would live.

Shortly after takeoff and as if I were zapped into another world, the Apache Indian, sitting one row back across the isle, in the same seat as before, began the mind-to-mind messages again. This time he added a new element. I felt as if his presence, his energy field, zoomed toward my body and entered it, while he was just happily sitting in his seat. As a foreign intrusive force, this energy swirled around certain areas in my body; my heart, my head, my stomach, my arms, my legs as if checking all this out. It startled me, and it was something I had never experienced. How could someone do this? While examining my body on the inside he continued to speak to me telepathically and explained to me how my mother's accident had to do with excess energy and an amount of blood had to leave her body. Though I understood the logic of what his message revealed to me at that moment, it is beyond me today. While this energy meandered throughout my body, I noticed a bear, a big old grizzly, walking around on his hind legs even entering my head space. I felt the body of that bear as if it was a component of my own body.

The Apache proclaimed: "This child needs a bear."

The shock of him entering my body while at the same time my childhood rolled like a scroll in front of my eyes made me cry and doubt my sanity. What happened here? I'm losing it. Yet, I knew it had to do with that Indian man one row over. I shyly dried my tears. I slowly moved my head back into the direction where he sat, and he gave me that same smile or was it a grin?

The plane landed in New York, where both of us changed airlines and without saying a word of goodbye he disappeared in the crowds at the airport. After all this we didn't even say goodbye or check out what happened here? Disappointed, no confused, I continued my travel to Houston.

In Houston, I began a search for the spirituality of my roots. Christine, my own German great-grandmother's gift for healing had skipped a generation and was surfacing both with my sister living in Holland and me in Texas. Christine was a well-known faith healer in the little village of Ulmbach and specialized in skin diseases and the healing of horses. I started to mix my Christianity with the ancient ways. Daily, I felt the spirit of an older Indian woman and intuitively felt it was the grandmother of Standing Eagle, the Apache medicine man. While her spirit's presence comforted me, what happened made no sense.

A fear crept up about embracing this new earthbound belief and the possibility of having to leave behind what I presently believed. It changed my linear thinking. Yet, I prayed and asked the universe for a teacher of the ancient ways. I began a search to reconnect with Standing Eagle, the Indian I met on the plane. After almost a year that we had met on the plane, we connected by phone through Judy Johnston, the marathon woman in California he had mentioned on the plane.

"I need a male teacher to bring balance in my life and to overcome my fears at a deeper level."

Five years ago, I began consciously to confront my response to different circumstances of fear in my life. I needed to raise my courage, my gut level on many fronts. I have so much more to give.

"I want to claim the strength within me and am in the process of doing so using my spirit guides. Standing Eagle, intuitively I feel that I need your thoughts and ideas to deepen out that experience, maybe mapping out a plan. I know our meeting was not coincidental nor was the fact that I felt the presence of your grandmother afterward."

"I will try to reciprocate and be a good hostess here in Houston, showing you the places in this area." I wrote him. I described his grandmother to him, her constant presence, her looks, her gentleness and because of that he agreed to come and teach me.

Before his arrival I mentioned four dreams of lizards. "Standing Eagle, in my dream I saw this lizard walk over the headboard of my bed while I lay sleeping," I told him.

"You need to make a lizard rattle from rawhide. Make the head and decorate it and use fringes for its feet. Inside the rattle you should put 405 crystallized white rocks from an anthill. As you make the rattle things will start happening. The rattle is charged with your subconscious using your energy combined with the earth. Use the rattle before you go to sleep singing a bedtime song, the rattle will help your dreaming. Now don't start analyzing, just accept the dream. How about if I make the head, so you will have male energy, and you finish making the rattle so the energy will be balanced?"

Not long thereafter this lizard head thing made from leather arrived in a box in the mail. It was dark brown with black designs resembling the skin of a lizard with a red-brown horsehair that came out of a red mouth. Its two feet had many leather fringes.

I projected so much on that lizard head that I needed all my might of creativity, for which I used heavy stones, to balance it out with my feminine side to stay grounded through it all. In meditation the words "unite my people" and "connect the stones" appeared.

I dreamed I traveled on the back of a huge lizard or iguana. The lizard took me to a clear lake. I got off his back and drank the water. I drank all the water in that pond and changed into a cocoon and then into a butterfly. I flew around. Later I wanted back, and I changed back into myself. I spat the water back into the pond and finished the vision of my work.

Standing Eagle appeared in dreams. He reminded me of my night song and before he left my semi-dream, he kissed my heart. I was surprised about the deep connection in that other dimension, and the closeness I felt with another person beyond the physical world I knew.

Standing Eagle, decided to spend time with me to reawaken more of the ancient ways. It wasn't long thereafter that packages with his belongings arrived by mail ahead of his arrival.

"Just think, you'll have your very own medicine man soon," he wrote. "It is a new time for all of us, a time of great change, expansion and personal fulfillment. I asked my grandmother to guide you until my arrival."

I didn't want Standing Eagle to become a guru person in my life. I sometimes lost energy in ways I didn't understand, especially with men and I was worried about that and told him so. Someway I was attracted to powerful men in my life yet was unable to claim that energy and power for myself.

He wrote: "We may lose our power by giving it away, but the guardians prevent anyone from taking it from us. Naturally, you are fearful because you are breaking away from the majority's belief system in a radical way. You don't know what might happen to you if you will lose control or what. Say goodbye to these fears. They are the personal demons of complacency that will now be removed, and they are fighting to stay by scaring you. They act quite like a creature that must protect its territory. A new and vibrant life is about to open for you. All it requires is patience and willingness to learn how to use the other side of you."

In this new way of being, I attempted to be true and stand up to my inner emotions, but the weeks of awaiting his arrival turned my stomach upside down and I lost a lot of weight.

Was I mad to invite a stranger, whom I met on the plane, to live with us? Could he relate to my two teenage children? Where was this desire coming from? Was it my adventurous spirit, or was it destiny? Or just G*d forbid, doing something on the edge, something scary? I didn't know and couldn't stop myself.

Sunday night with flight 794 he arrived at Hobby Airport. Would I recognize him? What had I begun? I hadn't seen him in one year and three months.

There was no mistake about it; there he was in shorts and sandals, loose long black hair and a necklace of small white snake vertebrae around his neck. In my mind I matched up the way he sounded over the phone with this smiling body in the flesh carrying a bottle of water, now walking toward me. I gave him a cautious glance. It felt like meeting a stranger, yet I felt that I knew him.

He looked darker and shorter than I remembered. I loved his voice and tried to draw him nearer into my reality. I felt music inside of me as we met.

We exchanged a timid greeting. "Did you have a good flight?" I asked.

At the luggage department he kept on looking around and around, mumbling something about awareness and being alert to your surroundings, while he spoke of water and the springs in Colorado he just visited. He mentioned that his knee on the right side was hurting. I noted: oh, his masculine side.

Upon arrival in our house in Clear Lake, Texas, he gifted me with a beautiful black raven feather. "You can always call on the magic of the raven when you need it," he said. He settled in the guest room next to Christa's room. He draped a Native American flag on the window. His beige leather jacket, loin cloth, moccasins, pipe in a leather bag with fringes, and various herbs he brought with him changed the energy and smell of the house. He opened the window in his room as wide as possible. And despite the humidity and heat, it remained open day and night. He used herbal supplements each day and his cooking seemed of a different way too. Cooking and healthy food was important to him, and he celebrated my culinary qualities with sometimes a kiss on my neck while I prepared a meal. Then he'd think out loud and say, "No, I must be a good teacher."

We set out to buy herbs for me as well, coriander, anise, black sesame, *ashwaganda*, *sarsaparilla*. Some herbs contained female hormones, and some would settle my nervous stomach. I found out that he trained the *Ayurvedic* Way as well, and that his Apache background included knowledge of the ancient ways of India.

I noticed that Patrick had a huge machete under his pillow. This stranger scared him. Had I not talked enough with my children to prepare them for this? I took a big risk with this medicine man. Yet something deep inside said, "All is well."

Our weeks were filled with laughter, confrontation, and emotion. Standing Eagle made space in the garage for huge wooden panels that he painted while I worked. He also set up a trial area to do eye exercises so he could do without glasses. I'd call him from the Art School at the University.

"Use your intuition and tell me where I am, what am I doing and which color of paint I am using?" he challenged me. Connecting with my intuition became routine.

At noon I came home to his cooking of *Miso* soup, vegetables, and rice. Each day I began with physical exercises he taught me. He began to teach me about herbs like Osha that could be smoked for different lung ailments. We'd go to Galveston Beach where he encouraged me to try to become one with the sea. Sometimes he told me to be quiet in a very stern almost angry way. That unsettled me then, and I'd be quiet for a long time until he spoke again.

My friends and neighbors were curious about the Indian at my house and stopped me to ask questions. They noticed how good I looked and that I had changed in appearance. They had never seen me so healthy. We'd get on with the teachings after I'd come from work and my energy became higher and higher, until I could not handle it anymore. He made jokes about shapeshifting, transforming into something else, and indicated it might come up soon.

'I need to write down your teachings," I'd tell him. He wouldn't want to hear about that.

"Put it in the *akash,* it'll resurface on its own later."

The only way to channel my energy those days would be to birth a clay sculpture totally guided by my inner spirit(s).

"You have to destroy to create," he said, while handing me a piece of red clay.

I birthed many pieces that way, including a woman birthing. Many were both male and female. Others were both human and eagle. Some included a snake. I remember crying throughout the process and many a time being at the breaking point of an amount of energy that I knew would make me crazy if I kept it inside. If I'd not carried on, I'm sure I would have started to yell or scream or run around and do all kinds of silly stuff. I'd probably tremble a lot, no, I had no choice but to create from a force that felt like 1000-volts within. These sculptures were created under the influence of hysteria, trance, or ecstasy. I couldn't do anything else but that or go mad.

"Your thoughts, feelings and actions need to become one, Ingeborg," he'd say. At times I'd be angry about the way he pushed my emotions.

"You are just feeling sorry for yourself, get off that couch," he'd say when I became depressed.

I realized that my mental breakdown after Toby died were recurring depressive or wild energies I could escape only through Shamanism and its outburst of artistic behavior and relationships with the spirits. The feeling was both compelling and frightening at the same time. I just had to go there, no choice!

This process deepened my understanding of others. My psychological defect began to embrace this only way out. A breaking point of my mind through physical and mental pain, retrieval of my power animal(s), telepathic phenomena, clairvoyance, dream journeys, it all came to the surface taking its rightful place.

We smoked the pipe while various spirits entered the room.

"Your grandmother is here," I'd say softly.

"I know," he said.

It gave me pleasure to communicate with someone able to see the same as I did. While sitting on the couch I felt my body being lifted off and weightless as if without the connection to gravity.

At night I'd be exhausted from it all. I had put all my energy in creating a statue of nine little babies coming out of a woman's womb, pushed out as it were by a strange creature. That creation alone came from a deep place inside of me and I cried throughout the whole process. I couldn't stop. As a mad woman this energy came out of me while my hands molded the clay. Nothing could interrupt that process, not even my children.

While I believe the creation of these statues saved my sanity it took an enormous amount of energy. At night I still had to teach German at the University.

"Go lay on the bed," he spoke. "This is only for tonight—a treat. Your body won't be able to handle many of these."

He worked with my body. He'd arrange the energy so I would be refreshed and highly energized and able to teach that night.

"You need to gain strength for the initiation," he said one day.

I began transcendental meditation. Early in the morning and in the evening we meditated together. He, however, would meditate for long periods and when ready he looked as if he came from another world. This centering assisted me in surrendering my life more. It too increased my creativity. I began rotating energy within my body. Touching my tongue against the palate in my mouth I circulated the energy in my body from energy center to energy center all the way around to the solar plexus. There I gave it a good swirl.

"This meditation changes your environment. It can change the energy in a plane, a street, or wherever you do it." And life did change around me; it became more harmonious, certainly within the home. Christa and Patrick, my two children, learned to respect that when the bedroom door was closed, and I was meditating they had to wait. To wait with their questions, their going out or whatever they needed. These times gave me space and calmness they'd benefit from.

I became celibate to contain the energies and increase my capacity for healing. People approached me for healing. Going out of my body to allow the universal energy to break through had become easier. I, however, remained shy about it. It would take a long time before I would understand when to do the energy healing work and when to back off. While teaching me he'd ask me to work on him to see how strong I had become. I felt nervous, but his humor always saved me. One day the atmosphere in the house changed. I came from work late that day and I found him not painting as usual but motionless sitting at the table.

"I'm not making any progress," he sighed, as his eyes stared into the void.

"Are you mad?" I asked him.

"I'm not mad, I'm serious. You are not getting the meaning of the exchange of energy. It's the very way nature works."

He wants money or sex, I thought. Later I would understand this teaching.

After a period of fasting, Standing Eagle initiated me at the altar I had in my bedroom. It was a beautiful ceremony. He used a pipe, water, song, and sage. Eager I anticipated the future. What had I been initiated into? Was it coming into my own and realizing my new path connected to the earth and ancient beings; was this about healing, or that grizzly bear I had experienced in the plane?

He concluded his visit creating a life size painting of me sleeping on the couch. A leopard sat in front of me, guarding my area. I longed to awaken myself in that picture.

"How long will it take until I'll be in my strength," I asked him on the way to the airport.

"It's different for everyone. You have to kill this large snake to become a warrior and leader," he responded.

After his departure he entered my dream again and told me to kill that big snake, I guess for courage. I saw the snake on my left female side. It scared me. Could the dream be metaphorical? How could I give birth to this enormous courage? It left me longing to spend more time with him in a cave, or maybe do a vision quest alone in nature to overcome my fears.

Thus, I began this path that some call one of Shamanism. I act in a state of trance in order to connect with the spirit world, to do the requested healing work. Could it be that I began this already at two years old sitting in the corner under that sink? Maybe I wasn't depressed but I was "dreaming."

With Standing Eagle, I consciously entered a path of indwelling spirits of the bear, the eagle, and the lizard. More were to come. As I continue to carve out the intention of my life, I have only a glimpse of the forces that pull me forward like a powerful magnet. Some call it destiny, the cycle of life, the sacred hoop.

The presence of Standing Eagle's grandmother, my grandmother Christine, and the experience of Standing Eagle kissing my heart were followed later by a heart catheterization. My heart procedure at the Houston medical center confirmed my mitral valve prolapse. And a few weeks later, as in a dream, I wasn't totally asleep yet, my inner grizzly appeared, ate my heart and gave me a child's heart.

Standing Eagle's teachings emphasized innocence and impeccability.

I realized I had been a warrior even before he came. As a child, I stood by my brother, and my mother. I stood by Toby, my husband through his death. I moved away from Holland and continued raising two children, often taking in other teenagers in crisis. I educated myself to the point that I can allow others the space to grow while holding on to my inner critic most of the time. I'm on the path with many.

My house remained full of spirits. The presence of the grandmother became powerful all day. Sometimes the grandmother changed my hands into powerful bird feet. The process of shapeshifting began. When my hands transformed into bird feet, I knew to stop what I was doing. It was grandmother's way to call me to a halt.

One day, I heard about a child I knew who couldn't walk anymore and had been hospitalized for a long period. That night the spirits approached me to help her. I prepared to travel to her in spirit. I entered the world of the child and encountered a very unfriendly male standing between the child and me. I began the process of freeing her from that spirit. The grandmother however protested and indicated it was too dangerous.

My anger towards that spirit and the compassion for the child couldn't stop me anymore and I proceeded to that dark force. As if on automatic I moved on strongly and roaring with my animals. I didn't even think about the fact, that I had surpassed Standing Eagle's grandmother who cautioned me not to go further. I completed the task, returned to the child and mentioned to her we'd meet one day.

The following days a dark energy force from the spirit world took its revenge. Coming home from work I found my house was full of gas fumes. A leak sprang in my house. The same happened for my daughter who lived in an apartment. It signaled repercussions of the spirit world for me. Did I cross a line?

However, I received a phone call about a miraculous healing of the child's illness in Belgium on the night that I did the ceremony and work. She walked out of the hospital a few days later.

Standing Eagle's grandmother's spirit said she now had to leave me. Had I been wrong to surpass her? Or was I ready for new teachings? I cried when I saw her off distancing away from me in the void. I just sat there confused, alone and sad. She promised me she'd be there once I passed.

Grandmother's healing songs were about frogs. Many a time she signals me through them but is never present as before. I remained grateful and missed her terribly. Standing Eagle on the other hand moved to Germany where he was asked to stay and teach.

Standing Eagle taught me the first conscious steps of connecting with my inner Muse, to believe in myself. The experience of birthing in a creative way, truly feeling that in my body helped me to write my Invocation to my Muse.

"That my child is the Holy Spirit," Sr. Margaret, a Catholic nun and treasured friend, remarked. These words and the awareness of the inner Holy Spirit under the veil of a Muse set me off to a new depth of mystery and adventure of gaining identity. I wrote an invocation.

"Divine Creative Spirit, help me express my uniqueness; that birthing energy that yearns to love, bring cultures together, write, paint, play, sing and get closer to the Earth. That seeks joy and innocence through new adventures and discoveries. Grant me the ability to recognize the stirrings of my Muse, that Holy Spirit, to act, and protect, so I may sink into the mystery of my core being. Show me how to integrate that which is, with that which is not yet.

Balance my Muse with respect for the Creative Spirit in others so I may humbly receive what others can teach me. Excited and grateful, I call You from the Heart of my being to be with me now and always."

VISIT BY A HUNGRY GHOST

My Spanish-style house in Houston, with its double arched entrance and two palm trees in the front yard, didn't fit the rest of the neighborhood's architecture. I turned the key of my front door and strolled into the living room. The sun was shining and cast beautiful shadows through the sliding glass doors that led to the backyard. With a deep sigh I plunked down onto the couch. Cree, the smart dog slept outside, her belly hit by the hot sun.

Breathe in, breathe out, deep nostril breathing. I recited my mantra, the one given to me by Standing Eagle at initiation and began my Transcendental Medication. My thoughts still wandered back to the office: Wild this morning at work, so many students, so much to coordinate.

Sunk into myself, about five minutes into it, Cree, with her black and white spots demonstrated her hyper-Dalmatian and black Lab character mix. She barked with a high pitch. Somebody will be arriving, I thought. Still barking, the dog jumped against the window of the glass doors, as if wanting to come through it and tell me more. Not her usual announcement when family or friends come.

I was both aware of my living room yet absent from it. Groggy, I opened my heavy eyes and was surprised. A mist appeared in front of me. It hovered. A dark blob, not very tall at all, floated maybe two feet in front of me. I, on the other hand, just had become relaxed away from the office. I planned to have lunch right after the fifteen minutes of inner silence.

"Hey, you, I want your bear. I want it NOW," the entity announced to me firmly and with a hungry desire. It spoke into my mind.

I sat up straight on the couch. Shocked by the intrusion, I became alert and present. No doubt, something, someone, a hungry ghost maybe, stood in front of me at close distance. There was no smell. It was daylight. The visual form was vague and appeared from another realm, somewhat grey in color, taller than I would be standing. I felt the strength of his spirit, especially since he was standing while I was sitting.

He was there for sure. Where did he come from? Who was this bizarre creature?

"I want your bear," he bellowed with a deep and stern voice showing his perseverance. Did I notice some movement, some pointing at me maybe? No, he was not planning to go away, to go anywhere before he'd possess what he wanted: mý bear.

I knew exactly what he was after. He wanted part of my inner spirit; yearned for my power animal "the grizzly bear." The bear was my teacher, my strength and my voice. That bear appeared in my dreams, directed my life, traveled with me. It was my companion. How dare he! How did he know about mý bear?

In front of me was the heavy oakwood coffee table. It was all that separated him from me. Where can I go? How can I walk away? To the right maybe? Go into the kitchen? Dang, this is mystifying, I'd better stay put. Hypnotized, now trembling and also getting angry, I firmly planted my feet on the ground. I sat up straight to think better. Would there be anything, anything else appropriate, that I could give this force instead?

My bewildered blue eyes glanced around. On the third shelf of the white bookshelf to my left, I spotted two small brown pottery figures. These two birds were special. I once purchased them in Caracas, Venezuela. They were handmade and precious. Should I give him those? Would that satisfy his hunger for power? In my mind I spoke to him firmly, "You will not get my bear, absolutely not! I will give you one of those clay brown birds over there on the third shelf. They are special to me."

It's a good and fair substitution for the bear, I thought. But will he accept?

An atmosphere of rage and disgust filled the room. Yet, I felt the ghost's presence weaken. He slowly disappeared.

Confused, I got up from the couch walked to the kitchen and prepared a peanut butter sandwich. Took my first bite but couldn't swallow. My hands trembled, I felt sick to my stomach. The experience lingered in my mind. After I returned to the office, all I could do is think of that hungry ghost. Damn, who could I tell, they'd think I'm out of my mind. I felt humiliated. My thoughts drifted to the upcoming peaceful weekend. Nancy, my stepdaughter, and Annie, her daughter, would be coming over. I'll tell Nancy before we go shop together.

That Saturday the three of us returned from the mall. "Let's have some hot chocolate and snacks." I opened the door. Casually, we carried the shopping bags to the kitchen when suddenly I glanced at a smashed clay bird in the corner of the dining room. Next to it was a small pin with the letters "Doc" on it. I panicked. This was evidence. I didn't imagine that first visit after all. It was more than I could handle. I ran for the phone to call the Cenacle.

"Hi, this is Ingeborg, Sister Mary, I have a very hard time telling you this, but I think I just had an entity in my house… twice now. Sister Mary was one of the spiritual directors and at the Cenacle, a Catholic retreat center. "He asked me to give him my bear, you know the one that's always in my dreams, my power animal." I continued my story and recalled the first visit of the entity a couple of days earlier. She understood.

"Yes Ingeborg, this is real, it happens. Don't be afraid. We have had it happen here. Do you have any incense in the house?" she responded gently.

"I do, I do, I will use it in every room I have to get rid of this thing …"

"Why don't you call your Dominican friend Cheryl and ask her to join you? She can stay the night, so you can tackle this together.

An hour later after Nancy and her daughter left the house, Cheryl arrived. She had brought cedar and a drum. "Let's bury your broken clay bird outside, off your premises. Not before dark— we don't want to alarm any of the neighbors. Then we'll drum. I feel a strange presence, especially in the room where that broken bird was."

Together we buried the broken bird and burned incense and cedar throughout the house. We chanted songs going from room to room. I had opened the windows. Nothing out of the ordinary occurred until we came to the dining room and focused the incense on the corner where the broken bird had been.

"Let's make sure each corner of this room is incensed well, I feel cold all of a sudden," Cheryl uttered while looking at me with frightened eyes. She continued to the bedroom where I had put up an altar in my house. There she sat for a couple of hours.

"You know, something strange happened while I prayed. My lower jaw became all stiff and I had a hard time closing my mouth." Puzzled we looked at each other. Then the phone rang. It was Teresa, a family member. "We just found Nanna," she sadly told me. The nurses found her with her mouth open. She must have been dead for a while and the nurses had a hard time closing her mouth."

A few days later I drove to the funeral in the little town of Trinity, Texas, where Nanna, Teresa's grandmother had lived and died. At the graveside, a man introduced himself to me, "Call me Doc," he said. "I'm Nanna's cousin."

The episode of a hungry ghost in my life propelled me to a darker side in me. This search presented itself in the form of a wolf teacher.

CHIEF HIDDEN WOLF,
THE SECOND MEDICINE MAN
1994

I HAD NOT EXPECTED TO go into the basement of the house with this man, Hidden Wolf. I hardly knew him. Yet here I was slowly walking down the stairs into this slightly lit area of his home in Vancouver, Canada. The smell of sage, juniper and cedar encircled me. I loved that smell. It came from a distance, all the way in the back behind a gated area filled with herbs.

I followed him under the low ceiling. He pointed to a room we passed on the right. I saw a small bed and a bathroom with an upper cellar window.

"Some patients need to recuperate for several days before they can go home after healing. I ask them to bring someone with them to stay overnight," he declared with a compassionate voice.

In an open area stood a large sewing machine where he worked with leather. There was a comfortable sitting spot with a couch as well. Patients could access the quarters directly from the outside. Close by a bench was placed against the wall.

Hidden Wolf was a busy man. He had the energy of a doer, always fixing and helping, healing people on the spot. Not shy or one to hold back. His hands and fingers showed hard work, his nails dirty. And while his hands were not huge, his nails and fingers were rounded somehow differently. They looked strong.

I contacted Hidden Wolf after I received the teachings from Standing Eagle, the Apache Medicine Man. Standing Eagle, after his stay with me in Houston, continued to connect with me in spirit. I was not ready to deal with his level of spirit intimacy and was unable to shield myself. I felt confused and felt a sexual connection. Unable to stop it I'd say in my mind, "No, my alliance is with Toby," even though he had passed.

These energy intrusions reminded me of the time I was raped. A mixed bag of emotions of guilt, anger arose and yet and yet... there was something in me that wanted to grasp this. What are the natural laws that allow this?

I looked for help and a solution. But with whom could I talk about this? I had entered a path not many had walked, certainly not any of my confidants. The spirit world had its own rules.

Many nights I just did not want to go to sleep, afraid of what would happen, and I grew embarrassed not able to tackle this myself. This mind to mind or should I call it spirit to spirit connection was new for me. I had no experience; I had barely begun and discovered my ability of spirit connection with Standing Eagle. You know, where you communicate your thoughts and feelings mind to mind, whatever your location. Quite similar as in our daily world where we physically see and communicate with words.

One day though, soon after I searched for help, I saw a poster of a Medicine Man, Hidden Wolf, being in Houston and paid him a visit. I had called and received directions to a church-like building on the south side of Houston, just off interstate I-45. That afternoon in the humid heat a few people waited outside on a small wooden bench to meet with him.

A door opened and a Caucasian lady wearing a long skirt motioned me to come in. I handed her a love offering. She hastily put the money away in her skirt pocket, as to not distract the visit from the money I gave. An Indigenous man swiftly followed her in my direction. He was short, maybe five foot six. He had his hair in a curly dark brown ponytail. It receded on top. He was well built, not overweight, and wore western clothing, black jeans, and a black T-shirt with a picture of a wolf on it. He smoked a cigarette. His brown eyes intently observed me.

On brown, well worn, moccasins he walked toward me in the large entrance room. "Come with me, there to the left," he said with a deep powerful voice that expressed authority and kindness. His body language expressed a manner of "I'm in charge." There was no hesitation or distance between action and words.

Still standing, I gathered my thoughts to express the motive of my visit. Before I even was able to, he addressed the issue calmly with a loud and strong voice.

"I'll take care of it tonight. You need a medicine bag, I will make it so no other spirit will be able to approach you unless they go through me. These approaches are wrong and shouldn't be happening to you."

It was a brief visit. He gave me his card when I left. It mentioned he was a Chief and drawings of various animals including the wolf and eagle were printed on the card in the red and black Pacific Northwestern Indigenous way.

I wanted more, wanted to know this man. How was he able to know things ahead of time? Yes, I was drawn to him, body, and spirit. It was mysterious and strong. His courage and strength attracted me. I wished for an opportunity to talk more at length with him or get some teachings. I didn't recognize that his wolf-like presence had touched my own inner wolf shadow still sound asleep.

Hidden Wolf had returned from Houston to his home in Vancouver. How could I reach him? I planned to trace him.

In prayer I called a second time for a teacher. Who could teach me about the ancient ways? Probing the quest for my past, and way beyond the culture of my parents, I unconditionally asked for this.

Thinking he'd be the one and guided only by my intuition, much like a lone wolf myself, I set out to Vancouver where I knew he lived. My children and some of my friends thought I was crazy. But I had this inner feeling. It was so strong. My passion for the ancient ways had a force that propelled me onto dangerous unknown roads. It unfolded my life in a weird and wonderful destiny. I had to do it. I took off a week from work and made the flight reservations.

At the Vancouver airport I rented a small red car, checked into a hotel and unsuccessfully called his house the following day, morning, afternoon and evening. Trusting my inner knowing, I gave myself two days to connect and then planned to take a tour for a few days in the beautiful British Colombia area.

The second night in a hotel in Vancouver I dreamed of Hidden Wolf. It was a signal to me that for sure I'd reach him by phone that morning.

"I already prepared a whole afternoon for you. I knew you were coming," said Hidden Wolf.

That morning in my rented red car I followed his directions to a residential area. He referred to a large pink school bus he drove in Canada and the US. I found it parked right in front of a row of houses.

Slowly and nervously, I crossed the street to the house. At the entrance I breathed deeply, a last attempt to keep my anxiety in check. My heart pounded. Was I out of my mind to follow this person all the way to Vancouver? Maybe this adventure equaled the excitement and danger I began craving since my brother's epilepsy as a child. Crazy it was. Look at that strange pink bus decorated with cacti and other images of the desert. The bus décor looked similar to the Taco Cabana restaurants in Texas. I walked closer to the entrance door of the house. My heart throbbed. I rang the bell.

Opening the front door, he welcomed me, gave me a strong embrace, as I immediately stood in his living room filled with Native American artifacts. In the corner on a special stand hung his large Chief-regalia of beautiful eagle feathers reaching from head to toe. I also saw a buffalo head hanging from the wall. Chimo, his large grey dog, checked me out.

"Half wolf, half dog, I saved his life. No one wanted him," he explained. "Come to the kitchen. I like to get people at ease first and offer them a cup of herb tea,"

His first and most important lesson I received, while nervously sipping his tea I would take to heart for years to come:

"Do not judge, Ingeborg. Allow things to happen." He went on, "I do a lot of my teachings at night. It's the easiest time."

Hidden Wolf explained to me that he was hereditary chief of the Paiute Nation. In that capacity he was responsible for their wellbeing. He told me about his lineage and his grandfather.

Hidden Wolf left for a minute. I put down an exchange for his teachings on a counter. Then I took the jade ancient tool out of my purse.

"I want to return this artifact. I received this in Guatemala from Mayan Indians. It is not right for me to keep, and it belongs to the Indigenous." I viewed all indigenous people in the world as keepers of the ancient knowledge and thus handed him, a Paiute, the Guatemalan object. The ancient green stone was made of raw jade in the form of an axe. "Mayans must have used it a long time ago as a tool."

Enjoying his stories, sipping my herb tea, I was surprised when he suddenly put out his cigarette in the ashtray and interrupted, "Are you ready to do some work downstairs now?"

I sat straight up. Nervous and frightened, my stomach turned into a knot. I was eager to learn, my brain said yes please let us do some work, while my body went into the flight position. "Can I use the restroom first?" My stomach was reacting; I wanted to buy some time before walking down into the basement. I looked at the pictures in the narrow bathroom area. Pictures of eagles and wolves looking at me hung on the wall. I washed my hands, took a deep breath, and left the bathroom ready to take on this experience.

He signaled me to come as he opened the door to his basement while I slowly followed him. There were rooms off the dark main central area. We entered one of them, a pleasantly heated room in which he did his healing. "Why don't you lie down?" He motioned me toward a self-built wooden table cushioned with a piece of foam and a blanket.

The table took most of the space in the room and above me were two lights giving off heat. One was a large red lamp, the other blue. The place had a pleasant earthy smell. A huge wolf hide, head and all, stared at me from a hanger a couple of feet away at the foot of the table bed. Drawers both on the right and in front of me were filled with various stones that he used for healing. I felt good and at home. I was at peace and now relaxed.

"Sometimes I put the wolf hide on for special healings and during ceremony I turn into the spirit of that wolf."

"Not on me." I thought. No, no, I probably would never be ready for that one.

He began on the left side of my body slowly scanning it with his two hands, starting at my left foot. At times I could feel the energy moving beneath his hands. I felt heat coming from his hands. "People must learn Reiki," he said."

That day and later through personal experience he taught me to find what is wrong with a person and how to use the stones. I too would be able to scan a body and pick up with my hands the blocked energy and take-out illness.

"Oh, a knee injury," he mentioned while touching my knees." I threw him a surprised look laying there on the table. He was right. I had many knee injuries. As a child I had been wild, did lots of climbing, jumped over fences and played soccer. My knees were often covered in bandages. I had also hit a car with my bike at some point.

Later Hidden Wolf would teach me at night, while he was in his house in Vancouver and I in mine in Houston.

At those times his spirit would pull me in. It was as if his mind flooded mine for attention. Then I would lie down on my bed to concentrate. He was then in my mind as if I stood right next to him and the person he was working on. It was like watching a movie. These teachings surprised me and I called him by phone asking whether he indeed had done that. He confirmed.

Now, still in his basement in Vancouver he worked on the right side of my body, touching my right collar bone and said, "I have to take something out of here. It will hurt. Here, put this black stone in your hand and hold on to my hand with all your might while I take the illness out."

I began to brace myself for the pain to come and as the deep hurt inside of that bone increased tears began to roll. "Aauuuuuw," I groaned while something utterly painful happened there.

Hidden Wolf assured me that he took out an illness and that it was very bad. Later however I wondered if he had not shot, much like with an arrow, energy into that area. How else could he, after my departure back to Houston, connect with my mind or spirit at all times and continue his teachings? Could it be the energy he put into my collar bone on the right that gave him the portal of connection? Or did he really extract something, possibly energy, on that right side.

They do not tell you everything, these medicine people. It is all by experience and simultaneously on different levels, emotionally, physically, and spiritually and who knows in what other parallel worlds as well. This way of teaching, figuring out for myself through experience, I had never found before in the world. Not in all my years of working at the University.

Risking, I learned and stretched myself. A continued seeking for an ancient way of knowing kept me going, because I felt it was right and lost to the world. With every teacher, every medicine person and experience in the ancient knowing, I became convinced that somehow large numbers of people in the world had detached themselves from the earth, this jewel. I too had separated from my inner knowing. I was willing to risk in order to reclaim this invisible path.

The small, gated area of that mysterious cellar bulged with herbs he had gathered, most significantly the juniper berry. It smelled great. He would explain the complexity of herbs. He emphasized how much there was to learn about one single herb. He taught me a combination of herbs that I would use later myself. It included special tobacco, sage, cedar, and juniper. Those I'd use to cleanse an area or people visiting my home when performing workshops. His use of these herbs, especially the juniper, persuaded me to find out more details about them. Some were complex some used for birth control.

250 · On Foreign Ground

Often when he talked, he got mad about what people are doing to the earth. Especially how people controlled the wolf population. He was also angry at the Catholic Church with regard to overpopulation in the world and explained how Paiute families had lived in groups in the past and took care not to get overpopulated.

"You whites can't leave anything alone; you have to change everything," he often said. I'd feel hurt and confused then. What was wrong with me being white? Were all whites wrong? Can white people not leave anything alone? Is it in our DNA? I began to ponder these questions. And I found that "control" is very much part of me and the Western world, whatever color the people are.

To correct myself I questioned where and when the entitlement to land and its resources came from. Some academics would point to religion. The false interpretations of belief systems may have been part of it. Human beings had drifted away from their earth connection; theirs and my umbilical cord was cut off from our earth mother in a profound way. It's tough to allow things to happen in life.

Through Hidden Wolf my connection with the wolf awoke. At that time, I didn't realize what exactly happened through his teachings. I hadn't reached a tipping point in my experience of Oneness in the world, even though his wolf dog, Chimo, entered my dreams together with his boss, Hidden Wolf while we were miles apart.

At the end of the visit, he handed me a medicine bag, which he had prepared for me ahead of time. "Keep this black stone for healing purposes." This showed me he somehow truly knew ahead of time that I would come to Vancouver for a visit.

I put the medicine bag around my neck and wore it day and night. It was made from dark brown smooth leather and about 1–2 inches large and sewn shut. What was in it? It smelled good and gave me a sense of security. It felt right to wear it at that time.

—m—

Not knowing what all had happened to me and pleased with the visit, I continued my vacation in Canada. I planned to explore a northern loop in British Colombia. I had invited Hidden Wolf to come along, but he declined. He would be with me though in another way.

While I slept in small hotels, the teachings from Hidden Wolf continued in my head day and night. It was as if a film rolled in my head with images of ancient people and teachings. Some of it I wrote down. Most of the time though it would go too fast, as if my mind was siphoned into a different consciousness. I just had to let go and endure it to continue in my head. I longed to call some of my friends in Houston about this spirit medicine but couldn't put what happened to me into words. Day by day the depth deepened in complexity, and any attempt to express it would be beyond me.

After a small breakfast in a hotel, I drove on early in the morning. A small flock of bald eagles started flying alongside of my car. They kept on hovering on the right, these powerful birds flapping large wings; they looked with their piercing eyes at me and my car.

Then in my head I experienced their energy and their speaking to me. No, they did not speak with their bird voice. I received it in human language: "There to that area with that sandy shore, you will go to gather stones for your healing work."

Earlier, Hidden Wolf, during our visit in Vancouver, told me not to pick stones by sight, but rather by feeling and intuition. Now the spirit of eagles guided me to an area close to the shore and water on the left. Further down were trees, most of them pines. Many logs and stones had washed up. I parked my car and continued on foot led by those huge bald eagles still hovering on the right and communicating with me. They motioned me to a spot on the left of them, close to the water shore. I saw an area where the washed-up tree trunks and stones captured between them were concentrated. To me it looked like a pretty good spot to gather stones as well.

I walked closer to the rough looking area, walking over large rocks that had washed ashore, continuously guided by that, for the eye invisible, eagle force. Yet playfully I let my own desires get in the way. I wanted to follow my own will. And as I struggled against the eagles' will I strolled a few yards further than intuitively the eagles had pointed to. I considered it a "better spot." As if by a stroke of lightning I was slapped to the ground of that rough terrain. Catching my breath in shock, I gasped with surprise. My back and legs hurt. Astonished, their force had startled me. And I could feel the anger of the eagles. What just happened here? What did I do or not do? I began to cry, my legs hurt, and my breath was swept away.

I understood. In my mind I spoke and apologized to the group of bald eagles. I crawled on my hands and knees back to the spot they initially communicated to go to. Sitting on the ground surrounded with washed up logs and stones, I concentrated now on finding the healing ones. With my eyes closed, I asked the stones to come to me. I scanned the ground with my hands still trembling from the whole ordeal. I felt energies coming from the stones and knew which ones to pick up. I had surrendered to the eagles and gathered exactly the amount they told me, not a single stone more, or less.

I don't cross eagles anymore. They are powerful and I welcome their help, guidance and protection gratefully with open arms.

Hidden Wolf's teachings went on especially at night for a year or so. At that time, he lived in Vancouver or wherever he traveled, and I lived and worked in Houston or wherever I traveled. I noticed every time I was tempted to go off the ancient path by connecting with a man, other than one on the Indigenous path, or make significant change in the road of my life, the image of this dancing medicine man in full regalia would flash in front of me dancing from the right to the left.

I knew this was my path.

After I returned from Canada to Houston, I woke up each night at the same hour. My dog would bark and there Hidden Wolf was in my mind, teaching again.

"That woman doesn't want to sleep on her right side," he'd complain. In my mind I could see him working on a person down in his cellar and then communicating to me what he'd do next and why. Later he would even enter my dreams. I'd ponder what he meant by me not wanting to sleep on my right side. Thus, I began sleeping on that side, the right area that many call the masculine side.

The specifics of my vigorous masculine side, enforced through a powerful dad in my youth, had no consciousness in me yet. It would take a lifetime to integrate these masculine positive and negative characteristics. They formed an integral part of gaining identity and authenticity. The wolf would come to my aid later.

There was no way out. I was on the path of orchestrating wolf traits. Others noticed it at work, my decisions became stronger. I was persuasive and asserted myself in ways I did not before. With Hidden Wolf's teachings I had entered the ancient ways and that is all that mattered to me, regardless of what others thought of me.

My hair grew longer. Hidden Wolf had reminded me of the importance of that when he visited Houston. The medicine bag I carried around my neck, always with me.

More people came to me for healing and spiritual direction. Many of them needed assistance in the spirit world, especially those who had experienced a suicide around them.

—⚭—

Hidden Wolf told me that he started his learning at the age of six from his grandfather. "I had to choose between the traditional and society teachings. He made me sit for four days in one spot and each day tell him what I learned about one single blade of grass. At the age of fifteen I joined the Canadian army. Even though I was too young, I sneaked in and was sent to West Africa. There I wandered away from my comrades and entered the villages and shared my knowledge with their medicine people. They shared theirs. It was in Africa that I learned the dark medicine ways. Ingeborg, you too must learn the dark side of life, so you can help people who have come in touch with black medicine. It's all part of the healing. There are many people that have come in touch with that in the world."

Years later I realized the power of his words and medicine. I too carried a dark side. From my youth on I had stuffed anger and transformed it into depression. I didn't know how to handle anger, and while the duration of falling into melancholy and depression would get shorter my anger flowed inward. Morally, rage wasn't what the world needed more of. Miserable in these low days, I wrestled in my head with whatever had me in its claws. I knew these were efforts toward a different consciousness.

I couldn't bare the unproductivity, the agony of being in the mind all the time. My head dizzy, on overload, I felt as if I was drifting somewhere in the cosmos, not grounded, not connected to anyone or anything. I needed to feel my body. Timothy Tate, a therapist in Bozeman, helped me work it through. He confronted some of my escapes like the manic traveling schedule I maintained to Europe, Asia, and Texas.

"I want to learn boxing. Not for competition, but to totally occupy my body, get out of my head," I told him.

It wasn't boxing that pulled in my balloon but strenuous daily physical activity, eating right, and choosing the right people around me. A vague memory whispered: surrender, be in the present. Think of others, it's all about you! What makes you happy, what makes you shine?

To work through these depressions had taken years of learning and courage. I trusted Timothy to explore the darker forces in me further. Dealing with my humanness, my shortcomings could bring me further in balance. Energized, a deeper reality of my options in life could be tackled.

I had to keep the overload of the masculine and my shadow side in check, those forces of greed for knowledge, my escapism through travel, my continued observing that led to judging instead of sharing my thoughts; the fear of cultural and academic rejection and most of all not being able to say no by giving others my power. I hated those parts of me, the time suckers, and I hated them in others ... except for the travel.

After Toby died, I had focused for years on conquering my fears.

"You are fearless" some commented—but periods of depression had not vanished. They'd surprise me. That roller coaster gained speed when someone had upset me, hurt me, and the martyrdom hoisted up again. I didn't say no, didn't speak up. Instead, I wolfed it down, first the food then the anger.

I'd observe the eating, the symptoms, and then maybe a few days later, I figured out what had occurred. At those times the wolf took over. I traveled long distances alone. It seemed that the universe and I needed to be realigned until I could join the pack of family and friends again. Driving the car, in the moment and free spirited I sensed freedom.

I had worked on my shadow aspects years ago. The hospitalization after Toby's death had ignited a desire to become a Jungian analyst and I began training and analysis, first in Holland, later in the US.

"You need to stick to the Native American road," a Jungian analyst mentioned. "That path fits you."

I continued my interest in both. The red road of the Native Americans however entered my heart. Their experiential learning kept me close to the earth and the spirit world.

Timothy's compass referenced both paths, too. My trust deepened. Determined to have the shadow surface and conscious once and for all, I reflected and meditated with pictures of wolves—so they'd teach me again what to look for, what qualities to expand on and which to call to a halt.

"People with a weak knowledge of their shadow tend to see themselves as victims," Timothy alerted me. I felt encouraged to dig in.

With my brother's numerous epilepsy attacks and the tense situation in the family and community growing up, I had begun the pattern of censoring my surroundings, pleasing others. I became an expert at sensing moods, specifically tension, anger, and pain.

Wanting to alleviate these, my feelings began working themselves from the outside in.

"Try to learn to love yourself first. Most learn to love their neighbors as themselves. You and some others must learn the opposite. Sacrificing yourself most often has roots in control," a Cenacle spiritual director pointed out."

Yes, those wolf dynamics are hidden. Hidden Wolf hid his too. His confusing tactics revealed some of mine through the years.

When I had returned to Houston, Hidden Wolf was hard to reach. Connecting with him by phone in Canada or getting a response by mail was nearly impossible. Yet during the day I felt his presence, I felt his connection. I even began to listen to different music. Something, no, someone was influencing my mind from afar. I felt it and knew it for sure. And then suddenly, after weeks and months of trying, a true earth connection was made by phone.

"Please come to Houston and teach me, I want to learn more about the ancient healing ways," I pleaded with him.

"I knew you would ask me and I have resisted it for a year now. Yes, I will come to see you and teach you," he said with his deep voice. "I'll get the bus ready."

"I'll send you some fliers so I can do some work down there as well."

I felt as if the man arrived "home" the day he entered my house. It surprised me and I told him so. Where were those feelings coming from? Were they a fantasy of a deeper ulterior longing? I showed him his room.

"I arrived already last night after driving the 610 loop four times around Houston. Finally, I parked the bus on the side of the 610 freeway. The police arrived quickly. They helped me find a place, so I stayed in the bus and cleaned up last night." I reflected on his words and asked, "Did I block you with my anxious and eager energy? Is that why you couldn't get here easily?"

"Yes," he said.

At my house in La Porte, Texas, or sometimes in the large, converted school bus parked in front of the house guarded by Chimo, his wolf dog, he taught me shapeshifting. Other healing ways were focused on the healing of my heart.

"Don't you want to distribute your posters?"

"Forget about doing extra work, I came because your heart needed healing. Sit down on the couch and lean into me, put your head and arms around my shoulders. Surrender, and allow things to happen." While I sat there his and my heartbeat became one. I could feel it. I surrendered more and more, encouraged by him and his guidance. Very slowly parts of me began to change into a black raven, or was it a crow? My feet changed as well. It was a strange and elated feeling at the same time. I was the black raven and at the same time I was able to observe what happened.

During one ceremony, as he drummed his large drum over me, I stopped breathing at times. "Oh, my G*d I'm in another world; did he just raise the upper part of my body with that sagebrush in his hand?"

"It is to help you over your anxiety and feelings that Helga will die, your friend in Germany with the Lou Gehrig disease, she will be all right while moving on to the other side. To stop breathing is not scary."

"I want to stop this, I can't go on with this, it is crazy. I will die right here when I stop breathing," I heard my inner voice. Yet there was this part of me that needed to know, needed to trust him and so I allowed it. I didn't die but stopped breathing for quite a time and now knew that Helga would be all right after all on the other side.

Hidden Wolf taught me to scan the energy body, do healing, and how to connect the heartbeat of a healthy heart with the heart of a person who has a heart attack until medics can take over. His teachings enhanced my capabilities to connect at a distance, yet most importantly I began a path to not judge and allow things to happen.

One morning however, everything shifted for me: "Don't look into my eyes, it will hypnotize you," said Hidden Wolf with a commanding voice.

"My G*d, you are not from here," I expressed with a silent breath and perplexed emotion, staring at the ancient presence, his face, of a being that looked as if it came from another world.

It happened unexpectedly one morning, while we talked about ceremony. I looked at him and experienced another way of seeing. His face was so old and deep bags under his ancient dark eyes, as if my view had gone backwards hundreds of years into his being. It was as if seeing his reincarnations through centuries all in one body. Was he from another planet? He looked so different from the person I knew up till that moment.

This experience quite shook me, and I kept on asking questions. I couldn't let go of what I had seen. Several days I pondered it. My head hurt thinking about it. He heard that and immediately walked toward me, put his forehead against mine and pulled out the pain that way.

"You must not talk about this anymore."

"Are you from another planet?" I asked.

"Yes, you and I both started out at planets close to each other."

We continued ceremonies after a few days of a break and decided not to talk about what I had observed seeing his face in this ancient way. Years later I learned about this way of seeing back in time and experienced this in a group under guidance.

"You have to come to me; I cannot come to you." Hidden Wolf said. He had talked about joining spirits. The day before in the park near the water, sitting on a bench, he had roughly sketched a picture of a tree trunk coming out of the earth and its crown consisted of an eagle head looking toward one side while attached to the eagle's head, a wolf head looked in the other direction. I wasn't sure about all this and decided to sleep on it.

The next morning still in my pajamas, I slowly walked toward the guest room at the other end of the hallway in my house, where he was still sleeping. I gently woke him up.

"I want to join our spirits the Eagle and the Wolf."

He motioned me to lie next to him on the double-sized bed. Both of us were dressed in our night clothes. No, it was not in a physical way, that spiritual union. I remember I was in deep prayer, asking for protection in my Catholic way from the Virgin Mary. At some point under his guidance I surrendered, and much like the energies of a physical union the spiritual union had taken place, not with orgasm, but with a sacred completion. I drew a large picture of the Wolf and Eagle now connected.

More and more, in a positive manner, I became aware of my own wolf spirit individuality. An inner vitality and courage now traveled with me.

During the day I went to work. In the evening, doing artwork, the fingers of my hands carved deep into the grey/white clay. The sculpture began to express the stronger lines of the vitality of the wolf. The front of the piece represented a cloaked woman holding the skull of a bird with two hands. I turned the clay statue of the woman around and formed eleven eagle heads where her spine was. Each eagle had attached to it wide spreading wings as in soaring flight. Possibly the woman statue, carrying the skull of a bird, represented the dark side of my personality, that endless grief of Toby's death. The eleven hidden eagles in the spine are still a mystery.

I don't believe the number eleven is considered a good number. These eagles might have indicated the eleven years of grieving that had gone by since Toby died in 1983.

At home, Patrick, my teenage son got along with Hidden Wolf and together they worked on projects in the yard. There Hidden Wolf let little things, mostly tools, disappear and laughingly blamed the teasing of his grandfather's spirit.

One day Patrick called home. "I need Hidden Wolf to pick me up from school, not you Mom, Hidden Wolf needs to come." Pat was disturbed about something; he didn't want to speak about it with me.

That afternoon, Hidden Wolf picked him up from school with his big bus, and the two had a conversation about Patrick's dad. Pat couldn't remember his dad well. Toby had died when he was six years old and all he could remember was seeing his dad in the Spring Branch Hospital Intensive Care unit connected to all kinds of gadgets that scared Pat. Hidden Wolf motioned Patrick to lie on his bed. And somehow brought him back to the time when his dad was so sick in the hospital. In a trance he assisted him to go past that terrible memory of the hospital and to connect with his dad in a different way in the home in Venezuela where we had lived. "It helped," said Patrick later.

Patrick met with friends to go fishing the following week. "Patrick, I'm so furious with you, I told you not to kill fish that are older than you. This garfish is at least 60 years old."

The first time he did this he brought the garfish home in a truck with his teenager buddies. It was nighttime and they moved the animal to the backyard. It looked like a fat alligator. Its head ferocious just like alligators have, ready to kill. Its body several feet long covered with scales, of course missing the alligator legs. That time they worked till mid night cleaning it, while I insisted upon putting every chunk of meat in the freezer. "You'll eat every piece of this, Pat. This is terrible." Late that night or better early in the morning around 3 a.m. much like shadows in the dark, we bagged all the excesses in garbage bags and dumped them in the bayou to recycle it to the fish.

A few weeks later Pat threw a garfish eating party. That was the first garfish.

"Mom, I sold it for a hundred dollars and I'm keeping its head."

"Damn, Patrick you cannot do this! You eat what you catch, but do not catch and kill fish that are taller and older than you are. I want you to stop it. This is the second time now."

Hidden Wolf entered the kitchen and saw the cut off head of the garfish and noticed my anger. Then both stood there holding the gar thing over the kitchen sink and the medicine man stated a prayer for the spirit of that fish. It would change the way Patrick related to animals, especially fish, forever.

Christa, my daughter who by that time was in college and out of the house most of the time, met Hidden Wolf and was not happy at all. She was distrustful and demanded in my absence that he show Patrick and her, his papers, driver's license, passport, and all. He did.

We performed many ceremonies, drummed with friends and some came for healing. His spirit was so strong during a drumming night with my friends that after I said I would like to dance my feet became so light I went into a trance. I lost myself in the drumming and I danced until I fell completely exhausted against the wall and unto the floor in the large living room. He made me dance all right and enjoyed that power. He was able to make people sit in their seat even though they wanted to get up. Hypnosis was a part of it. At times when I made him unhappy with something he warned "Be careful, don't wake up the wolf." That awakening wouldn't happen until a few months later.

Hidden Wolf conducted a sacred naming ceremony. I sat on the floor of my living room, dressed in a long colorful Guatemalan Indian skirt and a bright colored wool shawl that was similar to the one in which my husband was buried. The Guatemalan clothing held a special memory of the time I lived there with Toby and our daughter Christa.

We cleansed the living room area and ourselves with sage. Hidden Wolf dressed in Chief regalia with eagle feathers from his headdress reaching the ground, stood tall right in front of me, drummed and entered deep prayer and song. He sang loud in a language I didn't understand.

I received my name *Skw'a kwas'Skwu'Zat Saplil* meaning Sunshine Little Rose. This name became significant, a gift to me and those around me. My new name generated light like the sun. It steered me away from the sadness of my youth and the grief of Toby. Both names pushed me into a different meaning of life. One of lightness, discovery, and play. Their significance and connection with nature changed me.

Our closeness in Houston became more intimate; I loved his teachings, his attentiveness and authority. His eyes, his deep voice, his power, culture, and ancient connection all attracted me. "You need to grow your hair; it is appropriate in our culture. I expect you to follow me as a woman." He was one of those powerful men almost like my dad and I had become the child on some level. At other times, especially his generosity, would remind me of Toby my husband.

Laughter and fun filled our lives. I liked my life with him and his sleeping in the guestroom had transitioned by romance and our falling in love to my bedroom where he sometimes made vague remarks about being in the moment and not going to the future, something like, "We won't go there yet."

He often reminded me how he expressed his intimacy through love making and that it was his only way to do so.

Even though my children were suspicious of him we began to talk about which person and from what tribe could marry us, and in which manner we should do the traditional celebration. He gifted me with his father's silver ring, set with a large tiger eye stone. That stone and Hidden Wolf's spirit medicine would become important later in my life when I shifted in consciousness and began the *true* shadow work of the "Hidden Wolf" inside of me.

We prepared herbs together. I gifted him with return tickets to Canada so he could continue his work there as well.

—ɯ—

"You remind me of the story of Bluebeard," I told him once while walking on the beach in Galveston. You know the one who goes away and travels while telling her not to open a particular door. The room which of course she did open revealed to her the severed heads of women all lined up against the walls.

He stopped, looked at me and answered: "Yes, and I do leave you the key."

At other times he warned me again: "You better stop it, don't awaken the Wolf."

Hidden Wolf went back and forth twice from Houston to Vancouver to tend to clients. I too visited Vancouver again and met some of his children, his oldest daughter and a younger one with a young child. His youngest, Little Wolf, was off to work with chickens somewhere in another town. Hidden Wolf told stories about the spirit world and how his children would be afraid at night when the spirits came, and his grandfather teased them and pulled off their blankets.

I had similar experiences in my house at that time, when I went to bed trying to go to sleep, when suddenly a tall Indian with a large bold-shaped hat and so many other Indians filled my bedroom. It took me by surprise and scared me. I pulled the blankets over my head and thus fell asleep. This happened twice. The first time he stood close, the other a little further away from the bed to the left. Intuitively I felt they were Paiute.

In Canada though, during my visit Hidden Wolf generously prepared steaks to eat and we celebrated as a family. Lorna, Hidden Wolf's oldest daughter made note of a "bad" word I said, something that is never done in the traditional Indian language. It had slipped out. We had a good visit, and I later went into town to buy his grandchild some clothes. But at times during this visit his manner bordered on control and it began to bother me. I had been a single woman for a long time. Would I be willing to be the woman he demanded? I wasn't one to follow … anymore. I wanted to be equal and walk together, to share.

I went down into his cellar and just sat there on the couch. I reflected on dreams I was having while in his house. I felt warned especially since he quite often communicated with a lawyer friend.

"I want to show you something on a mountain," he said one day.

Interested and curious of course we drove in his daughter's small blue Hyundai on a lonely road toward the top of a mountain. I had no idea where I was, other than north of Vancouver somewhere in British Columbia. Chimo, his wolf dog was with us. The higher we went the deeper the snow on the road. It became so deep it reached the middle axel underneath the low car. He gave it a lot of gas to avoid being stuck in the deeper areas. I held my breath with his risk taking and the strange joy he seemed to express while he maneuvered the car at full speed. We were high up, but not at the summit yet.

We got stuck. I was not dressed for snow. It was close to four and darkness would set in soon. Scared, I walked down the road in the snow to find branches, anything to help him give the car some traction.

"Leave me alone. I'll get this fixed," he said with an angry voice.

My feet ached from the cold. He didn't want my help at all. Instead, he complained about an injury, a work-related fall he had experienced when he dropped on his back from an electric pole in the past. I began to pray. I begged him to let me help. After an hour we heard a car coming down the mountain. It was a large recreational vehicle high off the ground. They stopped and helped get our car out of the snowbank.

"Talk to him and if he wants to continue up the mountain do not do it. Don't go with him. It is dangerous; come with us," the woman insisted. And so, I ascertained we would be going back *down* the mountain and therefore asked the woman of the recreational vehicle "Would you and your husband stay around until we turn the car around in the snow to make sure we do not get stuck again?"

Hidden Wolf and I did not say anything to each other as we journeyed back down with the RV following us. I cried because my feet were frozen. He was angry, his back hurting from trying to move the car. He never told me what was up that mountain.

We continued the relationship. Back in Houston together again we celebrated Christmas. My kids and I were spoiled by him with nice presents wrapped in newspapers. I too bought nice presents for him. That winter we flew together to the Netherlands to visit my parents.

"You are not welcome," said my dad on the phone when I told him of my plans to visit them in Holland with Hidden Wolf. "I don't want to have anything to do with your Indians." That rejection felt familiar. I had heard it before in my early twenties when I was engaged to Victor, an Indonesian man from Sumatra. They just didn't like me to be romantically involved with people of color and were afraid I would not see myself in the children that would be born. This discrimination saddened me. It made no sense because they were close to my Indonesian Aunt Enny and several other Indonesian friends in Holland.

"You and your Indians; it is just not right," Dad proclaimed.

Somehow, I persevered and made the visit. Mom rather liked him, and Pa accepted the situation. Hidden Wolf and I even slept together in the bedroom next to my folks' room. It is there that I saw flashes of former lives of Hidden Wolf and me in old clothes working the land. In hindsight they were like a painting of Van Gogh, the first print Toby and I purchased when we began our lives together.

"I want you in the present," he said annoyed.

We continued our trip to Germany where we visited Helga, my friend and former colleague from years ago. She was well into her battle with A.L.S. (Lou Gehrig Disease.)

"I will lead you and Helga to a different place. When we come to the part where I take Helga to the other side, I will give you a sign and you are not to go there. You stop right there. It will be dangerous if you do not do so." He repeated the last several times.

During the ceremony Hidden Wolf took Helga to the other side to take away her fear of death, yet also assured her that she still had a choice to stay on earth and recuperate. He emphasized this by giving her energy to lift her hand and arm, which until then she was unable to do anymore. She was astonished; up till then two to three people visited her daily to feed her and bring her to the bathroom. She was able to sit, hold her head up, but unable to use her hand, and arms. Family members folded her arms and lifted and positioned them like heavy wet rags with no ability into her lap.

"You must find healthy unsprayed pine trees, cook the pine needles and drink the juice every day," he recommended to Helga.

We continued to visit Angela, Helga's daughter who was in a pediatric daycare mental hospital. She had observed the rapid decline of her mother's health from the age of four. Now at the age of nine she was not able to cope with her Mom's A.L.S. and escaped through sleeping all the time and sometimes becoming violent at home, throwing wheelchair parts in the direction of her mom. Our visit was important because I meant to eventually bring Angela to the US to take care of her. None of the family members wanted her or thought they'd be able to cope with her. Hidden Wolf brought her an Indian necklace with a bear that would remind her to be strong. They both got along.

Hidden Wolf and I continued our vacation in Germany. While shopping I had problems in busy and populated shopping areas. I felt dizzy and overwhelmed. He advised me to wear aluminum foil over my solar plexus area to expel it.

He spoiled me by buying clothes. When I found something, I liked he'd say, "get two of them, you like it." This threw me back to thoughts of my husband who treated me in a similar kind way. I was happy.

The day came that Hidden Wolf had to leave again to Canada to tend to his many clients and travel to towns throughout the Canadian interior for a while. In the morning, ready for departure with his bus, he handed me my house key and gifted me with a blanket.

We talked daily on the phone about how he would move to Houston. I purchased a white elk skin and filled my evenings with sewing by hand his traditional wedding regalia. The sleeves had to have long white leather fringes. The longer the better he had told me and promised he'd make me a white buckskin dress.

There were periods that I couldn't get in touch with him because he went to areas in the Canadian interior without phones. Then I spoke with his oldest daughter. By then I'd applied my remote viewing and was able to see who was in his house. Sometimes I'd see his son there, but I felt uncomfortable about this way of "seeing" and remembered how I felt with the Apache medicine man and so stopped it. It was not ethical, and it was intrusive.

It got harder and harder to reach Hidden Wolf by phone. Weeks went by until one day I had to make a business trip to Arizona. The Continental flight had just newly installed phones at each seat and passengers could make one free phone call. I wanted to know the truth why we did not connect any longer. I decided to call his house from the plane's phone where my ID would not show.

A woman identified herself as his wife, Morning Star. They had joined spirits too. She was from northern Texas. I remembered "seeing" her from my confused remote spirit connections I lately had with Hidden Wolf. The story sounded familiar. I assume he awakened the wolf in many women.

"He had to follow where spirit guided him," I remembered Hidden Wolf, the medicine man, saying often.

Those were the teachings from Hidden Wolf, the good and the bad medicine. A year later, while hiking in the Texas hill country, I took a break and sat on the sandy ground to do some reflection. When I got up, the ground fell apart with earth falling down the hill and a curious stone emerged. The stone I put on the area Hidden Wolf had worked on my color bone, the right shoulder area and used it to extract the energy he had put in that area.

—⟋⟋⟋—

After Hidden Wolf, I found stillness under a huge oak tree in Louisiana. Months had gone by when I felt paralyzed by the sudden break of our relationship. I often took down all memories of him in the house, and then later I would put them up again. My children were upset by my depression and disinterest in life. It felt as if I were dying. I totally withdrew from friends, went to bed early and kept on telling myself he would come back. This all was a mistake—in my stupidity, I even thought it was part of his teachings, to make me strong—to counter the dark side.

I sought refuge at the Cenacle, a Catholic retreat house in Metairie, a parish in New Orleans located next to Pontchartrain Lake.

I got up early that morning and lay on the grass, talking to the crows in a tree next to me. They came flying over me, a flock of them, and we cawed at each other while more curious ones came.

I stood up, walked to a large oak I had noticed the day before, and sat under that majestic large tree. At other times I met with a priest well-versed in the spirit world. He had experience in channeling, had an office with crystals and even a picture of a power animal, a whale on the wall!

I shared my story about love. "What love?" he asked.

That afternoon, I returned to the garden and walked the path on the levy at the water of Lake Pontchartrain. On my way to the levy, I again noticed the large oak tree on the left, its branches loaded with green leaves dancing playfully towards the light of the sun. The spirit of the tree began to talk to me and taught me my life song.

Peter V. Catches, a Lakota friend and medicine man, later translated it into the Lakota language. Whenever I sing it, I first do so in their language to honor the Lakota people:

Wací Can Oh Wací Can

A mun yus tan

A mun yus tan

Númpa nagí wanzí

Yámni nagí wanzí

Tópa nagí wanzí

Wací Can Oh Wací Can

A mun yus tan, a mun yus tan.

Dancing tree, Oh Dancing tree

set me free, set me free.

Dancing tree, oh dancing tree set me free.

two spirits as one,

three spirits as one,

four spirits as one,

dancing tree, oh dancing tree, set me free.

Sitting under that big old oak on Catholic grounds of the Cenacle, while the crows were cawing under the heat of the Louisiana sun, this tree spoke to me and said: "How can these dark spirits become light again, such a big part of you has died?" Then the oak told me to speak to them and tell them to help me live and breathe centered again. I heard in my mind the adapted verses from Ezekiel 37-1-11: "I will replace you with Light and dancing, sharing and courageous vulnerability. I will put breath into you, and you shall dance again and know that I Am."

I sat there holding these words mingling my earth spirituality with my Christian roots and saw the many branches of the oak tree, some big and strong. some tiny and light in the stillness not dancing. Then the Great Spirit told me to call on the winds from the four directions. "Oh, Spirit breathe upon my precious child her branches are ready to dance again with the wind" and soon that song came forth.

The sudden disappearance of Hidden Wolf took me to a dark place. Coming out from under that force took just about all I had. This path and the teachings of medicine men are going to kill me, I thought.

On the phone Helga warned me, don't become like me. "If you go too far into this darkness you come upon a place of no return." I think Helga's illness somehow had to do with the death of her husband and her being unable to let go. She wanted to join him. It also had to do with her incestuous father. No wonder the other side looked better to her.

Grace, the help and love from speaking with Fr. Larry Hein, helped me to own my inner strength and throw away the medicine bag that Hidden Wolf had made me into Lake Pontchartrain.

I was scared all right about the consequences of this act—messing with the spirit world. Would it summon the spirit of Hidden Wolf's powerful grandfather? Would it mean the end of my path in the ancient ways that brought me so close to this beautiful earth?

No, no, no—I threw far so I couldn't retrieve it even if I wanted to. I swung and let go, following the bag with my eyes into the water and beyond the stones on the side of the levy.

I vowed never to put someone else's medicine around my neck, only my own. What was it about me and medicine men? Was it addiction? Was it my destiny? What drew me into this path? Would it destroy me one day?

The buckskin Indian outfit I had prepared for him to wear at the wedding, I now changed into my very own and on it painted my spiritual journey to come.

Today, if necessary, I too can say: "Don't wake up the Wolf."

A time of leadership had begun. Something in me had shifted. I gave away most of the gifts Hidden Wolf gave me like the ring and a leather wolf bag. I kept an Indian neck band with a piece of jade corn. I destroyed the picture of the joined eagle and wolf I had made though it is engraved in my mind.

—⟶

At sixty I am shedding my persona and look to raise and express my inner energy in a totally different way. My own hidden wolf now is bubbling up in a devouring way. It shows itself through depression, deep falling in the nothing, the void that shows no end. A freefall if I don't watch it. This imbalance in me needs to be faced. A tiger eye is needed for a different journey I dreamed.

The disappearance of Hidden Wolf took me to a dark place. Integrating my shadow is of utmost importance. In 2012, a wolf in Yellowstone woke me up.

I noticed him eating on a carcass. He tried to haul it from the side of the river onto the bank. Halfway there, he spotted me and my family across the river. He swiftly fled halfway up the mountain and hid between the trees where his eyes fixated on the carcass and then on us. Not moving, standing tall, he contemplated his next move. I took out my binoculars and our eyes met.

We had linked up once again. "You haven't given the wolf much attention in years," I remembered. "You need the hidden wolf qualities for your identity, the wholeness of your good and negative side. You need it for balance," I reflected.

Ready with a picture of a wolf and the statue I had made when Hidden Wolf was there next to it, I began a ceremony asking the spirit of the wolf to help me, to help me remember what must be recalled for wholeness. With the penetrating smell of *Pom,* a Guatemalan resin from a tree used for prayer, I solicited help: "Teach me where I am vulnerable; teach about my sensitivity of what others think about me. Those habits rooted in that child of a *Mof* rejection; remind me of my wolf tracking, traveling alone long distances avoiding the pack, and my hesitance to say no to myself and others."

And thus, with the eyes of that wolf in Yellowstone fresh in my memory I also captured the wolf "strength"—the might it took to haul the carcass of an elk away from the riverbank, his attentiveness to what happened around him. He was invisible to many with the trees around. Most of all he didn't forget me. With our eyes connected he sent his love and healing message. I had remained part of the pack.

True, I had regained a lot of my identity messing in these murky waters of my hidden darkness. Where was love? The wolf had shown his loyalty, his patience, his caring. Love, the prime quality of my existence wrestled itself away with my illusions. Much of what I thought was love wasn't pure love after all. "Does the process and searching ever end? Contentment would be an act of grace in my life. "Do it before you die!" A friend's voice repeated in my mind.

"I don't want to die without truly and purely loving someone" like a parental tape it repeats in my brain. What does that mean anyway? I believe in the exchange of energy, in returning what you receive in some form. Basically, I'm pretty selfish. I like to express myself in art, in humor and in writing; Sensitivity toward others is important. That's part of love. Eventually I'll have to give up this life and face what I contributed, something other people can build on. Toby and I had a form of love in which both of us attempted to bring happiness. He shared a deeper insight into life, and me I had a good dose of compassion learned through challenges growing up. We had all these plans to set up life in a different way. No, that didn't work. He died.

There must be more. Love is on the spot in the here and now. I knew that this love essence existed in me. This love called me from deep inside and outside of myself. Yes, I knew for sure it was part of my essence, the person who I was. I had to get to this center of love and tap into it with the similar aggression of a wolf that feeds on its prey. Opportunity would show itself through the presence of a grizzly bear. Earlier the spirit of a woman had announced the first step.

GRAY WOMAN

FROM OUT OF NOWHERE THIS image appears, a presence of a standing grey woman emerges, a spirit maybe. She is very much alive. A woman with long hair, about six feet tall stands right next to me. I had not expected this. Did I tap into something evil here?

I sat peacefully in my living room that afternoon, a weekend with extra time. I had leaned back in my high-winged chair. Light of the afternoon sun fell in front of me on the floor. My thoughts drifted. The living room with its wooden walls felt embracing. Medicine men, the Apache and later the Paiute, had come and gone in this space. I had learned a lot from them about the place of innocence in life and the value of knowing my shadow or dark side.

The clay statues I created during that period in my life expressed my conquest of fear. Some of them foretold the future, such as the one, a woman, beholding a sun and with it several snakes. Snakes lived in this house through Patrick, my son, who raised them as pets. They had propelled me into a different learning, away from a fearful stance in Christian images. Snakes now embodied the metaphysical meaning of transformation and change.

These statues witnessed what had transpired on the inside of me. Their forms explained my spirit relationship with the bear, eagle, owl, snake and wolf, their presence in dreams. My bond with animals was intimate and immediate, a consciousness I could call on. It expanded an energetic connection with them and even with some plants.

Bright cloths purchased in Guatemala where we lived in earlier years bring contrast in my living room this afternoon. The red,
green, yellow, and blue threads woven by Mayan Indians bring
focus to the white porcelain statues.

I sense stillness around me. The woman, that female next to me,
is not one of porcelain. Her presence pours out a living form. This
gray woman does not resemble the Catholic Virgin Mary as she is
traditionally portrayed, nor is she cloaked in white, blue, nor gives
an inkling of a celestial being. I see gray, yes definitely light hazy
gray. Who is she? Why is she gray? Silent she stands awake and
aware. She emanates authority, a powerful poise. My father and
his brothers carry that kind of presence when they enter a room.
You can't ignore the eye contact, their measuring up of who and
how people are present. They don't have to say or do anything. You
expect something from them; something soon to come, not trivial.

Fear registers and confuses my body and mind. I want to get
away. However, encapsulated by the love from this gray woman on
my left side I stay put. My hand now holds on to the arm rests of
the chair. I'm perspiring a bit, my breathing is light, inaudible and
with expectation of what's to happen next.

She owns herself. Her aura of maturity and strength triggers
thoughts of receptivity, creativity and, yes, even the power to
destroy. Curious, I keep my attention with her. I realize my own
inability to reach such love. I intuit that this love beams and pene-
trates beyond expression, past all I know. She is not of this world…
or is she?

Tears begin rolling over my cheeks and drip off my face onto
my multi-colored jacket. It doesn't make any difference in the way
I experience her presence, good or bad. My awareness taps into a

love I cannot reach. Her presence touches my "divine or holy long-ing" as Ronald Rolleiser, OMI, so perfectly names this force.

"Ingeborg, to embrace this kind of love you will have to die," I tell myself. "It's the love of the afterlife. But I don't want to die yet!"

She foreshadows a death in me, to a lower self, the world, my ego that has to take place over and over again. A choice I have to make, to deepen my commitment to service and surrender. Where and what is it that must die in me to make space for it. But then she is gray. I bet it has to do with my capacity of seeing and experienc-ing. Would I be able to see and experience her full power, her full brightness?

"You saw your own potential," I told myself: "The potential of love that has not come to fruition. And the reason she is gray is showing you your own flaws and unfinished relationships in life."

I'm aware of my light breathing as if I don't want to disturb what's happening. Where did she come from on this clear day? I am compelled to go where she is. The vitality of her knowing and her might tug me into curiosity.

This straight standing woman doesn't look at me, she stares into the future, yet emanates this security of knowing what she wants. Once you taste, feel, and connect with this woman, there is no going back. You walk the path and live and die a bit each day. It's the price you pay for her love. She creates and destroys wherever she goes.

"You must breathe through your heart," the gray woman com-municates to me. That's all she says, her mind directly connecting to mine.

Breathe through my heart? I wonder.

I reflect on times when I meditate. I breathe all right, but chan-nel through the top of my head. She said to do it through my heart.

As suddenly as she had appeared, she disappeared. I wanted more, but she was gone. My thoughts drift to my mom. She had shown me some of this love with all her baking and patience with raising us and my challenged brother—not to speak of the rejections by people in Rotterdam on account of her being a *Mof*. However, I wanted more at that time: recognition, fierceness, a different kind of presence than that of Mom. I liked Aunt Enny, her presence to my emotions, her stepping out into the World Wildlife Fund, her continued studies of languages. I'm aware of how my friends love my Dad, his humor and his stories from World War II.

This all confused me. Surrounded by my longing for love, the love Gray Woman, whoever she was, just showed me. I immediately began to meditate, integrating her advice about the heart.

Not long after she appeared, I was able to ask Peter Catches, Jr., the Lakota medicine man, about her.

"You saw Buffalo Calf Woman." That's all he said. Peter doesn't explain much; you must figure it out yourself. Thus, I learned that Buffalo Calf Woman appeared to two Lakota and for one, brought the sacred rite of the pipe to the Lakota people.

A sacred summoning song came to me after seeing this Gray Woman. I sing it to other women and men. Voicing the spirit of Gray Woman through this song, I hope to inspire new wisdom and love.

I pick up my hand drum and chant while breathing my energy through where my heart beats. The words ignite strength and courage when this song ebbs from my life.

Woman, I'm calling you. Let's bring back the earth

Sister, I'm calling you. Let's bring back the earth

Brother, I'm calling you. Let's bring back the earth

Children let's celebrate. We are getting back the earth

Woman, I'm calling you

Singing the song and remembering her radiant spirit, as I experienced it, surfaces like water from a well. For a little while I'm back with her again and remember what I am about. I would like to do my part for the Heart of the world. I would summon that Gray Woman's love, fire and feminine awareness for this screaming heart of humanity while stretching mine and their love in relationship with others and creation.

I now believe the Gray Woman I saw was part of the feminine archetype. She contained the force of people that passed and those who are alive. She represents the intuition, the ability to receive for all humanity, maybe even all creation. I think I tapped into her courage, her truth, her fighting spirit, her birthing, but also her awareness of what's right and wrong in life. Otherwise, I wouldn't have been aware of the fact I had to die to myself.

So often I get pulled away by social media, my own distractions and insecurities, realization of my failings in life or participating in issues of control… it is tough to believe in your own potential and stay gray, stay humble, stay in the surrender mode.

My blind searching of the feminine joins that of others. I get caught up in the despair, knowing that we are raping this earth through our daily unawareness and arrogance. Then I read that researchers crashed an instrument into the moon to find out if there is water. Our moon regulates our menstrual cycles; it influences the tides of the water on this earth. My energy flows with her waxing and waning. I sing with that moon when it is full. This trespassing of research enters my body, I can feel its aggression, its rape.

I know that I long for that heart, that heart in everything, humans, and the earth—that drumbeat Indigenous talk about—my being wants to feel that beat. I want to experience it and pulse in this life as never before. I want my energy to be in harmony with this heartbeat.

This longing of my essence has been reignited by the Gray Woman. "Breath through the heart," she had said.

LAKOTA ZINTKALA OYATE, 38TH GENERATION MEDICINE MAN

Photo credit Debra Rueb

"WE ARE HUNGRY; WE LEFT two days ago. we walked in the snow to the bus stop at Pine Ridge in South Da- kota, then rode two days on the bus to get here" said Cindy, Peter's wife. I didn't realize their hardship. This long journey by bus from South Dakota to Houston took more than two days. I knew warm climates in the world, Houston, Guatemala, Indonesia. I didn't re- alize the poverty existing at Pine Ridge Reservation. The only cold weather I had experienced was in Holland. A walk to the bus stop during winter there implied ten minutes at the most. Peter and

Cindy had not eaten much in the last couple of days. I quickly prepared sandwiches to still their hunger and later a dinner.

During a presentation at the University where I worked, Peter V. Catches (Zintkala Oyate) taught the Seven Sacred Rites of the Lakota beginning with the *Inipi* the "sweat lodge" to purify yourself. This rite was followed by the *Hanblecha* or vision quest and the Sundance.

These teachings of Zintkala Oyate, Peter Van Catches, the third medicine man I encountered, reached the mystic core of who I am.

Every time I speak with someone who recognizes the core of my spiritual being and the longing to carry out my gifts in the world spins me into an emotional imbalance. It is triggered by the realization of a Oneness in the world. I become like a little child, not wanting to disappoint. This child falls in love. The adult in me disappears into the background.

Inspired by his talk I longed to do a vision quest, an *hanblecha*.

"I'm not one of those medicine men who take you right into four days." he said. It's like crossing a river, with me it takes four years. You'll have to craft a pipe in prayer—prayer for others. That will take up your first year." This selfless discipline pulled me like a magnet. It connected with a part of me that I wanted to expand and bring out into the world.

"Let's see if we can't divide this stone in half." And together with one of his friends in Houston, who had obtained some pipestone, they slashed off a piece of the stone and gifted me with it. In turn I presented the man who gave me the pipestone, a statue I had made. This nine-inch sculpture from white porcelain with undeveloped faces as that of spirits, represented a man and woman facing each other and holding hands. The woman did not look at the man; she faced into the future.

Peter's directives were minimal. I knew I had to craft the pipe by hand, yet how exactly I had to do this was pieced together from questions I asked him, his wife Cindy, and his close friends in Houston.

"I dreamed about the pipe and a ball," I told him.

"You must craft the pipe in however form you saw it during your dream," he responded.

After the two of them left Houston, I began to work with the pipestone every night until it was ready. A Mexican craftsman helped create the ball, that I "saw" in my dream, which needed to be fixed upon the pipe.

The four consecutive years of my pipe-fast unfolded differently from what I had expected. The first year, a one day fasting happened close to Pine Ridge. Much in fear, and after the full year of preparation I drove from Texas to Pine Ridge, South Dakota. During my drive I had strange forebodings through dreams. In my dream I saw someone, maybe myself, on a hospital bed breathing only through a straw, while the rest of the body was wrapped in white.

Upon arrival at Pine Ridge, Peter's sister alerted me that he was hospitalized in Rapid City. And thus, I set out to visit him there, driving the shortest road through the reservation. Because of the potholes then I couldn't drive faster than thirty miles an hour, sometimes less.

Arriving at the hospital, much to my shock, Peter was in a hospital bed much like in my dream and on a respirator. All his focus was on getting me to do my vision quest. Not able to speak he wrote things down encouraging me to do this with someone else on the reservation.

Confused, I rented a hotel room nearby and stayed until through prayer I got some clarity. Determined to do the quest, I nevertheless set out to drive back through Nebraska. En route I met a Lakota artist who encouraged me. "You will do this quest and find the right place, trust the Great Mystery." And thus, on my own, guided by my heart, a few miles outside Pine Ridge on strange lands, I set out to find a spot in a remote area.

Following what I learned from Cindy and Peter about the vision quest, I started with my pipe and positioned other parts necessary for the ritual in ceremony. Hundreds of grasshoppers and ticks lived on that land. "Please allow me to stay here for one night and share your home and space," I asked them.

That night, still much in fear of my surroundings, I prayed and prayed. A terrible thunderstorm came through and changed the weather to freezing temperatures. My sleeping bag was my only protection from the large hailstones that pounded my body. It felt as if these painful hail stones responded to some of my thoughts and gave me a warning message. "Don't share all of what you are learning; you know what the whites have done with information in the past."

Curled up like a baby in its womb I continued to pray while the sleeping bag and I became soaked. The snorting of a nearby animal shocked me. Again, my prayers intensified as I tried to make myself smaller. The dark night was long, I longed for the dawn to come.

The next morning a beautiful monarch butterfly kept circulating the praying area I had created. As if holding a knife, no, maybe a razor blade, it suddenly approached me and I felt as if it energetically sliced open my heart. Then it took off. It was after that I prayed with my heart, and the Sacred Pipe and I became one.

My life had changed forever.

The second year of the vision quest consisted of two days. I completed them in South Dakota after a sweat lodge directed by a Dakota Indian. The third year happened in Houston where I entered the three days fast at the Cenacle retreat center. During that fast, an insect bit me, maybe a spider, and I was in terrible pain for two days. In conclusion, the fourth year I took off from work and stayed at my home, sitting under an ash tree. These places I chose after prayer. I trusted the guidance. After four years I felt I had completed my promise to a greater Mystery and was grateful for the learning I had received during these times of fasting. In retrospect, I still had to overcome a lack of trust and surrender to a medicine man. The part of their tradition where a puppy goes to the dog-star on my behalf, felt foreign to me. I didn't understand. However, my loyalty, respect and connection with the Lakota people deepened during this time.

Glimpses of the awakening of the mysterious Inner Fire through the spiritual presence of Zintkala Oyate, the medicine man, I captured in a poem.

> Looking for lost love, drawn by your spirituality,
> my child awakens and I bury the wise woman
> with illusions of being whole.
> Your medicine induces my spirit's authenticity.
> Rudely awakened, I mourn.
> Our spirits connected and frozen in Oneness.

Even separated, your love and earth essence dives deep.

Humbly on the ground, you whisper into the womb of the
earth.

Yóur Spirituality

invokes a longing of me becoming whole.

My inner child and adult are at loss.

Your peace, presence and straight talk bewitch me into
adoration.

Storms, lightning, divine interventions …

I listen:

Self-nurturing, a mouth speaking pearls of truth,

giving true love, are essential to becoming whole.

I gently hold my inner child,

the sun, the earth, the stars, the moon, the wind,

my Spirituality.

Awakened I yearn to love others.

"Connect the stones and help my people," I dreamed long ago.

I gain strength in these moments,

celebrate each small part of me that trembles,

believing that this path will open in time.

My longing pulls me forward.

Its red road carries me, and I taste true love.

Moments of peace surprise me, thunder beings far away
confirm

you heard me.

I see and taste the Oneness now.

Yet memories of unbelief tease me, haunt my fragile walk.

Will I be able to grow into this fire

or in moments of weakness water these flames down

into oblivion, swept away by distractions.

Will I be courageous enough to give true Love?

Which path do I surrender to?

As feathers fall their lightness nectar me with gentleness,

birds continue to call.

When will I speak like you into the womb of the earth?

Deeper still my spirit needs to walk in authenticity.

You help me grow, soften my heart to surrender.

You devour my weakness, trick me to live and love.

Alone, I humbly ask that I too may reach

the top of that mountain nourished by a Great Mystery.

We shall celebrate leaving behind that ancient trail

which beckons others toward Truth, Love and Oneness.

As my realizations of the *Oceti Wakan*, that Inner Fire each one of us carry, deepens, Peter Catches and I continued to present experiential programs during International Education Week at the university. We also presented at the Rothko Chapel in Houston, together with Lee Standing Bear Moore from the Manataka Council. At these times I recognized what Peter's vision of Oceti Wakan, Sacred Fireplace, meant for me. Through him this holy inner fire becomes re-kindled again and again in many a person.

—⟨⟨⟨—

"I'd like to build a medicine wheel when you come for International Education Week," I mentioned to Peter. It took a while; he had to think, and then agreed quietly "ok". No directives.

I needed stones for the four directions, I knew that much. I set out by car each weekend to find the stones that were right for this ceremony. Finding stones on public property was not an easy task. After 800 miles of driving during four weekends I finally found a public access close to a bridge over the Blanco River in Texas. Lots of gorgeous stones were available. I loaded up my Toyota. Upon arrival in Houston and through negotiation with Peter's friends and followers, a plan was made for the ceremony.

On the day of the program, as part of the International Week's celebration, each visitor, mainly faculty and staff of the university, including the president, chose their own stone upon entering the large room. In the middle of the circular setting the Fire Keeper had created a fire that adhered to safety regulations. The four directions each had a large stone—colored in yellow, white, green and red.

Peter drummed and later used his eagle feather for blessings and one by one each person came forward with their stone. They created the medicine wheel.

Upon completion, participants were invited to enter the wheel. Each person wishing to do so could purify themselves with the sage and vapors lifting from the center fireplace. After the ceremony the wheel was picked up and I returned the stones with thanksgiving to the Blanco River in Texas.

EARNING THE NAME
"STANDING BEAR WOMAN"

M Y HEART WAS HARDENED. I felt heavy and restless. Father Stan, a 90-year-old, tall and warm smiling Benedictine monk, himself embraced by the South Dakota Native Americans, recommended I call Helmina, a Lakota woman.

I called Helmina Makes Him First from Texas, where I was living at the time. The soft-spoken Lakota Medicine woman, stated: "The spirits told me your Spirit name is to be *Mato Naji We* or Standing Bear Woman."

Heretofore, Native American names had been a touchy subject with my family in Holland.

"Why would you change your name, one your mom and I chose to baptize you with? Ingeborg Maria is a beautiful name," my irritated dad said during a phone call.

I felt compelled to tell my dad of my journeys. He lived in Holland and I, with an ocean between us, in Texas. I think I was driven by a sparkle of hope. Hope for a talk with him that explored interest and curiosity into my passions in life.

After my husband Toby died my dad and mom had supported me by taking care of the children during the long US summer vacations. Dad helped me with money when things broke in the old house I had purchased in Texas. It wasn't that he didn't love me or understand my challenges as a single mother. This was deeper.

I tried to share my feelings and longings with him, including those of a spiritual nature. After all, he was a spiritual man, following the Catholic faith.

"I'd make a good priest," he'd often joked. This was at times when he and Mom abstained from sex, so she would not get pregnant. It was for longer periods then he'd like. I found these jokes painful.

In spite of Dad's humor and obvious love for people I longed for a dialogue with him and hunted for our spirit-to-spirit communication. His spirit remained imprisoned. He defaulted to humor or sarcasm to escape a more intimate conversation. "You'll never earn a living with theology or Jungian psychology," he'd often say when I explored a new path.

Later I was drawn to the Native Americans, whose medicine people spoke my language and who gave me another name. Like me, they too had a strong connection to their dreams. In fact they referred to their dream world as being the more real form. They understood my connection with spirit encounters.

I didn't dislike my baptismal name. At thirty-six, I discovered the meaning of Ingeborg Maria. Inge comes from the German Goddess of Peace and "borg" is the boundary, sometimes a moat, around a castle. I translated the meaning of the name as being responsible for the protection of women.

Despite my father's objections and the occasional rolling of eyes by my friends, I celebrated my first Paiute given name of Sunshine Little Rose. It bonded me with the sun, with roses. It affirmed my increasing relatedness with people and nature around me. Most of all, the name Sunshine invited cheerfulness into my life. In the US people would say "You look like Sunshine, that name fits you perfectly." The Indian world related my name to a blonde, and blue-eyed woman.

However, after many years, through connecting with Helmina, the new Native name of Standing Bear Woman, entered my life. I was confused! A second Native name? What happened to the first? Indigenous often had multiple names in their lifetime.

Affirmed by my own inner world of bears in my dreams I asked Helmina if I could start using the new name. With uncertainty of what others would think, I occasionally began to sign my name with Standing Bear Woman. But at my work I was careful not to use or refer to it.

At the University of Houston-Clear Lake, where I worked, I focused on the concept of world citizenship from a Western perspective. Native Americans have a focus on harmony and relationship in contrast to the Western drive to change everything around us.

I was attracted to the Native American capacity to teach through experience and by their different concept of time. Their time follows natural and spiritual laws where Western thinking draws from science, economic, social and religious norms. Ideas for a certification program of world citizenship for the university unfolded. To organize it I wrote Helmina about the dates of my upcoming visit to the Standing Rock Reservation in South Dakota.

I planned to meet with several Lakota leaders to start developing a program honoring Native Americans at UH-Clear Lake. The program would attempt to convey the inter-connectedness in the world. Lakota use the words *Mitakuye Oyasin* which means "All my Relations" to describe the relationship of all creation.

I intended to bring awareness of a broader view. Responsibilities of citizens living in a country carrying a world power status should, in my opinion, be rooted in Oneness as a human race. Protection of the earth is an integral part of that. It should be done in a manner different than the usual "us versus them" thinking.

My friend Darlene in Ohio had similar views, so I invited her to join me at the reservation. I hoped she'd share my love of the Plains, the land that made me feel at home. Darlene and I began a close friendship in Houston years ago, where she practiced as a chiropractor before moving to Ohio. At that time, we shared dance, song, and creativity of all sorts. We both flew into Bismarck; she from Ohio and I from Houston. We rented a car and drove the straight and lonely road to Standing Rock Reservation in South Dakota's northern plains.

When we entered the reservation, our first stop was at the Sitting Bull monument. The large bust of *Tatanka Iyotake,* Sitting Bull, stood on a barren hill, which we reached by a winding road. It overlooked Lake Oahe and the rolling barren lands beyond. Sitting Bull's tombstone read 1834-1890. "Sitting Bull was born on the Grand River a few miles west of Mobridge. His tragic end came at the very place he was born. He was shot when being arrested because of his alleged involvement with the Ghost Dance craze," reads the tombstone.

I'm not sure whether Sitting Bull was actually buried there. I love the Lakota but am not Lakota. I am a white woman, from Holland. As such, I am a member of the dominant society.

A Cheyenne medicine man had once said to me years ago, "Oh, you belong to the dominant society." It was the first time I heard the word "dominant" in that context and was offended. In the days that followed I reflected on my language, my behavior, and my thoughts. Yes, I belonged to the dominant ones. That realization made my longing to get out and to be with Natives even stronger.

At times, I wondered about my path. I had stumbled upon the Lakota Nation and met various medicine men from other tribes after Toby died in 1983.

Perhaps I tried to retrieve some of his spirit through my connection with the Indian medicine people. Shortly after Toby died, I had seen a book of records at the Alabama Coushatta Indian Reservation. It had been laying on the counter of the visitors shop and mentioned the name Hayes. In the family it had been mentioned that his grandfather returned to the reservation in Broken Bow, Oklahoma. We later looked in that area but did not find any evidence on gravestones.

How did I get at this place of my life? This wasn't even my culture? Spirituality had been with me in my growing up years, something emphasized by my dad. Was I subconsciously trying to retrieve an emotional connection with him? Then there was the bonding with the earth by my grandfather on my mother's side— was that it?

One thing I do know is that after my psychological break through after Toby died, I found a parallel of how my brain worked congruently with that of the shamans and medicine men and women. The creativity and the continued deepening journey into the spirit world kept me sane. Sometimes, it frightened me too since every time I became restless and high in energy, my only way out was through journeying into the shamanic path, a path deeper into the world of spirits.

I recall one day in Texas; I attended a Native American gathering at the Brown Convention Center in Houston. After talking to many people, I noticed a group of Natives in a corner of the hall. They stood out to me, darker, taller than the rest of them.

Intuitively I knew that that group would be people I'd connect with in the future.

All the above are many pieces of a yet uncompleted mystery. I remembered the spiritual advice from one of my friends: "Delete the need to understand—No comparisons."

I knew my inner experience was one of destiny. It grew in peace with the Lakota and the Plains people. Here at Sitting Bull's grave site on their land, I felt at home. Together with them I believe that his remains are buried on the Standing Rock Reservation, his land of birth.

At the monument site the wind blew and moved the dry grasses and sage brush. The place appeared far from houses of the lower parts of the reservation. The direction in which Sitting Bull looked asked me to do the same. Beyond the river stretched rolling barren land, the Plains. The voices of small birds came to my attention.

My senses reminded me how I experienced the wind and silence in a different way here. I entered an unknown yet familiar silence, a void with presence. On a reservation the spirits roamed in that stillness. This feeling of awareness only moved me on Native American land. The silence and the wind on the land of non-Native people seems much different.

Several red cloths lay at the bottom of the monument. Pieces of glass from broken beer bottles were strewn all around the site—the broken glass left by those who were under the influence of alcohol and came for prayers. There were many people in distress. Their opportunities were dim. No jobs and plenty of alcohol sold by Americans just outside the reservation. The reservation itself was dry. The surroundings and vicious cycle often ended in suicide. All came to pray and plead for guidance. Darlene and I began to clean up.

I entered an inner peace and sensed the spirit presence of this land. I too made my offerings in the traditional Lakota way when I placed tobacco in a small packet of red cloth. I closed it then laid it down with the gifts others had left at the monument.

"Sitting Bull, please guide us on this trip. Help us to get clarity on the program," I asked. From his monument I looked toward the East, the South, the West and the North and I thanked the Great Mystery. As I felt a deep connection with the Spirit of Sitting Bull this spot would be a place I'd return to. Like others that visited here, I too would draw from his example of courage for many years to come. Repeatedly, I pleaded for his help from the spirit world when I faced difficult situations.

Ready for our visit to the reservation, Darlene and I set out for the village of Little Eagle to meet with Helmina. We slowly drove down the winding road from Sitting Bull's monument back to the main reservation route. The Standing Rock Reservation is large. The Plains, much like an ocean floor overgrown with grasses, stretched in front of us.

It took us a while to find the way to the small village. The rough one-hour ride on a wide dirt road wound down into a small settlement of prefabricated low-income houses with hardly any grass or trees around. Children played with old tricycles and balls in the sandy dusty streets. Men hung around the entrances of their houses. Thin dogs without obvious owners wandered around.

Of course, I observed my surroundings through Western eyes and perspective. I had learned that Native Americans are guided by different values and different connections. Their thousands of years-old culture and tradition, their connection with the ancestors and spirit of harmony keeps them close to the earth. Their perspective, as I understood it, included care of future generations. It was not a way of instant gratification nor was their concept of time congruent with the modern world. Their priority was spiritual, not the conquest of the material world.

This is not to say that they were not in need of improved housing, especially the insulation to lower their electric bills in the harsh winters. Or that they weren't in need of jobs to heighten their income. Spiritually, I observed that they didn't have that drive to conquer and change the earth they lived on. I wondered: Are Natives closer to the earth, therefore less restless? Are Natives closer to their cultural identity? Are the indigenous in the world connected to their land to a degree, that I can't even recall in myself? I do remember that my mom's dad was one with the land. He didn't follow material pursuits.

"Helmina left for Pennsylvania," the tall Lakota man hanging out in front of her house told us. He had long black hair and wore an armless blue T-shirt with an Indian design. His left upper arm had a tattoo. He wore the dark sunglasses often worn by a drunk. His height reminded me of my dad. He, joined by another tall young teenager, seemed to know that we'd be coming.

"Come in," he motioned kindly, as he opened the door to the small house.

"Helmina told us you can stay and to give you a key to her room. Carla, her daughter, is on the way."

The unexpected news, that Helmina had departed for Pennsylvania shocked me. I had come far. I tensed up, but at the same time explained it away as "meant to be" in the spirit world.

The house was well kept, had a small kitchen and an annex living room. Above a couch was a piece of leather with several

Indian symbols. A tipi and arrows drew my attention. I noticed the repeated four directions in all. A large circular shield hung next to it. A fly swatter hung on the same wall.

Darlene's and my eyes met silently, agreeing we would not stay. Our intuition did not confirm our safety. It could be safe in the house, I thought, but in the village...? Why did Helmina keep her bedroom door locked?

The front door of the house opened. Carla, Helmina's daughter, entered. She was short, had long black hair worn in a ponytail. Our eyes met, her black ones and mine blue. She had a welcoming smile. I felt connected. The presence of Carla, who I guessed to be in her mid-forties, immediately changed our conversation from the program to the personal and spiritual. We spoke the same language. She understood the language of Spirit and why I had come.

We all sat down in the living room. Darlene sang some fun songs for the children. "I'm a little teapot … For the adults I sang the only song I knew in the Lakota language. It was a song about a dancing tree, *Waci Can.*

Then I said, "My heart is hardened. I have become less empathetic, quick to anger. I'd like to become lighter, share laughter and encourage people. I need to do something before I continue on this trip and create the program for the university."

Carla immediately focused in: "Our people go to Bear Butte, a sacred mountain, and offer Tobacco. You need to keep on going, keep on going. Why don't you go there? It will help in your journey. You will find a medicine woman there and an opportunity to pray. If you ask in the right way you will be able to attend an *Inipi* sweat lodge, there. Bring an offering."

With encouragement from Carla, and precise directions from the tall Lakota man with the dark glasses, we set out to Bear Butte, a three-hour trip from Little Eagle. I noticed a sign riddled with bullet holes. It read "Leaving Standing Rock Indian Reservation." I was somber about missing a visit with Helmina.

When we got to the Bear Butte parking area, I saw an older man sitting in his car smoking a cigarette. He pointed to the mountain. "I have two people on the mountain. Can you see them?"

"No," I said, just as Darlene also joined.

"What are you girls doing here?" he asked.

Since he was Native American and had two people on the mountain to pray, I explained I was looking for a medicine woman.

"Carla, a Lakota woman, had previously mentioned the possibility of attending a sweat. I hope to attend a sweat lodge here," I answered him.

"I'm not a medicine woman," he laughed out loud. He paused, took a puff of his cigarette and continued, "But I'll build a sweat. Why don't you and your friend come back here tomorrow? You can join the sweat. Fast overnight think about it. Think about how you will continue to pray. Be here tomorrow at 10 a.m. and I will send for you."

He handed me a picture of himself in full regalia. I found out the man with the ponytail and the strong Roman nose, was Eugene Black Bear, Sr., a medicine man. In the picture he gave me, he posed at a movie location where he had acted as the Cheyenne Chief in the movie The Last of the Dog Men.

When I walked away toward my car he called out laughing: "I'm not a medicine woman…" Don't know why he thinks that's so funny, I thought. Encouraged Darlene and I went to the hotel and prepared for the sweat the next day. I made prayer ties. We purchased tobacco as a gift to the medicine man. We hunted for some clothes to cover the *Inipi* and wood for the fire.

The next day we returned to the parking area. It was empty. We waited and waited. We had not eaten since we had met Eugene Black Bear, the Southern Cheyenne medicine man the night before. We had welcomed his invitation to join into a sweat. Will he show up?

While waiting in the parking area close to the Park's headquarters, I checked out the statue of Fools Crow, a Lakota Holy Man and Storyteller. His large bust, draped with yellow, black, and red prayer flags, quoted his 1975 prayer before the United State's Senate: "Give us a blessing so that our words and actions be one in unity, and that we will be able to listen to each other. In doing so, we shall with good heart walk hand in hand to face the future."

"How long shall we wait?" Darlene asked, getting restless. Aware of the different notion of time Native Americans have I decided to add another hour. Soon a car slowly drove up the winding road and a woman driver looked around. "Are you waiting to join us in a sweat?" she asked and motioned us to follow her to a different area.

At our destination the medicine man Eugene Black Bear Sr., who I had met the day before stood in front of a small wooden bridge we had to cross to the *Inipi* (sweat lodge) site. He leaned on a walking stick and motioned me for help as all of us continued a trail. "You're flexible," he uttered. "Me flexible? "That thought came as a surprise.

I was nervous. My stomach growled. I was hungry. How would he lead the sweat? Would he be gentle, or would he fire up the stones to the point of being unbearable? I worried. Would the Southern Cheyenne ways be much different from the Lakota ways of doing a sweat? Was I dressed appropriately? I fretted about making mistakes and offending Southern Cheyenne tradition. I was not familiar with their nation.

We spent the rest of the day helping to prepare for the sweat. We covered the structure, hauled water and wood for the ceremony.

The experience of the sweat I cannot share. I don't feel qualified as a non-Indian. Nor is it in line with the teachings of Sweet Medicine, the spiritual leader of the Cheyenne. Sweet Medicine discouraged sharing through writing.

I remember the kindness that surrounded me, a different way of entering the sweat, and the gentleness by the medicine man in leading us. He spoke to and connected with each one of us. He smiled a lot. When he told stories, I also experienced another side with strong boundaries.

He sat in the shade. Close by some put blankets on the skeleton of the sweat branches and tended to the stones and fire. Eugene Black Bear began his story. Briefly into it one of us interrupted him and asked for some detail. "If I get interrupted another time I will not tell the story," he responded firmly. Disruption during a story was not appreciated. The honoring of a century old story in this way made sense to me.

After the ceremony was over we had dinner at a casino in a nearby town. Here the medicine man obviously enjoyed the slot machines. Excited and with a cigarette hanging from his mouth he pulled the levers in that noisy establishment. As soon as he had used up all the quarters Darlene had given him he joined us again at the table.

"That's how we get your white people's money back," he joked. He referred to the casinos many of the Indian nations possess today.

—∿—

Just as this trip turned out to be geographically counterclock-wise, it indicated a different turn in my own life. The planned uni-versity program which I had been working on for UHCL did not come to pass. It had to do with living out my Native name which up till then had been Sunshine Little Rose. The new name, Standing Bear Woman, required turning around on the inside also. This new name required a change in my life I could not grasp at the time.

I knew Helmina was right when the spirits told her about this name. For decades' grizzly bears had been in my dreams, giving me messages about healing work. Roaming through empty rooms in the house on the left, they showed my emptiness on the cre-ative side. I recalled dreams of twenty-five years ago when a grizzly repeatedly stood upright roaring at the edge of a canyon.

It felt scary to bring this out, the part of me voicing truth, regard-less of what others thought or how they'd react. Confrontation I learned early as a child did not pay off. It was a weak part in me. How could I manifest this? Could I bring the bears that lived in my dreams out into the public world?

Traditionally, receiving a spirit name comes with a ceremony. However, I felt intuitively guided to accept, integrate and celebrate my new name in a different way. I made a promise to visit the Sacred Mountain of Bear Butte, *Mato Paha,* for the next four years on the day of my birth. Unexpectedly something happened during the summer of that fourth year, 2011. I became worthy of my name Standing Bear Woman while in Waterton Lakes National Park.

Glacier National Park is in the State of Montana. Waterton Lakes is on the Canadian side, where it's called Waterton Glacier International Peace Park. A week before the Waterton trip I had called Helmina, the Lakota medicine woman, who had given me my name.

"I'd like to learn more about the bear spirit," I said.

"Well, you are going to Canada, the land of the grizzly bears," she responded.

I left for Canada, where I met my friend, Anne, a blonde Dutch woman. We shared a love for adventure in nature. Our backgrounds in psychology, she through Gestalt and I through my Jungian perspectives, grounded us in decades of friendship, and led us across oceans to visit with each other. After spending some days in Calgary, Anne and I drove for a visit to Waterton Lakes National Park. There we followed the narrow winding sixteen-mile Akamin Parkway, a gorgeous one lane mountain road. On the south side, was a rock-filled stream. Enticed by the beautiful creek and the easy access, I veered off to the right into a perfect small parking area. I noted a family from India having a picnic on the black pavement. Anne and I had stopped at an historic site of Canada's first oil rig dating back to 1902.

Across the road, close to the monument, was the first fast-running clear water stream we had found on our vacation in the Rockies. The beautiful body of moving water, several yards wide, and its surroundings was quite the contrast with the flat land of the Netherlands Anne had come from only a few days ago.

Immediately, Anne walked through the small meadow area and headed for some big boulders which crossed the stream where the woods began. Several people were around us; a young couple sunbathed in the grass near the monument. Since we didn't plan to hike, I decided not to take the bear spray. On one of the large boulders Anne took up a contemplative pose. I was about 100 yards away, still close to the monument, exploring rocks in the stream. I took my first pictures of the stream.

The split second that followed changed my sense of security. Feelings of shock, like when one is hit by a car that you don't see coming, struck me like a thunder bolt.

"There's a bear!" I heard someone shout. A woman and a small child carried by a man in his arms dashed away from behind Anne. They ran up the hill to the road.

"I need to get Anne away from there," was my first thought, "but where is the bear?" Scanning our surroundings, not seeing the bear, I headed toward Anne.

"Anne, stay calm, get up immediately. Slowly walk toward me," I told her.

She gave me a funny look as if I were joking but followed my directions anyway. Still searching for the bear, I didn't notice one. I thought the bear must be somewhere behind her, in the woods and brush where the people ran away from. Facing that direction, I walked backward. "Don't run, Anne, don't run. Whatever you do, don't run".

Anne moved forward along the stream and headed toward me, now realizing the seriousness of our situation. I spotted the grizzly bear walking out of the woods on the downstream side of the meadow behind Anne. It was about 100 yards away from me. It appeared to be a young blond grizzly around 250 pounds. Anne moved toward me. With the stream on our side, we both attempted to move closer to the monument and closer to the hill toward the road. The bear diagonally approached and almost cornered us. The relatively small monument was now only yards away from me. Anne walked faster, getting closer to where I stood. I observed the moving grizzly. I wondered where it was headed next and tried to figure out where we could escape to. I avoided eye contact with the bear while I repeated to Anne, "Don't run, do not run," to slow her walking down.

Anne walked more rapidly after spotting the bear herself. Suddenly the grizzly, head down, its eyes focused on us, increased the pace, and approached faster and faster.

With the stream on the right, the road up the hill on the left and no means of escape, the distance between the grizzly became less and less ... 30 yards, 20 yards ... we continued to take steps backwards very slowly.

"Don't run, stand still." Suddenly the grizzly bear charged us. I felt we had no chance. We froze. "No eye contact," I commanded in a low voice again.

Anne and I stood near each other with about nine feet separating us. On the other side of Anne was the Black Gold (oil) marker. The fast young grizzly got closer as if in a line of attack, headed straight toward me, its fur rolling rhythmically.

I was focused on the bear, totally in the present, not conscious of fear. It helped that I had my spiritual experience from the past. For decades I had observed bears in my dreams. I had painted a grizzly only months before. Maybe all this kept the edge of fear under control. It kept me from running.

The grizzly bear charged straight at me. Directly in front of me, the bear suddenly diverted, went between the two of us and made a run for the woods behind us. This was our chance. Anne and I ran past the Black Gold marker up the hill where around sixteen people stood in the parking area. People congratulated us for being alive. It was then that I began to tremble and noticed my fast strong heartbeat.

Seconds later an even bigger grizzly came out of the woods and followed the path of the first grizzly.

What had just happened here? Was it a coincidence? Or had it to do with my name? It had been twenty years ago since the Paiute medicine man had given me the name Sunshine Little Rose. Even then the dreams of the bear were present. At times I was confused about receiving a new name and learned that once given a name we were to grow into it until such time as it no longer applied. .

My Paiute name had flourished through the creation of international and cultural programs at UHCL. They had come to full success and fruition. Internationalization of the faculty and administration had become a success over the years. I had orchestrated many international and cultural immersions on countries from across the world. The House of Representatives, District 149 of the State of Texas wrote a resolution recognizing the program and esteemed individuals participating in the 2007 UHCL immersion on Vietnam. These individuals included speakers of the Smithsonian Asian Pacific American program, the president of the Vietnamese Culture and Science Association among others.

I received university recognition for my efforts on world citizenship. Inwardly, however I felt times had changed. I felt completeness. The programs had come to a certain height. Maybe, I had earned my Paiute name. One more immersion on Turkey and then it was time to move on.

With the geographical turn around in South Dakota four years previously, a new path unfolded. I had received my new name but began owning it when I faced that grizzly. From that moment on I carried myself differently.

What is the task of a Standing Bear Woman, I wondered? That Standing Bear had to become manifest. "How courageous would I need to become?" After all, since my breakthrough in the hospital, I had followed a path of overcoming fear. I became known as being fearless. Was there more to conquer to become courageous?

I felt overwhelmed and set out to fulfill my fourth year of commitment to the sacred Bear Butte Mountain in South Dakota. In September of 2011, when I saw the familiar form of the Sacred Bear Butte, it gave me a joyful feeling. I looked forward to the familiar depth of connection with the spirit world there.

I searched for the hotel in Sturgis where I would stay for two nights. I had a longing for Chinese food and hoped to find it in the small town of Deadwood nearby. The sight of bars, casino's, men, and women smoking, tourists with raw voices walking the street, hurried me back to the hotel in Sturgis where I mentally and spiritually prepared for my visit to Bear Butte.

The next morning, I signed in at the park's office and education center at Bear Butte. "I'll be spending most of the day here," I said to the Native woman behind the counter. Shortly I left heading to the familiar grounds on the foothills of that sacred mountain *Mato Paha*.

A quiet area became my prayer site. A small rabbit and dove met me at the entry. I was alone; alone with the grasshoppers, butterflies and birds, the trees, and colorful flags that moved in the wind. I spotted a bald eagle in the north, the place of wisdom. I smoked my pipe in thanksgiving. It was a day of many insights and gifts. As a closure I laid down on the ground, honoring the many had prayed here thousands of years before me. But something was not right.

I stood up and heard a pounding. It startled me. I looked around, searching for a person running down off the mountain. There was no one. Thump, thump, thump… I heard big steps at regular intervals. It was as if someone leaped off the mountain. Again, I looked around me. I stood very still to hear better, waiting for the next sound when I realized it was my heart pounding in my body and connecting with that of the Mountain. Could that be? Does a mountain have a heartbeat? Did I hear the heartbeat of the earth that the Indians often talk about? If not that, did my heart join the Bear Butte Heart and its mysteries? I smiled, grateful for the moment.

Thankfully, I walked to my car. My heart had become less hardened. It captured a harmony with something much larger in this universe. I, Standing Bear Woman, returned to the hotel.

—◆◆◆—

The years of connecting with the Indigenous ran parallel with my long-range foundation building through international and cultural immersion programs at the university. It began during a National Association for Study Abroad conference where I met Dr. Verghese Chirayath from John Carroll University, Cleveland Ohio. He introduced me to the concept of a daylong immersion. We co-facilitated the first one on India, his country of birth at UHCL. Thereafter, I became certified in Spiral Dynamics integral and tweaked the immersion program to address various levels of consciousness. Programs on China, Indonesia, Iraq, Africa, Turkey, and others offered the faculty and staff an authentic experience with leaders of the country represented in the Houston community and US. These programs for many did away with stereotypical notions.

The Indigenous also helped me focus on the primordial force—Water. Our sacred relationship with waters of the womb, and its ancient force as part of Mother Earth capable of bringing us life or death. These programs became integrated through experiential teachings of the participants during yearly International Awards, again involving the Houston international community and programs with Peter Catches.

My experience in various countries with Toby and the children in early years, while I lived in Guatemala, Iraq, Germany, the U.K., Indonesia, and Venezuela, empowered me to offer experiential education and bring my personal life full circle through the university. The programs were an opportunity to set the record straight and heal some unfinished wounding that had occurred while living on foreign ground in earlier years. I made my peace and could celebrate all aspects of the country, as well as expand the international connection of the university in the Houston community and offer friendship with people from other countries.

Slowly the picture of E Pluribus Unum as on the US nickel—Out of Many, One, was brought a bit closer. The buffalo, represented on some of the older nickels reminds me of that strength of *Tatanka*, the Lakota word for buffalo. Together with the Indigenous and their relationship with all creation we might save our life on this planet. That *tatanka* which carries the strength the backbone of the US. We must understand we are all part of the human race. As immigration heightens through change in weather across the globe, we all will encounter some form of culture shock. We must learn about the origins of people who immigrate or ask for asylum here in the US, the Middle East, Asia or across the world. We might even be forced to find ourselves in a place elsewhere, a culture different from our own. Either way integrating another culture here or there we will experience culture shock.

FOUR

WORLD CITIZENSHIP

UNCOVERING CULTURE SHOCK-
VOICES OF IRAQ

T wo men with cloths wrapped around their heads and faces, pointed machine guns at us. They blocked the road. Toby slowed down and brought the car to a halt.

"Did we do something wrong?"

The two men did not approach the car. They seemed angry. Stark motions with their guns signaled us to turn around. We did!

Such became life around Basrah in the time that Saddam Hussein came to power 1976. There were different rules, unexpected ones, no cameras allowed for pictures, and always a sense of being watched. The border with Iran opened and closed every few months then.

Power and control ruled this regime; such a contrast with where we came from.

We had come from Guatemala where we lived for two years close to Lake Izabal in El Estor. The village of a colorful Mayan community was wedged between a large lake and the jungle mountains. My thoughts recalled beautiful Guatemala and culture shock experienced there. Families used to arrive from the US or elsewhere. I dreaded newcomers, the negativity, the newcomer's complaints about food, housing, school, and people. Darn, their arrival infects the community to culture shock and anxiety all over again. Don't they have Kraft mayonnaise here, breakfast sausage, and iceberg salad? There's nothing on television … on and on it went, blinded by what they lacked and missing the gifts the country had to offer.

They didn't notice the various kind of bananas, oranges, mangos. The culture shock of expats missed out on their music, the wild jungle, most of all the people and their challenge with poverty. The Mayans were the ones living without water and electricity on a dirt floor. These Indigenous slept in hammocks and lived under often broken thatched roofs.

Yet, the moment these new families in Guatemala embraced the sparkle of another culture and worked through the shock of a different land and people, moods shifted. We'd explore fish in the river, visit villages or in my case purchase a motor bike so I'd have transportation on the dirt roads. Life became a celebration. Differences became a challenge, a new language to learn. We expats began to understand that there are different ways to do and be in this world. I wake up from my dream-like reminiscing.

We had moved to Iraq. No bright colors of clothing, happy Marimba music, or the smiles of people. In Iraq, the endless desert took the place of the Guatemalan green mountain jungle. It had a nakedness and was disorienting. The desert seemed to me the most disorienting and vulnerable place I had ever lived in my life. Aloneness forged my soul in a silent inner scream. Fear of the desert became my companion.

"*As-Salam Alaikum* Madam, *Alla bil-kheir*," Mohamed, my driver greeted me with a smile. In his mid-twenties, with long black sideburns, dressed in a Western jacket, Mohamed's face always shared a kindness toward me and a love of Christa. He was peaceful to be with, attentive and ready to take me anywhere. Shopping, he walked behind me, giving me my space.

I scanned the streets of my new surroundings. "Are those round pinkish balls pomegranates?" A mountain of them were placed on the ground at a corner of a street. I had never seen this fruit before, didn't know what to do with it. I tried to handle the many pits but found the red juice too tart. A bakery had a low and wide window-sill with plates of Iraqi flat breads, spicy breads, platters of halva (a candy like cookie,) and baklavas. The smell of dates, almonds, sesame seeds, cardamom, rosewater, and the clay oven made it the best bakery in my world, right there in Basrah.

One day in the fall, Mohamed drove us to my favorite spot, the *souk*, an ancient marketplace. Sounds of hammering on copper and a musky smell coming from the Basrah *souk* greeted us. It was a buzzing, dark and old area.

I looked around me. I felt disconnected from the women with long black robes, their heads covered. Many of them only showed their eyes. I could see the black lines that accentuated their black eyes. I felt no kinship with them. Both of us knew that we came from different worlds with different symbols and societal norms. The black they wore didn't look practical, comfortable, or attractive.

Mohamed and I headed to the street with the Mandean silver and goldsmith shops. I found many silver antiques. Circular daggers hung on the wall adorned with gemstones, silver worked with detailed craftsmanship. Some were hundreds of years old. I found antique arm and ankle bracelets. I purchased an ankle set for Christa to cast off the evil eye. The bracelet had several bells. One bell that had a strange face embedded would stop the evil eye of onlookers. It would block bad thoughts such as envy while looking at Christa. Mohamed told me.

"Would you make me a golden necklace with my daughter's and my name?" I asked in one of these shops. I wrote out *Inge* as well as *Christa* on a piece of paper. Embarrassed, I grasped that the man was able to write in my language, even in gold. I could barely say the word "thank you," *Shukran* in Arabic. Later, finding out more about Arabic poets and the spiritual roots of this language, I would regret not learning and exploring Arabic while I lived there.

We moved on to that part of the *souk* where carpets were sold.

"I'd like to buy an Iraqi carpet, Mohamed." I had no idea what rugs would be typical for Iraq. I expected to see a stack of Persian carpets, similar to those sold in the West.

Mohamed pointed to a couple of men dressed in long dark grey shirts all the way to the tip of their black dusty shoes. They smiled. Surrounded with stacks of colorful carpets they welcomed us, *Salamat*. The older male had a white circular cap on top of his head. A manly tobacco smell came from their cigarettes.

A high-volume exchange with Mohamed in Arabic followed. I liked the sound of their language; it had a power and directness to it. Curious about what exactly they talked about I examined the pulled-out carpets. Are these done by the Marsh people? I wondered. The people that lived close by in the marshlands with its reeds and waterways to the south and east of where we lived? Its crude thread, possibly wool, had been died in earthy colors of red and greens. A pattern of birds stood out. The fabric felt rough almost like rope.

The price haggling began. Mohamed screamed back and forth with the two Iraqi salesmen. Different amounts of Iraqi dinars were mentioned until I saw each one of them with smiles. The deal was closed. I delighted in the carpet and the price!

—◊◊◊—

Christa and I had followed Toby, my husband, to a job in Iraq. We had flown from Amsterdam into Bagdad by way of Damascus. In Damascus the plane stopped for new passengers. Armed Syrian soldiers came aboard the plane. They had walked up and down the aisle, looking left and right staring at us passengers. Nowhere to go, but to stay put in our chair. What did they look for? What were they after? After they left, the Dutch plane left for Bagdad where Toby would welcome us. Going through customs at the *Matar Baghdad id-Duwali* I was surrounded by a world of men with long white dresses and the *keffiyeh* traditional headdress with ropes in colors of red and black. I showed our passport and visas. Several stamps were put in them with few communications.

It was a different world; all men, where were the women?

Toby had been happy to see us, but his mood seemed to be flat. "I haven't been able to find us a hotel yet. Let's try out the Baghdad Hotel. It's not far from here." He sounded a bit frustrated.

After an overnight and somewhat in shock with the minimal sandy comfort of my surroundings, we now traveled through the desert to Basrah, about a six-hour trip. We would make one stop to get something to drink and buy some Iraqi flat circular bread, *Khubuz al-Tannour*. People fought off the flies that were big, hungry, and plentiful at such a sandy spot in the middle of the desert.

Vendors selling drinks sat in front of the one shop. They swatted their faces with a piece of flat bread to keep those flies off. Other people on the road had stopped and purchased some food. Most stood around or found a place to sit on a bench and similarly ate their food while swatting the flies.

"In Basrah we will temporarily live in a large company house. We can use the entire house except for the offices, and we have a very large bedroom," Toby said. The plan was that we would move out into the desert close to where the petrochemical plant and our compound were to be built.

After arrival at the mansion, I walked through this new place. The welcome of the office people was cool. I had the feeling they were frustrated with the presence of a child in their working quarters. Iraqi men did not shake my hand. It is because I'm a Christian or Western, I thought.

Curious I moseyed through the large square living room. It had a red and blue Middle Eastern carpet on the floor. Against the wall were seating and coffee tables, some copper trays. The middle of the room was vacant. How would one entertain in such a setting?

Our bedroom had a queen-size bed. In a corner I noticed the crib for Christa. "What? No mattress for her?"

"No," Toby answered." I tried to get a mattress at the state store in town. I couldn't find one anywhere here in Basrah. We will have to go to Kuwait for that."

"How far is that? Why on earth are there no mattresses here in Basrah?" More questions popped in my head. What about mail delivery? How would I connect with my family and friends abroad?

I had heard rumors that the mail at the Basrah Post Office was way behind in delivery, and that letters were spread and stacked on floors everywhere. International calls were easy to make. There was one problem though. The government would cancel our phone a few days after each call abroad.

After seeing parts of Baghdad and Basrah and our long trek through the desert between those two cities, the thought of moving to the desert suffocated me.

In Iraq, Christa and I stood out with our blonde hair. I made it a point to dress culturally appropriately, long sleeves and slacks or a skirt covering my knees. It wasn't as hot as I thought it would be so close to the desert. Our house had some heaters. It was late fall, 1976. I spent time reading while Christa took naps and Toby worked. I went to shops and tried to connect with neighbors or foreign people living in Basrah. Contact with our direct neighbors I made connecting with the husband talking across a garden wall. He invited me to tea and meet his wife. He and I sat on the floor drinking tea while his wife sat away from us in the room at a distance. She never engaged in the conversation.

Foreign women from East Germany and Russia who had married Iraqi men stood out. I spoke German and was eager to connect. One East German woman was happy to visit her family at home but didn't receive a passport for her kids, to assure she'd be coming back to Iraq. "We were told to avoid questions and were discouraged from connecting with Westerners," one said in German.

Toby helped by introducing me to Iraqi colleagues. One, an engineer, had studied in Russia, as many of them did at that time, and was obliged to volunteer in Iraq at the university for a couple of years. This was in return for the opportunity of studying in Russia. I found that a good rule. Later we connected with an Armenian family. I felt a kinship since they were practicing Orthodox Christianity. We tried to fit in and make friends and go on outings.

"Let's get some Iraqi pennies at the bank to play poker at home."

The bank located in the center of Basrah seemed to be surrounded by people. People, all men, were screaming and had anti-Israeli posters. The mass of people felt more like a riot than a demonstration. I could sense the hate in the air. Israel seemed so far to me. Had these young people even met an Israeli? Their anger and voices terrified me. We quickly went back home. Yet during weekdays, I was thankful to have Mohamed, my driver, to venture out a bit each day. *Inshalla.*

—m—

"What's that Mohamed?" I pointed into the distance to a standing handcar without an animal attached to it. It was pitch black and looked somewhat bumpy. "Those are dates, Madam." We drove closer, maybe too close, because once my eyes focused on the black I saw it would forever change my relationship with dates. In front of us stood the buzzing silhouette of the cart, formed by fat black busy flies.

"Those dates are exported to East Germany to feed the pigs," he said.

We parked the car to do some shopping, but I couldn't get those dates out of my head. The look of that wooden cart would continue to reappear each time I would eat dates. The image had entered my DNA yet didn't keep me from eating that delicious fruit.

In the *souk* Christa rattled around with the two ankle bracelets made from tin and was not troubled by the evil eye. I could hear her through the sound of the bells, wherever she went. The *souk* was always crowded. I enjoyed the sound of banging on copper and was amazed by the delicate and ancient craftsmanship of men carving lines and images on large copper serving plates, pots and vases. I preferred the red copper, especially the old-fashioned coffeepots standing tall with a huge spout and decorated top, used to brew coffee directly sitting in glowing coals. These would hold hundred cups of coffee at least I thought. Indeed, the large pot with its round belly would sit in a bed of coals one could grill a steak on.

En route home, I picked up a delicious, scented flavor. Soon we passed the store where outside on the dusty gravel racks of rotating chickens grilled in gas flames. We bought a couple. I noticed a long line of people.

"If you see one of those lines you probably want to get in it," Toby often said. "They have something we need."

Later I remembered and motioned Mohamed to stop when I would see one and got in line, curious what would be sold and checking if Toby had been right. Getting closer to the front after quite a wait with Mohamed attending to Christa in the car, I saw a middle-aged man. He sat next to a huge brown cotton bag with potatoes in it … we hadn't eaten potatoes for a month now. I was tired of all the rice at each meal. My mouth watered with thoughts of Dutch French fries with mayonnaise.

It was my turn and while the man was filling up a small bag with potatoes, the amount of which he decided, I motioned if I could get some large ones for fries. Not looking up he emptied my bag in response. I pleaded in my minimum Arabic, said that any size was ok. He complied. *Shukran shukran*. It was a good day.

We turned the car into the dirt lane to our house. Sheep led by an older man were grazing through the compost outside the wall of our house. That's where our cook threw the peelings over the wall.

That night I noticed again a group of men dressed in suits sitting under the palm trees across from our walled and guarded house. Who were they? What were they watching for? Oh no, they are government people, I felt intimidated, what would I ever do wrong here?

The gardener opened the gate. Distracted, I noticed our beautiful red roses, the size I would never see again in my life. Glad to be home I prepared some Turkish coffee. It smelled good in the house. The cook was preparing rice with curry and raisins. He cooked spicy. I handed him my treasure—the potatoes.

Toby had just arrived home ahead of us. "I invited an Armenian colleague and his wife tonight. You will like them," he said. I was ready to make new friends.

At seven our gardener announced the visitors. There were about nine of them standing at the door: Armand, Toby's colleague and his wife, parents, aunts, and brothers. This became my first experience of having guests in Iraq and the way people welcome and greet one another. Iraqis and Armenians come as a family when invited! They expect the same of you.

"Come to our house for a dinner of lamb," The Armenian said.

We arrived and were welcomed by plenty of family all living in the same house. One child opened a room to announce to his napping uncle that we had arrived. I counted five single beds lined up. When it came time to eat our host motioned us to the dining room where a whole grilled lamb, head and all, stood on the table. Many dishes of rice, pureed eggplant, and chick peas surrounded the lamb, and there were truffles from the desert as well. The desert, that site of fear, had truffles? Large black delicacies sniffed out by pigs from deep under the sand. They tasted good. No, I would not move to that desert despite them. Every time Armand or his wife offered me the truffles my mind saw the desert. If I'd had to flee from the desert, I wouldn't know what direction to go. It seemed so endless, without limit, no hiding place. No borders. I'd lose all interior orientation with the exterior isolation.

While ten to fifteen family and friends stood in a room close to the dining table, each of us received a plate with a very big piece of lamb to eat. Our host, as is the custom, took the head and sucked out the brains and other parts in that lamb's head. We joked around. No, they don't eat the eyeballs.

—␣—

We attended a Catholic Church on a Sunday. I understood Catholics were not popular. Should I even go? Maybe the government will harass us because we are Catholics. I'd heard about the small group of nuns who had started an orphanage and were harassed. Details I didn't know. Why could I not practice what I believed? I didn't come to convert anyone.

We continued our day with a stroll in an area close to the port of Basrah on the Shatt El Arab. It's where the Tigris and the Euphrates come together. We passed beautiful palm groves on the way. Many people gathered at the harbor for a walk, some as a family but in general I saw mostly men. Men who were holding each other's hand like friends.

I learned from other expats that the Catholic hospital, and the only clean one in Basrah, had run out of anesthesia in Iraq. They were short on sheets as well. With Christa being small this worried me. I needed to find out how safe we would be in case of an emergency and thought of Kuwait again.

"Lets' soon drive to Kuwait and do some shopping, get bananas, oranges and a small mattress for Christa," I suggested while walking. We lived close to both the Kuwaiti and Iranian borders. The Iranian border was somewhat tricky because Iraq was on and off in war with Iran. Sometimes the border would be open for a few days or weeks, then closed again. No, we didn't want to get stuck in Iran and not be able to return to Basrah because they closed the borders once again. We chose to go to Kuwait instead. I planned to purchase some China since most of the cups and glasses in the furnished and elegant house were plastic. Not much was available at the state store. Christmas was coming and we needed some toys for Christa and presents for Toby and me.

"Don't do anything wrong," someone at work had mentioned to Toby. "If you do we will catch you at the border." The Kuwaiti border was not far from Basrah and it was easy to go through the checkpoints. We had reserved a room in the Hilton. Kuwait seemed rich and busy. I noticed an abundance of expensive cars, especially Mercedes Benz. I don't remember how many millionaires lived there at the time, but it was an unbelievably high number and it showed. I felt a sense of freedom. It made me feel less alone and connected with the people.

The spices smelled strong. Whiffs of curry, cardamom, coffee, and unknown scents transported me to curiosity and wanting to buy and try some. All were sold loose by the pound and visible, a delight for the eyes, pounds and pounds of pistachios also. The split open nuts could be easily opened. And the small greenish salty and toasted nut was addictive.

Let's drive all the way to the tip of Kuwait, close to the water." We walked on the sea wall, inhaled the water on one side. It felt good to be away from the desert even though I was probably right in it because there was plenty of sand all around.

In the Hilton, we drank a *Cuba libra*, a nice Coke with rum and lemon we used to drink in Guatemala. Drinking alcohol felt strange and made me uneasy. You couldn't purchase alcohol in Kuwait, but our Kuwaiti friend had brought some in for us. He had also purchased bananas for us to take home. While in Kuwait we saw a pediatrician for Christa and noted that the hospital was in very good shape.

Back home in Basrah going through winter, I longed for the summer. Our second temporary house in Basrah had a huge terrace on the roof with a high wall surrounding it. It was built that way because of the heat. Many families would set up beds there in the summer and sleep or visit outside at night on the roof. I looked forward to that experience, seeing the stars, observing them together with Toby and Christa. This house was located not far from the company's house. A long narrow elevated road gave us access. The sand on both sides of that narrow strip would flood during certain seasons. Standing on top of the roof, I investigated a walled village of people maybe from the surrounding marshes, fishermen, or were they gypsies? The women wore a lot of gold, earrings, bracelets, and rings. Their rooftops were made of thatched material. I sneaked some movies even though the government didn't allow it. With my film camera barely noticeable resting on the wall of the rooftop, I shot home movies during the time that the sun went down, often changing position or interrupting the filming with holding Christa in my arms.

It was getting colder now, and we would not use the rooftop for quite a while. Instead, we needed a small gas heater to heat up the rooms in the house.

Our final house, a large home formerly rented by a dentist to the German ambassador to Iraq, was the largest place we lived in Basrah. Two male helpers lived in the house.

"Could you clean the carpet. They are so dusty," I asked one of the helpers. His body language showed resentment. There was no communication or eye contact back from him. He mumbled something in Arabic and began sweeping. There were no vacuums, and cleaning carpets was done with a small hand broom and dustbin. The dust and sand everywhere were frustrating.

I began to prepare the house for Christmas with minimal communication with the men who worked for us. Resentment was in the air. We shopped for Christmas presents in Kuwait. Toby purchased a watch for me that wouldn't work when he gave it to me at Christmas. He angrily threw it across the room. It was not like him to be so impatient or angry. I just didn't know what was going on with him.

There was another present, a surprise from our early nights in a crazy double bed with a hard wooden strip in the middle. Naturally, we'd end up on one side of that bed.

"Hon, I think I am pregnant," I told him at Christmas.

My fear of the desert compounded with questions on how to deliver our next baby.

Toby was not happy. His unhappiness surprised me. He had lived in Banda Shapur, Iran, before and always talked highly about his friends and his experience there. But Iran and its people were not respected where we lived now. Later I learned that the government advised Iraqi men who were married with Iranian women to seek a divorce. Maybe that's why Toby was upset a lot. Maybe his colleagues didn't respect the fact that he had worked in Iran who after all was their enemy. Our moods were not upbeat like they used to be. Usually we ventured out, couldn't wait to explore. It just was not happening now.

Years later I realized that both of us were deeply trapped in culture shock. Unaware and deep into negativity we totally missed the history, museums, the famous place of Ur, the shrines at Warka dedicated to the Goddess of Love, not to mention Samarra or an in-depth experience with the Marshlands and its people. Our heads were disconnected from the land of Iraq and its people. Toby was unhappy, I was pregnant and there was no anesthesia available should something happen. Hospitals were dirty. We wanted to leave and that was easier said than done.

"Do you think they will issue me an exit visa?" I asked nervously. Iraq did not have an American embassy and all passport and visa issues were done through the Swiss Embassy. Iraqi exit visas were hard to get. Decisions on an exit were of course handled by the government and I remembered the internationals where the parent and children would be split up.

Everything went smoothly though, and Toby planned to resign from his job a few months later once we could transfer to another assignment.

I, pregnant, left with Christa before Toby under the disguise of going on vacation to the Netherlands. Again, we drove the long way to Bagdad. Mohamed drove us. No bathrooms on the way. Out of the car I could only see sand on the right and sand on the left. No trees to hide behind and being pregnant I had to go, despite the row of cars behind us and the presence of Mohamed, our driver. I went between two open doors of the car along the road.

A long slow caravan of cars on their way to Mecca had joined us.

Toby visited Ur after I left and at least he had seen that place. His successor, an Englishman, soon arrived. The Englishman later was incarcerated for a year because he couldn't stop talking about Christianity. The plant in the desert was built to completion. Much later, after two years in Germany where Patrick was born and by the time we would live in Indonesia, there was war again between Iran and Iraq. Iran bombed the plant in Iraq, and in turn Iraq bombed the plant that Toby directed in Banda Shapur, Iran. With that war, the US government would wait too long to evacuate people, and a few died.

We on the other hand ended up with a pregnancy that started in Basrah. Patrick, our son, was born in Heidelberg after a very complex delivery. Antibodies due to my RH negative had formed and the doctor spoke about an inter uterus blood transfusion for the baby, to be performed in Frankfurt. Taking a needle straight into my belly monitoring the water surrounding Patrick in my uterus became a routine. The plan changed with an early delivery after ascertaining the baby's lung capacity. Patrick would need special care for months on account of cerebral palsy symptoms. He'd be hundred percent alright after seven months of intense daily alternative physical treatment. We had made the right choice leaving Iraq for Germany.

Years later in the nineties long after Toby's passing, and while working at the university in the cosmopolitan city of Houston a yearning for Iraq and the Middle East continued. Feelings and questions about the desert, the Iraqi people, and their history lingered on. My love for the sound of the Arabic language continued. I became curious about their poetry, music, and history.

While it was easy for me to recognize culture shock in others when we all lived in Basrah, I had missed my own that lasted much longer than two months. Toby and I had been deeply stuck in negativity, opinions, and inflexibilities. And mostly my fear.

I would be able to re-address and search anew for that which I lost through culture shock.

In 2005 after the US initiated the war on Iraq. I attempted to give a glimpse into the culture and history of that country for faculty and staff at the University of Houston-Clear Lake. I created an all-day program and opportunity to connect with leaders of the more than 5000 Iraqi families living in the Houston area and other Iraqi scholars in the US. As a world citizen concerned for the future of the Iraqi people, I pondered how I could be a catalyst for supporting cross cultural communication without imposing my own thoughts. This was my way to bring a human face to the Iraqi people in the terrible war I didn't agree with. It was also an opportunity to rekindle my experiences of living for almost a year in Basrah, Iraq in the 70s.

Meeting Iraqis in Iraq, Jordan, in the US and in my homeland of the Netherlands created a deep-seated curiosity to learn about their history and preservation of their cultures formed by numerous invasions over centuries of time. It changed the way I watch the news and I eagerly receive documentaries from the Middle East. It also educated me about the human fear and cultural disconnect people have.

I reconnected with leaders of Iraqi immigrants now living in Houston.

Iraqis live exiled from their homelands in Jordan, the United States, Canada, the United Kingdom, the Netherlands, and other countries. Most people living in Iraq did not have the financial capacity to leave the war in their country, and thus endured the daily challenges which some call worse than the time living under the rule of Saddam Hussein.

On a positive note, the marshlands once destroyed by the government of Sadam Hussain, could slowly be accessed, and developed by returning Kurds. Dr. Jawdat born in Nassrya, Iraq, started his medical career serving the people in the marshlands of Iraq, visiting them by boat. Dr. Jawdat's career brought him to Houston where he practices as a notable US cardiologist at St. Luke's hospital. I wonder if he could elaborate on the present marshlands and how his family spread around the world. Do they plan to ever return? How does he, a Sabean Mandean Iraqi, continue family relationships? How does he support his country from afar?

From a Sabean Mandaean Iraqi family living in the Netherlands I learned that being a Sabean Mandaean Iraqi is a whole different story. In 2005 a group of around 40,000 Mandaeans remained in Iraq in the Basrah area. Their faith is an ancient Gnostic religion following John the Baptist and is still in existence. This religion originated in southwest Mesopotamia well before the Christian era. They are pacifists and have suffered discrimination and human rights violations. Traditionally they are silver and gold smiths. I remembered visiting their shops while I lived in Basrah. Under persecution many fled to Iran, Indonesia, Jordan, Yemen, Australia, Holland and elsewhere. I wonder how many of them remain in Iraq today. Will a potential new constitution after the war in Iraq allow them a safe life in their homeland?

That international and cultural immersion of Iraq at UH-Clear Lake in 2005 began with an Iraqi breakfast; the traditional flat bread, dates, omelets, sweets, and watermelon accompanied with strong coffee and sweetened tea. Nawal Nasrallah, who wrote a cookbook and history of Iraqi cuisine "Delights from the Garden of Eden" presented in a long green traditional gold—embroidered dress. "These are date-filled traditional *kleicha's* made with *dihin hur* (clarified butter.) It's the national cookie of Iraq. Yes, even in the time of the Mesopotamians such a cookie was popular. I baked them last night for you and brought them on the plane." I smiled at her hospitality. I recognized it from living in Iraq and especially now since I am no longer in the claws of culture shock. Today I welcomed the warm reception by the Iraqi people in Houston.

Her husband, Shakir Mustafa from Boston University, read Iraqi short stories written by female writers, and guided us in a very basic understanding of the Arabic language.

UH-Clear Lake welcomed the Khudairi family and together with them and others we set the agenda for the immersion. Mrs. Sawsen Khudairi addressed two misconceptions about women. "Not all women are veiled, and women can get a divorce when men choose multiple marriages." Their son discussed do's and don'ts in Iraq. "Now that billions of dollars are allocated to reconstruct Iraq, business must appreciate the dynamics of the Iraqi culture. Always err on the formal when addressing Iraqi people in business." Iraqis are more emotional when it comes to business. The latter became reality during the immersion when the owner of the Khudairi Trading Group gave an overview of oil wealth in the Middle East. An emotional reaction followed when an Iraqi oil consultant elaborated on the suffering the oil had caused the people of Iraq. "War after war we have suffered and all because we have oil. The people of Iraq have not benefited at all."

This is what cultural immersions are about. A chilling air was in the room, truth had been spoken and I needed a shift to take place. It was time for the oud, Iraqi's oldest instrument. With great tenderness Rahim Al Haj played his piece named "Childhood" from his album "The Second Baghdad." It filled the room with childlike tunes that healed for a moment the heavy exchange that had taken place. People listened in silence. I traveled from the head to the heart.

Who will help those left behind? What happened to the widows of the men that died? Can they remarry? Who takes care of them? A question that lingers till today.

Each country we lived in reached deep into our memory and the people living there had entered our hearts. Indonesia carved deeply as well.

EAST KALIMANTAN, BORNEO INDONESIA

S TOP," I YELLED TO THE driver, pointing at the snake. The cobra hissed and pulled his body straight up, while his hooded head ferociously concentrated on us at the height of the jeep's window. People had told me they spit and would make you blind. It was awesome to exchange relationships safely sitting in that jeep behind the window and observe a dangerous snake in its own environment.

Kalimantan, formerly named Borneo, is known as "Snake Mecca." It inhabits the largest amount and variety of snakes in the world, three hundred different kinds.

The first day we moved into our house, Christa, my daughter, found a three-foot green snake. The guards, killed the snake with a stick. Snakes curled up inside the air conditioning window units. There were special snake people in Indonesia, *Orang Pintar*, who'd come to your house and do a ritual to chase them off.

During trips through the jungle, Toby spotted several on the road and a wild energy would get hold of my husband. His large boots would hit the brakes of the jeep and he'd jump out, run after one and squash its head with the heel of his boot. Other times he'd drive over it. I would constantly check inside the jeep to see if they had crawled into it.

Workers in Indonesia, while bulldozing the road through the jungle, would spot snakes that were big enough to eat pigs. Their bodies were as wide as a big person's thigh. Sometimes they came too close to the compound where we lived, and kids were not allowed to play in those areas.

I didn't want my kids to grow up distant toward animals. In Indonesia we created a sea aquarium, catching clown fish, stone fish, and a variety of tropical species in the salt water on the edge of the jungle. Later we found a trapped mouse deer. It got hurt and we consulted the company's doctor to help it. Just outside of the location with our group of houses, right smack in the jungle in Loktuan, lived orangutans. At night, afraid of the orangutans, the help didn't want to go home.

"We noticed two large boas hanging from the tree where now your yard is," workers told me when we moved in. It didn't make me uncomfortable, just aware.

After thirteen hours of flying, London, Amsterdam and a stop in Singapore, we had arrived at our new destination in East Asia. The airport in Jakarta was warm and tropical and had a sense of Dutch organization to it. Some of the words had their Dutch roots. I understood them. They carefully checked our immunizations: Cholera, BCG and then some.

"*Selamat Datang.*" At the Hotel Horizon, a bell boy carried our six suitcases to a large suite on the fourth floor. The hotel stood on the outskirts of Jakarta on the black beach of the island of Java, Indonesia.

The welcome by the Indonesians at the hotel, dressed in orange and black batik clothing, snapped up my weariness of the trip after we left our last residence in England. On a table we found a bowl with exotic fruit. Next to it stood a vase with hundreds of small purple orchids. We felt embraced in this new yet *déjà vu* country. Another construction job, a fertilizer plant needed to be built for Pupuk Kaltim in the jungle of Kalimantan also called Borneo.

Borneo is a huge island 830 miles long, 600 miles wide, where the gentle and misunderstood Dayak headhunters live. The land has thick jungles, wild cats, red-haired orangutans, and fascinating tapirs; monkeys, exotic birds, ancient dragons, and flying lizards; impressive and aggressive king cobras. Majestic trees edge into mangroves. At the coast I noticed mudskippers rolling their bulging eyes. Torrential rains, water buffalos, and much more hid in that unfathomable work of creation. As for the people, they were ancient ones as I experienced them, those that lived in the longhouses. I felt they were not as innocent as I had previously experienced the Mayans in Guatemala.

Many of the Dayaks, the Indigenous of this island, still preserved their "price" from times not long ago when headhunting was legal. One of them brought me unearthed antique vessels and Durian fruit. Some of the vessels, unknown to me then, came from cemeteries disturbed by the Canadian logging companies. The Durian smelled up the house something terrible. I became interested in the antique Celadon vessels they offered me to purchase. Were they real?

I had always wanted to go to Indonesia. Aunt Enny, my foster mom, came from the island of Java. Opa, my Dad's father, lived as a soldier in Aceh on the island of Sumatra during World War I. I observed the old sailboats in the harbor and tried to imagine how he had sailed to Indie from the Netherlands.

While the children and I explored our new surroundings, Toby flew off to meetings on the islands of Celebes and the southern part of Kalimantan. He returned with stories of eating the cold food with his hands and how he flew in planes that landed on water.

My life in contrast to his at the hotel had a sense of luxury. I taught the children to swim in the pool of the hotel and met

Indonesian people who joined me exploring shops and antique markets in Jakarta. We indulged in the authentic Indonesian food of *satay ramas, sajur lodeh, sambal goreng,* food wrapped in coconut leaves and always drank *klapper*—coconut juice. Many a night we returned to Indonesian gamelan music and traditional dance at the hotel.

"It hurts Mom." Said Christa, upset. after Indonesians affectionately squeezed Patrick's and Christa's cheeks while we walked around. Their fairness, in contrast with the dark hair and eyes of the local people attracted them. At night we walked the black beach and noticed *Krakatau*, the volcano, in a distance. Toby announced he would be gone for a while to Celebes.

Unlike in the early months of arrival at a new destination, here in Jakarta I immediately sensed freedom to go around and explore our new space on Java. I connected with the current of my dad's father having lived and fought here. I recalled the sweet attention my Indonesian foster mom gave me when I was young.

Indonesia had been a colony of the Netherlands. I even had an opportunity to talk some Dutch with older Javanese and discovered a dark side of my country of birth.

I was terribly embarrassed, no ashamed, when I heard some of the stories. What had overcome Dutch colonizers to expect the Indonesian people to fall on their knees when Dutch rulers drove their cars through the streets in Jakarta? Why wasn't there an even exchange of goods and knowledge for all? Why had an abyss existed in education between the wealthy and the poor? These thoughts and many more bubbled up in my awareness while living in Indonesia, especially when alone with our children Christa and Patrick, with Toby often leaving to different parts of Indonesia for meetings.

—⁕—

Toby was gone on a business trip, I didn't feel good, and my moon cycle had acted funny. I began searching for a doctor in this crowded city of millions, Jakarta.

"There is nothing wrong with your cycle, woman—you are pregnant." The Indonesian female doctor glanced at me from behind her desk.

The ground underneath me disappeared. Darkness enveloped me. The problems with antibodies, huge needles going straight into my pregnant belly, puncturing the water during my last pregnancy, still hovered in my mind. In panic I began to sob.

When did this happen? When and where did I get pregnant? I am RH negative. This cannot be. I just arrived here. I am not even at our final Borneo destination, where our house had to build. My G*d, I am not yet over the last birth. I felt like I just came up from under the water to breath and I am being pushed down again.

"Have an abortion. So many women here have an abortion; you have two children, that is enough. You don't need the complications of this one," the person behind the desk said.

"Me, have an abortion?"

She went on: "You are not ready for this child. Two are enough. Two are enough," she repeats in English with her Indonesian accent.

Images of the complications with Patrick, our youngest, his cerebral palsy, his early birth, the discussion about inter-uterus blood transfusions flashed through my mind. Again, she said,

"Have an abortion."

"Shut up woman," I thought then, not accepting the norms of this country which were so foreign to my own values.

The darkness around me tightened—where had I come? What place was this, what people? They talked so easily about abortions. Aunt Enny where are you—is this your country? Is it some sack of rice they talked about? They all did it, abortions everywhere, I saw it clearly. Here in a different world, they emphasized abortion, not life. Toby, where are you? I feel trapped. I will not have an abortion. I must get out of here.

That afternoon on my way to the hotel I saw many women walking around pregnant. I don't want an abortion. I don't want this child; I am not ready. I do not want an abortion. I do not want an abortion.

So, I'm pregnant in late 1978, number three. Each two years now I had been pregnant; 1975 Christa in Guatemala, 1977 Patrick in Germany and now in Indonesia number three to be born in 1979. "What's up with the two-year thing?" What happened with me when I was two? What am I trying to birth every two years? Could it be that at two years old I became a mother and stopped being a child? What became locked or blocked in my subconscious?

A few days later Toby arrived at the hotel. I shared the news. He was not thrilled but didn't express a lot of his emotions or feelings. I was unable to share mine either. It happened, so be it.

We moved to Bontang, on the island of Kalimantan. An hour plane ride took us from Jakarta to Balikpapan, a harbor town with a small airport and refinery on the west coast of Kalimantan. From there we took a two-propeller plane built in Spain to Bontang.

We temporarily lived in a house on the established refinery compound at Bontang. Meanwhile our housing would be carved out of the jungle across the equator, a 30-mile car trip near a short one road local village, Loktuan.

The jungles appeared thick and strong. An inner voice said: Don't go in there—you won't come out alive. The local people walked into these jungles holding up a sharp long blade like a machete turned outward in front of their head and chest. Thus, they avoided becoming strangled by boas hanging from tree trunks. There were leeches abound. Voracious large dragons or ancient lizards rested along the mud road.

We bought our food at a small company grocery store. The only way out of this place had to be by plane on that dusty airstrip. Visits to the nearby coast became my means to see a little further and shake the psychological clench of the surrounding jungle. We had come to the end of the world.

Our temporary house had two bedrooms, no quarters for the *babu*, the help. The house was simple. Western people, Americans, and Europeans, lived in simple wooden housing, while most Indonesians lived at the other side of the compound in large bungalows. I picked up their quiet resistance toward people from the West. "Can't blame them," I think. Hauling off the lumber from their jungles, humanity satisfied our excess need of wood. In later years the area supplied cottonseed oil for export and cattle graze the now barren land to satisfy meat diets all over the world. The Orangutans would lose these jungles and end up living on protected acreage to survive. Twenty-five years after our family lived in deep jungles, lungs of creation, they had disappeared from the world forever.

The Indonesians needed our expertise yet resented it. I'm on their side, especially after the history of colonization by the Dutch and occupation by the Japanese.

The government of President Suharto dictated that all foreign countries needed to buy their building products from the local economy first. It created a challenge for the companies that had to construct their plants. He organized an emigration plan to spread the overpopulation in Jakarta to the various islands. Some, with the promise of a free piece of land, ended up in Kalimantan.

Each day, Toby crossed the equator. He drove in a jeep to the new site that had to be cleared for the construction of the fertilizer plant, including a small housing area. Temporarily living in Bontang, I spent time with the children and with Bertha, the Christian Torajan *babu*.

Bertha traveled from the Indonesian island of Celebes to Kalimantan for work. We didn't understand each other; she spoke Indonesian with possibly a Torajan dialect. Instead of teaching her the Western way of cooking we adapted to the local cuisine that she knew well to prepare. All of us enjoyed it. Our bodies slowly shared that typical odor of Indonesians rather than that of Western people.

Bertha carried Patrick around on her hip. He began to eat the local way, cupping his little hands and picking up his food instead of with a spoon. Christa found an Australian boy and a girl from India her age to play with. As a family we became even closer. Each night Toby read stories to the children. Bertha put them to bed and sat next to their little beds while she rubbed their back until they fell asleep.

My pregnancy advanced. I had not told anybody. I was over three months now and didn't show too much. Did I feel the baby move? Toby had left on a trip for meetings in Celebes again. I became lonely.

That Sunday, with Toby in Celebes, a jeep stopped at our house and a man from India walked to the door. "Come we'll show you the new site where the Pupuk Kaltim fertilizer plant will be built. The place where you will live."

Grateful and curious I accepted. Pat, Christa, and I, and one of the wives stepped through the backdoor of the dusty jeep. We sat down on the metal benches that hung on both sides. The man from India and a large-built American sat in front. They had flapped up the side windows for air.

After about a mile, leaving the compound, we started on a wet red clay trail. It wasn't a road, just a path created by Canadian trucks excavating logs in the middle of the jungle. The driver drove fast, not wanting to get stuck. Ahead I noticed the rolling hills with the Kalimantan jungles hugging us on both sides. An endless route curved like a snake through the jungle.

The Canadian logging company had illegally cut the wood of this last rainforest, which I later found out fell under the protection of the World Wildlife Fund.

During the week, our company's bulldozer followed the logging trucks, taking advantage of the newly carved area through the jungle. Later it helped jeeps like the one we were in to pass.

King cobras, orangutans, boas, dragons robbed of their habitat found another space to live. Upset with our invading presence, cobras raised up their triangular head and hissed at our slow moving jeep while we passed. We crossed the equator. In the back of the jeep, we were thrown from one side to the other. I hit my head against the ceiling of the Toyota jeep several times. The guys in the front had fun being challenged by the road. They manly conquered the endless path ahead of us. They had no clue that I carried a baby.

I felt sick to my stomach. Inside of me I screamed "please slow down I am scared, I am pregnant," but overridden by my need for acceptance and love I kept quiet. I became emotionally paralyzed. I held unto my belly and tried to catch each bump, reaching out and protecting Christa and Patrick at the same time. We all bumped up and down on the hard seats. With fear I shut down. I didn't want to tell. I felt embarrassed that I got pregnant just as we had arrived at a new jobsite. It was not a convenient time.

The jeep stopped. We had arrived at our future place of habitat. It looked desolate, ugly, with steel beams thrown around. I saw some old barracks that had to become offices. I could not imagine that we'd live here soon. Numb, I walked around in that barren area with fewer trees in the middle of the jungle. I felt low and headed to the jeep ready for the long road back.

That evening I laid down, held my belly, and cried. I longed for Toby. Three days after that trip to Loktuan I began to bleed. G*d, I prayed, let me keep this baby. Toby arranged a plane and I departed with Christa and Patrick to Jakarta. We checked into the Horizon Hotel again. Together with my newfound Chinese doctor, I began the fight of keeping the baby. My antibodies are too high already as they should have given me higher anti-RH doses after Christa was born when we lived in Guatemala. I did not want to lose this baby. I felt contractions. The doctor confined me to the hotel room with total bed rest.

We watched the Indonesian TV programs, and I entertained Pat and Christa with games and room service. Once a week I took a taxi to the doctor to receive injections. I rested six weeks, maybe eight. On the weekends Toby arrived from Kalimantan.

Over five months pregnant now, the contractions sat in every ten minutes. I began losing my baby. In a small hospital, the Chinese doctor gives me anesthesia and I soon recuperated in a nice room.

"What was it, a boy or girl?" I asked the doctor. He shrugged his shoulders nonchalant.

"I couldn't tell; it came out in pieces."

He had done an abortion!

That afternoon I went back to the hotel. "Let's get some groceries," Toby said on the way. Stacks and stacks of diapers I noticed in the store. In the streets every woman looked pregnant. Numb, my eyes followed where these women walked.

With a hollow feeling, we flew home from Jakarta to Balikpapan and again in the small prop to Bontang. Doctors assured me that there were other factors than the road that caused the contractions; still, I am laden with guilt. "It's your fault. Verdict guilty. Give her a life sentence."

What did they do with my baby? All in pieces... Which pieces? Where are the pieces...? How did they dispose of my baby? Was it their baby to dispose of? Did that doctor carry my baby in hís belly? Were it hís genes? Was it his heartbeat that was separated? What kind of animal tears babies apart to get them out? Tearing apart in pieces? Who gave him that right?

I didn't understand, didn't understand the culture, and didn't understand about miscarriages and how they happen.

None of my neighbors said anything. Nobody commented. They avoided the issue. Toby and I had no dialogue about it either. He was warm and sweet, held me close, but there was not discussion. Shortly thereafter he had a vasectomy. It never dawned on me that our John would have been his child number seven. With no dialogue it seemed as if the vasectomy was his part of the miscarriage.

Unable to process we talked about adopting an Indonesian child. And started the process. Doctors had to agree to such an adoption and having already two children worked not into our favor in Indonesia.

I felt alone. Then Fatima's baby was born. She, my good friend living in Jakarta, who had become pregnant together with me. I had strange feelings but became able to set it apart, her baby and mine. Our little baby entered my dreams. A boy, I named him John. Sometimes I think Toby crossed because of John, to be with him. Why did that doctor pull my baby apart? I want my baby back!

Spiritually, I had not discovered a tangible hold that could guide me through the grief of losing a baby. My faith simply hadn't matured yet. My trust in life had no road to go on. And while I thought I knew about love through loving Toby, the children and my family, I hadn't taken ownership of that love, nor did I recognize love.

In Bontang, I did experience the spirit presence of my dad's mother, my Oma. This comforted me, but when it kept on for a long time it scared me.

"Please go away." I asked her. She did, but not before she brought into my awareness that I had been depressed and for years had been carrying the anger of my dad. His accumulated anger from WWII, the suicide of his dad at the end of that war, and the death of my parents' first child after birth. She thanked me for that and mentioned that my dad wouldn't have made it without me carrying his anger. I understood.

A small Catholic church had been established at the Bontang site. Toby and I attended mass when a priest could be there. I liked the simple English songs they sang. It gave some comfort. One of the quiet women who lived in Bontang mentioned, "In hard times, I always use my Bible." I took note of this, I heard her.

Other expats had a tough time too living in such isolation. "I just think about the dollars that are going into my account, the amount

I save through living here," many said. Such thoughts didn't help me. I didn't think that way.

"Let's go to Samarinda," Toby said one Sunday. "Fatima and Fernando are visiting, and this is a great time to gather up some people for a trip."

I became excited. What could be in Samarinda?

Five families each with their own jeep lined up at our house. Samarinda connected with a similar red clay road through the jungle. The clay appeared wet and soft, but it didn't rain.

Excited and curious we began our trip through the jungle. Our son Patrick, two years old at the time, managed to open the back-door of the dusty jeep on a regular basis. He had no fear. We stopped the caravan, took a break, and secured it so that Pat wouldn't do that again. A drizzle began outside, and the wet clay became wetter. Some motorbikes passed us, and two cars were stuck in the mud along the way.

The guys were challenged but all of us kept going. An hour into our ride we noticed a break in the jungle where a dark body of water appeared at the edge. The caravan stopped. People got out of their jeeps to examine the place closer. A small dock of about five yards long drifted on the side. People had been here before!

Toby with Patrick on his arm, and Fernando with his son on his, walked toward the dock and stepped onto the wooden planks. Suddenly they noticed something large and moving. The two men barely kept their balance on the wobbly old deck and were able to step off. They managed to stay upright, neither one dropped their kids.

Right at the bank of the water, fully stretched, mouth closed, his big head resting halfway in the water, eyes fixed upon us, lay a caiman crocodile the size of which I have only seen in jungles. We held our breath. Quiet, we realized we just escaped something big.

Samarinda appeared in the distance. We noticed some radio towers. Our jeeps made some long slides in the muddy clay, but none of us became stuck. Getting closer and excited, we observed on the side of the jungle a little house or office. A metal beam blocked the road. Edges on the side did not allow enough space for the jeeps to pass. All of us got out, checked out our surroundings and decided to head back before dark.

Close to Bontang, we stopped. Christa and Patrick selected some plants at the rim of the jungle. Toby cut them with a machete as we planned to create a garden with them.

"We have to move first," Toby said one day. He reflected on the other employees who too lived temporarily in Bontang. The houses in Loktuan were finalized yet few wished to move and give up the conveniences of a store and a swimming pool.

"I'll go first," I said. That afternoon a truck came to pick up our belongings and the trek through the jungle to Loktuan began. Bertha and I cleaned and created our new home in a much smaller compound of about forty houses in Loktuan. It would be a while until others followed.

Since we were the only family living in the Loktuan jungle, I rejoiced when a German friend from Bontang visited. Christa sang and danced from excitement. She lost her balance and fell through the glass door that led from the living room to the porch. We had not realized that the quality of the glass in Indonesia, did not resemble the strong quality of glass doors elsewhere.

"I want a bandage," Christa screamed, while I put tourniquets around her arm to stop the wounds from bleeding.

With Christa in my arms, I ran toward my friend's jeep. I slipped, got up again and climbed into the back, holding Christa. We rushed to the company doctor of Pupuk Kaltim, who frightened by the extent of the damage, and not being experienced or capable panicked. Someone had called Toby and as he stepped into the doctor's office, he immediately carried Christa to his jeep. We rushed to the small hospital in Bontang. There a capable doctor, through thirty-six stitches sewed various places of her arms and back together. Gratefully he had done all under full anesthesia.

Two days later Christa and I drove back to Loktuan again. The stitches could be removed later in Jakarta.

From a karmic perspective, if one believes in that, Indonesia didn't prove itself the highpoint of our lives. I lived a life without reflection. Unaware, I moved my life from one day into the next.

Toby and I gave full attention to our family life. At night, our togetherness flourished. We took time sitting on the screened porch, observing the locusts. The company had exchanged our glass door for a wooden one.

Sometimes we entertained. We brought the employees together and served the local saté, the meat on bamboo sticks. We laughed seeing the flying lizards land from one tree branch onto the other. We battled crops of locusts that invaded our site in the jungle at regular times. With surprise we noticed one night a group of people walking ceremoniously from the Loktuan little village, the medicine man at the front. I didn't understand it, just observed.

Toby kept watch of the tides so we could visit a small island that emerged off the coast when the tide was out. A company boat brought three to four families out to the islands which every day emerged in new ways. We admired the forty cm large seashells and took pleasure in the tropical fish shooting away when we swam.

Once the tide changed the company boat returned for us and brought us all home from our magical white beach island with its crystal-clear water.

Each five to six months every family could go out of the jungle and get some fresh air in Singapore or Jakarta. We alternated visiting Portuguese friends in Jakarta and at other times we flew directly from Balikpapan to Singapore. In Singapore we matched our visit with my sister Ilse's flights and together we stayed in the Good Wood Park hotel. These luxurious occasions with Ilse, who flew for the Royal Dutch Airlines, kept us close to my parents. Ilse could relate how we were doing in the East Indies.

Returned to Loktuan, one day around lunch time I heard an unexpected rumble coming from the area where the offices were located. It seemed immense. Swiftly I noticed several Indonesian soldiers surrounding our house. "Go inside, go inside," people ordered me and the children. I had no clue what happened.

Thousands of workers had lined up at the Pupuk Kaltim construction site to get their meal. It happened every day. Lines became long and people became impatient. Each day workers from various tribes and islands lined up a bit earlier. At 11:00 they were ready to eat. Toby had to put a stop to it. The workers became angry. They had stoned his office. As a protection someone sent the soldiers to our house. After everyone had their lunch, it ended. Toby ordered the reorganization of the midday meal. It became calm again. The soldiers guarding our house left the next day except the usual one who guarded the compound in general.

I hadn't noticed how Toby stressed during our time in Indonesia. It only occurred to me later when I looked at some of our pictures. Building a plant that size with thousands of workers became a tremendous responsibility. The challenges to use local supplies and his desire to complete the construction before the time scheduled mounted. The events at home, losing a baby, the accident with Christa, and an urgent gall bladder operation on my part didn't help.

After almost two years we earned a trip home and scheduled a vacation in the Netherlands. We used the regular route, Balikpapan, Jakarta, from there to Amsterdam.

—ᴡ—

After two weeks of reuniting with my parents we returned to Indonesia, the regular route and long trip in reverse. Stepping out of the jeep in Loktuan, we learned that Ursula, our German friend in Bontang had been murdered while we visited our family at home.

Perplexed and with anxiety we walked into our house. I pondered the many rumors that had surfaced with the announcement of her death. One suspect became her husband, who had just secured large insurance on her. The other suspect, the yard man, had had an argument with Ursula on the day it happened. She had made a dumb mistake in that she didn't pay him his small salary because he hadn't done his job right. And while the little money the man earned didn't have a significant amount in our eyes, it was his livelihood.

It became all people talked about. Long after we left Indonesia, we learned that her husband after an investigation, served time in prison in the States.

The final blow of our challenges in Indonesia came close to the end of the year and the completion of the plant. Christmas, which we celebrated with a Santa Claus who arrived in a cart pulled by a water buffalo, happily framed our mind.

Toby walked into the house. "I have just been fired," he said, his head down and eyes focused on the floor.

He told me the story. "A contract needed to be signed. I had to agree to it. I noticed such a large amount as a payoff to managers, the government and more, I couldn't do it. I couldn't be responsible for that amount and refused." They fired me.

The next day, office employees purchased tickets for us. We'd depart from Balikpapan straight into Singapore. I became scared. I realized that the plane, an old Pan Am plane, flying into Singapore belonged to the son of Suharto. Would we get out of here alive?

We filled our days packing. We became isolated. Colleagues didn't know us anymore. Toby had led the successful construction for almost two years. Close to completion and not aware of the true reasons for our departure they didn't know us anymore, with one US family and an Indonesian being the exception.

New Years' Eve Toby courageously gave a general speech to his employees. Quietly we left, trusting that the truth might surface. In Balikpapan at the airport three of the Indonesian directors met us. A brief conversation between Toby and them took place. I couldn't help but feel angry. Also, I was afraid about what could potentially happen to us leaving Indonesia and flying with Geruda Airlines. Both parties knew that the firing of Toby was unjust and based on a sizable corruption which Toby did not want to take part in. I began to see corruption in many countries. Wrapped in different packages each country deals with them. It's up to us to change that. The American construction company we worked for in Indonesia found another US director willing to sign the bribes. The final completion of the plant took place. We heard that three months later the true reason for Toby's firing became known at the construction site. Integrity is sometimes hard to come by.

—⚒—

The feelings of living on foreign ground, not having a sense of belonging, began with the marriage of my mom and dad. A marriage of two people each born in different countries at war with each other during World War II. This feeling of being on foreign soil, a not being anchored, deepened with each foreign country I lived in. I seek refuge in a common humanity to open a perspective for myself and others. Every country and culture had to be integrated in my inner world, because I tried to discern my contribution on this planet. For years my thoughts wandered in this bathtub of a common humanity longing and grasping for love and life's meaning.

I go frequently back and forth in time, seeing what had happened in each country we lived in. A need to understand the carving of a red road, red thread of a worldview unfolded. The containing of such spaciousness takes an inner refuge of beliefs that one must hold like a feather—lightly! A surrender of sorts.

—⚒—

My experiences with Toby, after traveling and living in many countries had become the foundation of my later work at the university. I knew I carried something special, something that others who had not had those experiences could benefit from. I became aware of my ease in connecting with people from various cultures, be they from South or Central America, Muslim countries like

Indonesia and those in the Middle East. This could be beneficial. Making friends across borders reduces war. The Houston location with eighty-plus consulates had become a superb experiential ground to connect leaders from the university with consulates and other institutions representing their country in Houston. I felt complete.

Family circumstances and leadership changes at the university brought me retirement which became a culture shock as well. I left the cosmopolitan city of Houston and settled close to our daughter and family in Montana. It was tough to bring myself to an international halt. My nomadic blood had been running its course I thought. During a family visit to Texas, I lucked out when Peter Bowman, a friend and former colleague, invited me to meet him in Vietnam. A professor of environmental management, he retired a bit earlier than I did. He supported my international magazine and programs at the university. His help to Vietnamese students while they studied in Houston had been extraordinary. Over time he began visits to Vietnam and connected with students' families there. He often helped them out financially. "I can connect you with Vietnamese students in Hanoi," he said.

Challenged with a transition from Houston, a large international community, to life in Montana, I explored my own motto and possible karma "I have more to give," I eagerly accepted.

KARMA IN VIETNAM

2010–2012

Thich Kiên Nguyêt, Thiền Viện Trúc Lâm Tây Thiên

T HE OLD WOMAN CHEWED BETEL nut. A status symbol, it had colored her teeth shiny black.   It made me want to smile back to those black teeth.

She squatted on a stool, her back against a colonial building in the French Quarter of Hanoi. Her face looked earthy. A shawl with flowers printed on it covered her grey hair. Motioning with her hand she invited me to buy some of her tropical fruits on the sidewalk a few feet away from the hotel entrance. Other vendors carrying two large baskets, each balanced with a stick on their shoulders, hurried to their areas. I handed the woman 50,000 Vietnamese *Dong* as she dropped a mango, some red bananas and a soft fruit with a skin that resembled a turtle shell in a plastic bag.

I didn't buy from her each time I returned to the hotel, although I wanted to. Understanding, she smiled. She could be part of that Asian family of Aunt Enny, my foster mom, I thought for a moment. Unlikely, but I liked to dream it could be. Enny came from a rich family from tea plantations in Indonesia. Her Asian side came from a Chinese Indonesian mom and Dutch colonial dad. This was Vietnam, a totally different population in Asia. Vietnamese people with Communist political views, which included Buddhist and Christian spirituality, had their belief in connecting with the ancestors. They harbored a complex history, especially in Hanoi where I visited, the North of Vietnam. Foreign countries dominated Vietnam's past, among them the Chinese and the French. This led to centuries of cultural integrations and covered up parts of their true identity. Their writing and educational flux is evident in Hanoi in the Temple of Literature. Chinese writings at old pagodas show this foreign influence as well.

The woman sat in cold and hot weather. I wondered how she kept herself clean. This was February and the sun hid for weeks behind clouds and fog. Old, she had to work to survive while other women her age sat against a tree, socialized or simply knitted. She didn't seem alone however, like many older people in Western individualistic society.

There was plenty for her to see. Foreigners strolled through the old French area of Hanoi. I breathed what she must have breathed every day, the exhaust from hundreds of motor bikes. Drivers covered their mouths and noses with pollution mask. The traffic, a steady river, created an unrelenting flow through the web of small streets. Motors puffed by gasoline, with pedestrians jumping away, people on loaded motor bikes sporadically brushed one of them with their wheel or handlebars.

The poignant smell of incense blended and covered the various smells. It came from old pagodas and incense that burned at individual stalls. This fragrance had a power to transform the psyche of a person. It put me in a different space, that of spirituality. I didn't need a picture; all I needed was the smell of the incense. In the States where I live, it was the sage and cedar that propelled me into the spiritual world, a world of the heart.

Sidewalks, small tables, and chairs where people ate Pho soup brought calmness among the turbulence of bikes. Pho broth with its mix of vegetables, soy, garlic and sesame smelled inviting. A few times the mingling of odors made me gag, probably from the sewer. In general, the streets were clean, and the French quarter smelled like incense. As an added mystery, a black web of electrical wires with bundles knotted like hair dangled above me. The population moved and traveled energetically forward. Forward to what, echoed in my mind.

"Don't mess with it," a Vietnamese told me. "If the river stops, there will be accidents."

Can I take your picture? I motion with my camera. The old woman nods. Later, after developing, I offer her the photo. Embarrassed, she puts her hand over her face, she looks at herself. The other merchants sitting next to her chime in, too. Their eyes lit up. They begin a conversation among them. Smiles and laughter follow. I don't understand a word they say. But they are happy something had brightened their day.

This was my first visit ever to Vietnam. The reality of a war that took place here had unexpectedly entered my consciousness. Here in 2011, years after that terrible war, my reckless political thoughts at the time resurfaced. As a Dutch woman listening to news, my brain had formed an opinion.

Now in Hanoi, the people linked my heart to my compassionate foster Mom from Indonesia. The horror of that warfare hit upon my essence. On Sunday in the cathedral located in the French Quarter, surrounded by Vietnamese, tears of grief welled up for fighting I had never been a part of ... not physically. Yet, at twenty-four years old when the atrocities took place, I had judged who was right and blamed those who I thought wrong, and what should be done—as if I was qualified to do so. Now I experienced the guilt of my brainless ego at that time, the negative attitude added to many others that contributed to a huge war. Shame and sorrow welled up inside.

Is this what the Buddhist in Vietnam call karma? Was it karma that brought me to Vietnam? Life is circular, my Indigenous friends in the US where I now live often said. Look at the sun, the moon, and the seasons. And it did feel circular; my judgment about the war did come around.

Some karmic thoughts seemed bizarre to me. I heard about the revisiting of illnesses from other lifetimes. Then the likelihood that our energy after deaths checks out couples where to possibly incarnate. It felt over the top. It didn't rhyme with my world of an all-loving Mystery who forgives. But then, I did believe we are all energy and that this force goes somewhere. Miniscule parts of me in this mammoth universe, maybe multi-verse, had a place in a Providence that's beyond me.

My thoughts wandered to my Catholic upbringing. The saints held my expectations of intercessions. They included my mom, dad and friends who had crossed over. I knew I could count on them. Their consciousness still floated out there in a different form.

In my opinion, it's not only the good, but also the bad of consciousness that floats the universal boat. Centuries ago, many Catholics had been injected with missionary zeal. I bet that's part of my karma as well. In fact, today I experience that zeal as a darkness of my consciousness. Buddhism, like other religions, evolved through many centuries no doubt holds its own karma.

Karma, the cause, and effect had shifted over the centuries. Priests and nuns gave their lives for love and justice, especially in the countries where I used to live, Guatemala, Venezuela, Indonesia, and Iraq. Rather than rooted in that false zeal of having to change others, including their spiritual search and reality, many now came from a healthy love perspective. Catholics, Buddhists, Jews and Muslims had true heroes.

In my travels I observed that Buddhism, like Christianity, Islam, and other religions, cultured its people through its values, customs, ceremonies, and symbols... and possibly karma... I added in my mind.

People I had met in my life, the ones I had fallen in love with, could be acquaintances, family maybe, from past lives, I pondered. Maybe they were my previous brothers, sisters, aunts, uncles, lovers. After all, many of my close friends were brown in color, be they from Indonesia, India, Indigenous like Peter Catches in the US. From a Buddhist perspective I could have had past lives in Asia.

—⅏—

Destiny had pulled me now to Asia. Karma and Providence had surfaced into my awareness.

It all began when my belief in myself had taken a blow. The direction of my life as a cultural and international program director had come to a halt. And even though this ending was the result of an intuitive decision to take early retirement and move to Montana, I now felt like I was in the midst of an identity crisis. These people who enjoy retirement are spreading a myth. It's damned hard to reinvent oneself, to be content and optimistic. I need meaning... I don't want to die without truly loving someone, something. Not solely the romantic layer of love, though I'm ready again to include that too. This unreserved love held a deeper plane.

I questioned if Vietnam would bring me closer. It better not be a notion of self-importance, dominance and missionary zeal or, G*d forbid, writer's ego.

On the shadow side, my new environment, Bozeman, Montana, a small intellectual community that was not diverse, ebbed away my international reach. This foreign ground of mountains around me stifled my flow. After all, the pulse of my land by birth, Holland, was close to salty seas. I had moved away from water and a cosmopolitan city.

At sixty-three I had lived a full life. I had tasted joy and freedom. I have had adventures, lived in jungles, received teachings from medicine people, and had an exciting career; more than many have in one lifetime. At the university I had built my career on the experiences I had lived with Toby, my husband, on foreign grounds. It had built on my sense of self. Now an invisible undercurrent ripped me off my feet. I wanted more and thinking of my Indonesian foster mom, I had intuited this trip to Vietnam correctly. Korean Airlines brought me all the way from Seattle, Washington to Hanoi, Vietnam, where Peter Bowman my colleague, and a former student picked me up. At the airport I recognized women of Vietnam Airlines dressed in their traditional *Ao Dai*. Their elegance and flow of colors, white and soft grey, reminded me of the way Aunt Enny had dressed.

Each night students invited us into their homes. "Come upstairs, I'll show you our altar and praying area." I followed the mother of a student up the stairs where in a room she had a statue of Buddha and pictures of her passed family members. Incense burned and food had been put on the altar. They honored their family members in other worlds. They respected food and placed it on the altar in thanksgiving before eating it.

The following day Phuong's family arranged a car and invited Peter and me to visit a temple northwest of Hanoi. The prominent architecture of the *Thiền Viện Trúc Lâm Tây Thiên* Zen Monastery nested, halfway up a forested mountain about 85 kilometers west of Hanoi looked impressive. The entrance with 150 steps up to the temple, the bell and drum towers, called me with expectation. Nuns walked by. They walked slowly and smiled while they folded their hands in a gesture of greeting. A tall nun offered to show us around. She took us on a steep hike to their gardens with spinach, unknown greens and papaya. She talked in Vietnamese, sometimes some English, and smiled a lot.

Looking down, I noticed in a distance a line of orange robes with Vietnamese straw conical hats, moving forward. They were monks, each one of them holding a bowl in their hands. They paced one sandal in front of the other, a silent processional to a large building. Their presence pointed to something that's bigger than I and them together.

Lunch time took us to the same central hall. A soft breeze moved through the dark wooden openings into the hall. Long tables for hundreds of people stretched out in front of us. A statue of a large Buddha oversaw it all.

"*Xin mời thầy cô dùng cơm với chúng tôi.*" Please join us for food she says in Vietnamese. Bowing and with folded hands she motions us into the dining hall. We each receive a large and small bowl. Standing in line at the tables with food, our group copies the nuns. I put rice in my big bowl, cover it with tofu, spinach and something wrapped in seaweed. Like them I fill my small bowl with soup. The tall nun points to a table in the hall quite far from the monks and the nuns. It has large thermos flasks with hot green tea and pots with salted peanuts. Peter takes off his hat. The monks and nuns begin to chant, I close my eyes, sometimes peeking to see if I am doing the right thing. One table over, Peter's head is sunk forward in thought. I wonder what he is thinking about so deeply.

"I'm so grateful for the kindness I receive here," he explained later. I too felt this thankfulness when students welcomed us and took us on trips. Their joy, their spirit of experiencing life together stages a different consciousness. People shared their lives, their stories; there was a "we-ness" about it all. As I experienced it, the Vietnamese have such a sense of togetherness. The students we visited and who joined on this trip brought their brothers and sisters. This atmosphere of support held the opportunity for a different awakening.

A table bell with a high sound ring rhythmically chimes while the master chants. Then all of us take a small bite, a few grains of rice, part of the reverence for the food, I think. We put down our spoon and hold our big bowl. A monk steps outside of the hall onto the balcony. He stands tall in his orange robe, looking into the fog and void in front of him. His hands and bowl extend to the sky. He offers the universe a prayer. Somewhat impatient, I worry that my food will get cold. The chanting took long. What did they chant in these long prayers? Finally, from a distance one of the nuns' gestures for us to start eating. We eat slowly and in silence. And there, for the first time, I participated in the liturgy of food from a Buddhist perspective.

I could use a different focus on food. Here I'm eating vegetarian, maybe vegan food. The thought of food as medicine, as these Buddhist believe, throws me off. On altars I noticed fruit, cookies, candy, tea surrounded by incense burning right in front of the Buddha. Later it would be consumed in a quiet and grateful manner.

The Vietnamese people began to enter my heart. I loved their respect for and connection with the ancestors, their altars and incense burning in their pagodas, homes, shops, and parks. They seemed direct and had no problem approaching me, a stranger. Photo Miss, photo Miss, while they gently pulled me next to them and made pictures. They celebrated their ancestors, not only in their homes, but outside in town as well, in the pagodas, their shops, the parks and especially during the celebrations of their new year. Their ideas matched what the Native Americans and I too believe. I felt an allegiance on a spiritual level with young and old. It was a different perception than most people held where I came from. People did so much together here—even exercised in the park on the lake. "Look, there goes a Western older couple hand in hand. They imitated the Vietnamese. They seem happy."

From my hotel I heard music. It came from the lake where at 6 a.m. everyone joined in to do Tai Chi on music by a battery-powered CD player. At outings in museums, Vietnamese people reached out to meet visitors. "Can I take your picture?" Before I knew it, I was part of a family picture. This happened often. Eating Pho together with others on the sidewalk or in a small restaurant would bring about a conversation. And let's not forget the traffic, each person or family driving their own way, making their own rules, with lots of beeping but never upset, just finding their way in a heap of vehicles of all kinds. It seemed that despite my aloneness, I never felt lonely. The Vietnamese were busy. They were busy together. And never too occupied to smile and connect with a visitor.

In the US I did a lot by myself. I lived alone, pursued my goals, even though I came from a close-knit German and Dutch family that over the years adjusted to cultural consumerism. Present economics had promoted values of self-interest with strong individualism. My value system in contrast with what I observed in Vietnam lingered in my mind. Their supportive "we society" was something I longed for.

I soon pursued a second visit to Vietnam. This visit connected with a dream about a stone I needed for life's journey. I wondered if the Vietnamese, like the Native Americans, believe in the dream world. Do Buddhists?

In a habit of reflecting on my dreams from a Jungian perspective, this one mystified me. It stood out from the rest of them. "You need this for the journey," a kind brown man said while he handed me a stone that to me looked like a tiger eye. Who was this man? How could I find him? Eugene Blackbear, Sr., whom I knew from Oklahoma, could he be the man in my dream?

I later, therefore, invited Eugene, a Southern Cheyenne medicine man, to visit me in Montana. He and I had been friends ever since we met at Bear Butte, the sacred mountain in South Dakota. But I soon realized it wasn't him in my dream. Eugene talked about arrows and not about stones.

From an Indigenous perspective, our dreams are considered more of a real world than our daily life. It was my perspective too. This dream stood out from my other dreams. Who was the person who handed me the stone in my dream? Why did I need it? Intuitively my link went to the Buddhist temple I visited my first trip to Vietnam, especially since the Buddhist nun at the temple had spoken about multiplications of stones, which were carefully placed in front of the Buddha. It persuaded me to test my dream in the reality of this world.

"May I come and visit your temple? I'd like to write the tougher chapters of my memoir there," I wrote from Montana to Master Kien Nguyet of the *Trúc Lâm* Temple, that same Zen Monastery I had visited with the students as a tourist the year before. The passionate image of the gentle man in my dream lingered: "You need this for the journey."

Waiting for his reply I became discouraged. Comparing the people from Vietnam to those of the Indian Nations in the US my thoughts wandered to my teachers of the past. My friend Peter Catches, the Lakota medicine man, often made me aware of food and whose food you eat.

"I wouldn't eat that food," he said during a luncheon meeting of a country's ethnic food made by people of a land that was at war," or "my father discouraged people to eat food prepared by angry people."

Now wait a minute—is part of the Native and Buddhist religion, connected? Was it karma or destiny that I met all these medicine people earlier in my life and that I now connected with Vietnam? How did all this fit my spiritual journey? Their belief in the ancestors was similar to the US Natives. Like the First Nation people in the US, the Buddhist monks also offered food to the spirit world. Could they, like medicine men, enter my dream? There seemed to be similarities between the two cultures. Both practiced the ancestral belief, the honoring of food, even sharing it with the spirit world. With thoughts spiraling up then down I even toss in the community of the saints from my Catholic roots. I remained indecisive. The only way was to step out in faith. I wanted to return to that temple.

My trip tested my dream world as never before. "The dream world is the real word," I remembered again the words a Native American woman had told me. This other world challenged me to the core.

The response of the master encouraged me. "We will do everything possible. Your book will be a success." Thích Kiến Nguyệt, the master of the temple wrote back.

I sent the requested references and felt supported in moving forward on my spiritual journey and left for Hanoi in January of 2012.

Chúc Mừng Năm Móy. (Happy New Year.) Red letters on yellow flags announced TET, the New Year in accord with their lunar calendar.

Going through customs went well. I had sent my paperwork ahead of time to receive my visa upon arrival. I paid $ 25.00 to the immigration officer and received the stamp in my passport for this, my second visit to Vietnam.

Who'll be waiting for me here in Hanoi? "Mr. Tu, our teacher, will pick you up from the airport on my behalf," advised the master of the temple by email. Yet I didn't know Mr. Tu and I didn't want to be hauled off by a stranger. Exhausted I walk through the doors into the arrival hall. It's crowded. I look around for someone waiting… A man, dressed like a monk smiles at me… Ms. Ingeborg? Mr. Tu?

Another nun and monk walk up and welcome me with an attractive multicolored bouquet of flowers the size you only receive in Asia. They wear grey and brown monastery clothing. Thick woolen hats cover their bald heads. They smile and are soft spoken. "Please follow us to the car. Here's a bottle of water." A cell phone rings. "It's the master; he wants to know if you arrived OK. Here talk to him," the teacher Mr. Tu says.

"Oh no, you answer him." I felt shy. They confirm my arrival in Vietnamese.

"Where can I get some Vietnamese money from an ATM?"

The monk takes me back into the terminal. I choose one of the several ATM machines. Insert my US bankcard. It asks me how many *Dong*. What's the exchange again … two million, hundred million? I call out to Mr. Tu.

"You cannot get more than 200 US dollars' worth of *Dong*."

"That's all? Three months on 200 dollars? When will I come here again?" Panicky, I wonder if there are ATM's close to the monastery. Tense, I await the millions of *Dongs* and take a sigh of relief when the machine spits out my debit card. Just to make sure I'd have access to money I had brought three different credit cards and some dollars in cash.

"You won't need any money at the temple anyway," he remarks smiling from underneath his thick beard.

The loaded Toyota Highlander took off. Ten carton boxes are loaded in the back. We are on our way to the temple. Curiously, I observed my new surroundings and laugh loudly as on the road in front of us a huge mama water buffalo with her little one made her way toward us.

"In Vietnam animals have as much a right to the road as people," Hang Tinh, the young nun sitting next to me, gently corrects me. A cultural trade I'd find repeated in the future.

Ah, there's Vĩnh Yen, the city we had to drive through to reach the Buddhist temple. The streets were well-maintained. Many dogs roamed around. Our car swayed around the masses of motorcycles and cars. We drove as if in a maze, always finding a way to continue driving either going around the right or the left to keep on moving. Our young driver honked constantly. I marveled at the sight of the dense Vietnamese mountains. These rainforests emerge in low hanging clouds. Around them are agricultural fields kilometer after kilometer.

Farmers, men, women, and some children, tended the rice fields. Barefooted or in thin plastic boots they stood ankle deep in water, bending over to plant the rice. A *nón lá* conical Asian hat protected them from weather. Elsewhere some tilled the soil behind a water buffalo. As testimony of their bond with the land they burned incense in the little houses created as tombstones. On the side of the road families had built a stall with a thatched roof. Under it they roasted corn to sell for a few *Dongs*. A bit further dozens of shoes on the sidewalk, mostly black and made for men were offered.

Briefly the Toyota traveled through water that flooded the road when we entered a village.

"That yellow building is the police station and the jail in our province. You might end up there," Mr. Tu teased. His joke made me uneasy. It felt quite different traveling on my own. Last year I had met Peter Bowman in Hanoi.

Are these people to be trusted? Will they help me in case of an emergency? After all, this ís a different regime, a different culture, I am on foreign soil, don't know much about them. From the States, I had registered with the Dutch Embassy to put me at ease. In the years before, my travels had been with my husband. A big company backed us in case of emergency. What could a small country embassy like mine do if I got in a fix? Mr. Tu interrupted my reactive distrusting preoccupations: "There are some troubles with your papers. You might have to stay at a small hotel instead of at the temple. Our master must go to Hanoi to make another request for you to stay. But don't worry, you can always stay at a hotel, and we can visit you there."

My eyes searched for hotels in this poor area. Unsettled, I recalled Mr. Tu's joke about the yellow police building. I felt uncertain and questioned what on earth I would do for three months in a remote hotel.

With the car circling up the mountain on steep S-curves we left behind people, shops, traffic, and houses, I felt familiarity but did not know why. The temple was close now. Driving through the fog, we entered a quiet world; the pine trees and stillness embraced us in a similar way a forest does. The car came to a halt on the pedestrian circle in front of the dining hall, the very spot where last year I had lunch. Stepping out of the car, I looked around. Through the fog I cannot see the little village in the valley we just drove through. It's almost as if the fog touches the building. It flows into it.

Hang Tinh, the nun who had accompanied me with needed translation last year, and I walk down a steep sloping concrete road on the side of the dining hall. As if in a tunnel daylight pours in at a distance. Halfway into the tunnel we pass through carved wooden doors, into an area where guests stay overnight. Through another set of doors, we end up on a balcony. From the balcony I can now almost touch the fog.

She unbolts the doors of the room on the corner and opens the tall wood carved door. I like the room; it has a high ceiling. In the corner a bookshelf, two large wooden chests on each side of the room and a small table and chair. The room has a window. I have my own water cooker and a brown pottery tea set. Someone staying there before me had stretched an iron wire across the room for clothing. I notice another painted door. A metal hitch keeps it closed. That must be the bathroom, I think.

"It's simple, things are simple here," Hang Tinh says while Mr. Tu rolls my suitcase into my appointed room. He shakes my hand, and on account of being in the quarters for women, he immediately disappears.

"Where do I sleep?"

Hang Tinh points to the wooden chests, one on each side, two pillows and a blanket. The chests have plastic mats on top of them. She notices my worried face as she responds: "I get you an additional blanket to sleep on. Tomorrow at 6 a.m. is breakfast. We eat vegetarian. You will get used to it. At 3 a.m. we get up for meditation. Come and join us. On the table is a flashlight." Hang Tinh, ready to leave me, explains the lock and bolt.

"Many people visit here. It's better to lock things up, day and night."

My room feels damp and cold. No heater! The wind comes through the doors. Darn, I brought the wrong clothes.

The flights, the change of time and the cold I felt affects my body. I tremble. Nervous, I take in my bare surroundings and open the door to the bathroom. Mold is on the walls. Thank G*d, a western toilet. Noticing the black mold and in denial I tell myself it's not as dangerous as the mold they talk about in the US.

I dig out the pictures of my family, my kids and grandchildren at home and put them up on the bookshelf. Looking at them the distance between the US and Vietnam sinks in. I put my medicine on the table, so I won't forget to take it in the morning. I detect something out of the corner of my eye, something brown, black moving from under the bookshelf. It cannot be… a roach—a Texas-size pine roach. "You're not supposed to kill anything," I say to myself. "It's against their belief." I step out onto the balcony and find a stink bug—belly up. I will not kill them. They don't come around or bother me. It was the last time I'd see them during my stay. It feels good not to kill them, to just co-exist. Secretly, I wonder, do they not bother me because I don't kill them… Good karma.

"Ms. Ingeborg?" A soft-spoken Hang Tinh knocks on my door. "Made you some soup. We only eat twice a day here. You might be hungry. Another question: Can I have your passport? The master needs it to go to Hanoi early in the morning. He wants to see you in a while and welcome you. I'll go with you after you eat your soup."

We meet the master in a room with a large conference table. Another monk serves us green tea. The master's reception of me in Vietnamese translated by Hang Tinh is warmhearted. "All will be well with your visa and your passport, he assures. "The nuns will take good care of you. While you are here open your heart," he repeats "open you heart." Tired, I return to my room. How do I open my heart, I question? I think about it, try to imagine it—but don't know how or where to start. What happens to my heart when I open it, I think? I feel my heart and don't want to have a hardened heart. I want to make my heart softer and bigger. With the Native Americans I'd attend a sweat lodge, where I pray and am sorry, become humble again. I wonder how a Buddhist opens their heart. This question of the heart hangs on while Hang Tinh and I slowly walk back to the room.

"We take off our shoes, "Hang Tinh says. She hands me some slippers. Still in a daze from the flight, I forgot, and I had tracked the wet floor with my shoes." That floor would be cold and damp on account of the daily fog for the rest of my stay. "Come to meditation in the morning, it will warm your body."

At 3 a.m., still with my clothes on, I get up from my wooden bed. My elbow, knee, hips and shoulders remember the hard wood of the trunk I slept on. Equipped with my flashlight I unlock the bolts of my door on the inside, and step into the fog on the balcony. In the dark my hands uncover the metal bars to lock the place up again. Spooky, my feet follow the neon flashlight up the narrow-wet road along the dining hall. The image of a dungeon appears in my mind, until I reach the open area. Fog and a light drizzle drip on my coat. It is pitch dark. Construction in preparation for TET had made the climbing and descending roads muddy. I try to recall where the nuns live, and I should meditate. It is still as a mouse, no insect to be heard, except for the fog and rain not even the trees and bushes ruffle. It seems spooky. My flashlight illuminates the two roads in front of me, one going up, another going down. One leads to the men's quarters, the other to the nuns housing and meditation area; which one? I choose the wrong one. It keeps on going up and up; though I recall that somewhere I have to go down. Something moves on the road below. Dressed in grey and brown, a woman walks as if she knows where she is heading at 3 a.m. My feet hurry down the steep and slippery stairs to follow her. A sharp bell sounds through the valley from a hall in front of me. Dozens of plastic women shoes stand outside on the wet pavement. Incense pours out of the hall. Nuns, facing each other, hands folded bow. Then they turn to face the Buddha and bow again. Next, they prostrate. It is the end of a ritual in preparation for the meditation.

"There's your mat," one of them points. My mat, a cushion to sit on, and a blanket are ready for me. Grateful for the spot in front with the prospect of fresh air from an open door makes me smile. With my legs crossed I tuck the woolen blanket around for support.

Thirty nuns are now quiet and together with me form a silent union. "Oh no, three wooden sticks, hanging on the wall, the ones shown in movies from Asia used for discipline." The clock indicates 3:30 a.m. You can't even hear us breathe except for one nun, who bare-footed, step by step, one foot in front of the other, snails her way to me. In silence, she squats in front of me and takes my hands as they lay in my lap, fingers crossed and thumbs touching. Repeatedly she repositions the way my thumbs touch. I don't see the difference. It's important. Oh no, my legs too? Gently she tries to put one of my crossed legs to rest on my other thigh. It's not going to happen—she realizes it too. We both tuck back the blanket around my legs. With a last glance at the clock, I close my eyes.

My trance awakens when the deep sound of an outside drum vibrates like gentle thunder all around us. My heart is happy. I'm in the experience and out of my head. This is my liberty bell; it reaches my bones and every cell of my body. My trance deepens.

Around 5 a.m. a faraway bell, probably from the monks' quarters, awakens us from the spell where each one of us went. The spongy sound of people slowly moving their bodies fills up the room. All of us, now awake, sit on our mats. Someone in the back of the room speaks softly and serenely in Vietnamese. Hers are the first words crossing the threshold of the morning of a clean new day.

With a glance at my neighbor, I too put my hands, which had laid palms up for two hours in my lap, onto my eyes. Next, we swirl energy with our hands at the mid area of our body. I copy the self-massage of head, shoulder, face and legs, there is a faint recognition of what Standing Eagle, the first medicine man, once taught me. Outside it's still dark. We stand up and face each other. Chanting begins again. We prostrate and bow again and again.

I cannot bow to the Buddha, even though I wish I could. Something inside of me just won't have it. I don't know why or what keeps me. Maybe my heart is closed, I think. Maybe you are not humble enough. It really doesn't matter from a faith perspective. It's all one, I tell myself. Yet, I go through the motion as a physical exercise. The ritual is complete, and we leave to find our shoes outside. With a changed inner rhythm my feet follow the flashlight back to my room. In one-hour breakfast is served. I lie down for a bit when the buzzing of a mosquito alarms me. Buddhist teaching instructs not to kill anything. Restless my mind wanders. I sure hope it doesn't have a disease. There is no malaria here and I hope no dengue fever either. Just in case I put "Off" on my hands, feet, and neck. After breakfast a knock on the door takes me out of my trance.

"The master wants to see you." Hang Tinh wakes me up from my doze. Together we walk up the steep roads where I arrive out of breath. A tiled balcony has carved chairs, a table and a couch. My shoes I leave at the step up. With each step on the marble-like floor, my socks become wetter and my feet colder. In front of the seating area a large mat was placed, and slowly more and more people arrive. They quietly sit down in the lotus position. We all wait for the master. Hot tea warms each one of us. The master, a tall warm and fatherly Vietnamese robed in orange clothes and long saffron colored woolen coat sits down in front of us. He smiles extending a welcome. In Vietnamese, soft spoken and calm, the master elucidated his views on karma. Hang Tinh next to me patiently translates into English. "Do you agree, do you agree?" he'd often interrupt himself. But I don't know if it's polite to give my opinion, as no one else does, so I keep quiet.

I don't share all these karmic thoughts. "Don't make comparisons with your own belief. You want to learn and be open," I reprimand my mind.

But after four hours, I don't have the discipline to keep my own opinion. A story about fish, Christopher Cooke, a teacher on consciousness, once told bubbles up. "But Master it can't be all karma; I'm also formed by my surroundings. You know like the fish in the water. If the water is dirty the fish get sick." It can't be all karma. Slowly, still smiling, the master gets up. It's foggy, cold, and some of the men shiver while listening to him. He invites some questions from them as well and then walks into his residence.

We had touched each other's environment; he with the karma and I with the fish. And I knew this was not the end of this story. Frozen, all of us returned to wherever we came from. The men walked with the men and the women with the women. Two monks crossed our path.

"What's the most important lesson I need to bring from here?" I asked.

"Believe in yourself," they both answered.

It intrigued me.

My relationship with the new surroundings and fog had eased a bit. That day the fog slept a bit higher on the mountain. I even could see the vague green outline of the mountains from the balcony in front of my room. One level below, Hang Tinh noticed me.

"The master invites you to the big hall this evening. There are university students from Hanoi he'd like you to meet."

Together with Hang Tinh I find a place and squat on the ground around one of the low tables. Initially it's challenging to sit in the lotus position which others do so naturally. Immediately one of the nuns pours some green tea for me. From a distance Mr. Tu gives me two thumbs up indicating that the master had been successful with the government, and I can stay at the temple.

It's mystical to sit in a room on the floor and see the fog flow in. Young people visiting from the university sing, taking turns and encouraging each other with clapping. I reposition my legs, put them straight out in front of me. They hurt; my feet are numb. I recognize a playfulness and innocence of the Vietnamese youth. Hundreds of motorcycles are parked in the parking lot. They drive them with two to four people on each. In contrast I can't imagine thousands of youths visiting their churches for New Year elsewhere in the world, making pictures, hanging out, bringing plants and flowers.

"Will you sing for us?" one of the nuns asks. Impressed with the simple joy and enthusiasm of hundreds of students I accept and honor the first Nation people in the US with an Eagle song. "We need a drum. The US Natives use a drum to resemble the earth's heartbeat," I explain. Immediately, one person creates a drum beat while others chime in with rhythmic clapping. Karaoke was a favorite pastime in the temple, and I got to sing American Indian songs thus connecting the two cultures.

—ᨏ—

While I longed for the quiet environment of the temple, it took getting used to. Most visitors had surrendered their computer and cell phones upon arrival. However, Hang Tinh had given me a cell phone so I could always connect with her. Even a Vietnamese cell phone seemed intimidating to me. Uneasy to be without a passport, I'd ask her about it every day.

"Hang Tinh, it's five days now. Where is my passport?"

"They need it, they need to make copies, don't worry Ms. Ingeborg." I had no idea where it was or who had it. Where I came from the handing over of your passport was unimaginable, a big no no.

"How can I leave this place, go to the village?" Something in me needed a break from the isolation. It could make me grounded to know what was here other than the temple.

"We need permission. The master usually knows when one is ready to leave the temple for town."

This is crazy; I want to be able to leave on my own accord. I felt confined. I'm ready to go home, I panicked. I have no passport… "You are in culture shock, relax," I told myself.

Eventually Hang Tinh handed me my passport and it was probably good I didn't have it for five days. I would have been out of there at the rate my negative and reactive feelings went.

—ᨏ—

The first couple of weeks I didn't fully shower. I didn't understand the setup of a shower hose coming out of the wall next to the toilet. I washed my hair over a large plastic bowl and reused the water to wash myself and my dirty clothes. Since I didn't trust the water, which I boiled, I did not drink enough. Tired of the mold on the walls I washed it off, careful not to touch it with my hands. I took possession of the bathroom with a mop.

The Buddhist Zen monastery with its silence and the daily meditation gave space to reflect, to discover a greater mystery of life. My dreams were strange. All kinds of people popped up in images. I began getting used to sleeping on the hard wood. In fact, I liked it. I didn't eat meat now for three weeks already and worked hard to finish my autobiography. I longed to start a fresh chapter of my life, creating a container for helping people to bring life forward in a beautiful way. Finishing my book would allow a new focus. This stay in the monastery was a gift. The silence helped me to stay focused and write the toughest chapters of my book, those where Toby died, and where I was hospitalized. They were tipping points of my search for meaning and identity in my life. It's when I began to recognize who I was and where I came from. It's where my identity began to take roots. Grateful, my thoughts drifted back to the dream I had:

"You need this stone for the journey," I recalled.

The warm and safe container, which living in a temple created, became a sacred mystery. It was too large to express in words, but my heart could touch it. I began to feel part of the spiritual community and their Buddhist temple. Freshness, silence and innocence after early meditation each day felt similar to walking barefoot in the dew of grass. It transmitted to a presence. A sense of contentment came over me. Sometimes with alarm I sensed my detachment from family and friends. This utopia could cut me off. And that didn't strike me as love.

The rhythm of going to bed early at seven and rising at three came easy in the beginning. In bed, all tucked in under the blankets with my socks still on I'd be thankful. Some nights, after looking at the pictures of my grandchildren, I cried. Gone were the feelings of utopia. Aloneness had set in. "I am far, far away from my family," I panicked.

Daily encounters of kindness began tearing at my heart when I became aware that small thoughts I had were answered quickly... I wish I had a flower to put with my pictures. That afternoon one of the nuns, while creating a flower arrangement for the Buddha, with no words but a smile offered me two roses!

My body needs some more fruit I thought, so I maintain my weight and health ... "I bought this for you. Can you share it with Minh?" Hang Tinh handed me a bag of fruit for me and a guest.

One morning, a visiting Dharma teacher approached me. "Come to my room after breakfast," she said with authority in broken English. I'm in trouble, I emoted in a mode of child-like regression. After the breakfast food liturgy, I located Hang Tinh and together we knocked on the head nun's door.

"We have decided to invite you to join us on an important trip. In two days, we will leave at four in the morning together with all the nuns." I accepted. Happily, I recalled my desire to make at least one trip while at the monastery. Then she looked me over, her bald head moving up and down, and with a friendly smile she noted, "You need different clothes."

What was the matter with my clothes? They had only seen me in a coat, long pants; was I out of line?

That afternoon in a sewing room one of the nuns took my measure. The following day my outfit was ready. It consisted of a pair of grey, wide pants with an elastic waist, and a jacket that reached the middle of my thighs. "From now on you wear this every day so other people know you belong here," chippered Hang Tinh. Three other nuns, seeing me in the new outfit ran up, touched, and turned me around to see whether it all fitted right. Confirmed smiles followed. This would be my casual wear during the day. "Eating is a liturgy here. You need to wear this long gown over it whenever you eat breakfast or lunch. Put it on over that other tunic. Wear it during all ceremonies."

And that was that. I didn't need any of my clothing from the US. I'd become a nun. So that's how people join a cult—you strip away their clothes to begin with and keep their passport, a quiet rite of passage. It jolted in my head.

But my passport was returned, and I did like the clothing. I had my own identity, my own inner compass and wanted to learn. The next day, properly dressed with the only distinction of not having shaved my hair off, we all answered the breakfast call.

Seated at long tables, all dressed the same and silent, covered with hats and coats because of the cold, a nun made rhythmic sounds with a bell. With folded hands, chanting in Vietnamese followed. Our hands now touched our bowl. Each one of us put a small piece of rice in our mouth. The Dharma teacher shared the English translation of the liturgy. In English it's sinking in. Vows are repeated: "Commit no evil, do good deeds and save living beings." We contemplated the work and growing of our food, reflected on greed, and wondered if we deserved it. This was medicine for the body. Four bells rang—ready to eat. My food was cold!

Then after four weeks it happened. Just for a second I'm in the present. Not thinking all over the place, a flash. I tasted the food, saw its gift, felt the joy, the gratefulness. I was in the moment … until I recognize what happened … Then my thoughts wander again and in my mind's eye I saw the rice fields, the people standing in the water. I had returned into my head.

At 11 a.m. the ritual began again. Sometimes the dogs came during lunch. They walked under the long tables where about 20-30 people ate and had a happy vegetarian life. They protected the area. One dog came to my room. Very shy, he wanted a cookie. I didn't know how he got to the 3rd floor. The dogs watched as we recited *Namo Sakyamuni Buddha* for the lunch.

This would be the last meal for the day. With my two bowls filled I sat down. The head nun approached my neighbor on the left. "You should sit more to the end on the right of her, she's older," she told her. Embarrassed for her I moved a bit toward the middle to where the nuns sit. Laypeople and nuns sit at the same table but were still separated. During this lunch I pondered the Vietnamese cultural respect for the elder. I liked to be the recipient.

She was not the only one corrected; I too, experienced a push on my arm as a young nun motioned to fold my hands in a different way. I smile. People from Rotterdam like me, are not the only ones in the world who are direct. I moved my folded hands back and forth in a thank you. My thoughts wandered: Tomorrow is the trip. What should I bring along? My neighbor pushes against my arm. A young nun, twenty maybe, motioned me not to make such noise with my spoon against the bowl. We smile at each other, and I held my spoon lighter.

Quietly she put an extra piece of fruit on my plate. She bowed with her hands folded in prayer. I smiled. It is tasty, not too spicy. Again, I want to only think about the food, but the upcoming trip kept on chasing my thoughts.

The pilgrimage to the 700-year-old site included hiking over three mountains and walking around one mountain through a bamboo forest.

"Let your feet do the walking. Slow down, don't ponder how far and high we still have to go," Hang Tinh said. Easy for you to say, I thought. Then far, very far away halfway up a mountain in front of me I noticed a small shed. I can do this, I thought. But then they told me that shed is the midpoint, a place to rest for a while on this rocky path.

"Here take some water, let's sing some songs" another tall nun encouraged me while I fell behind the rest of the group. "Use your bamboo stick to lean on."

The statue of a golden body lay on its right side adorned with flowers and offerings of those that had made it on the all-day trek up there. We sat down at a wooden makeshift table, shielded from the weather, and ate all we had brought along for a meal, rice, tea, fruit, tofu and veggies. Then all nuns put on their orange clothing over their usual grey ones—they were ready to pay homage to the king and the sacred place he had chosen to die. This man, a king, had lived as a hermit. Entering the small and old chapel that only gave room to one at a time I thanked him for this journey. Confused but in honesty I still could not fall on my knees and bow unto the statue like the other nuns did before me. The remote spot marked the place where the king had gone to die. At this site, in the North of Vietnam and not far from the Chinese border and the coast, we paid homage to *Trần Nhan Tong*, the king who defeated the Mongols. His success and ultimate retreat in a hermitage high in the mountains began Buddhism in Vietnam. Arrival at the small chapel-like building reminded me why I had come a second time to Vietnam. I needed this for the next step of my journey in life. I felt that my belief in my dream had affirmed my faith. Others might think of me as crazy, but I truly wanted to follow my inner guidance life. It felt like a spiritual adventure. I wondered if it would move me to deeper unconditional love, a softer and bigger heart maybe. I hope it's not some selfish escapism, an adventure of independent searching for my own benefit. I'm curious about this karma. With this trip to Asia, its culture, and its people, I had followed my own spirit and the one of Aunt Enny.

Our group descended from the mountain to the spot where our bus and driver waited to bring us to a sister temple close by. There we'd spend the night.

On our way to the temple, in the middle of nowhere, our bus got stuck with its axel on a slab of concrete.

"We have to get out of the bus, so it becomes lighter," I told everyone. It didn't help.

"Push, push the bus forward." Thirty nuns, some local people and I pushed a red bus that would not budge. We spread out to various sites while four men, all with smiles, pursued different ways to move the bus. One nun squatted close by and entered meditation. Another joined a local woman cleaning her vegetables. Locals offered us a plastic chair to sit on.

After thirty minutes, never losing his smile, the bus driver set the bus in motion. Squeaking, the now raised axel broke free from the slab of concrete. We rejoiced, hopped on the bus and happily continued.

Not one person mentioned or showed a sign of anger about why we had gotten into this situation in the first place: A parked expensive car, whose driver refused to move it, had caused the police to come. The policeman, rather than have the car move that blocked the road for everyone but the motorcycles, insisted the bus drive backward. Our bus driver had done so for a couple of kilometers and then decided to angle off the concrete and onto the mud road next to it. That's where the back axels had become stuck. The bus hung with two wheels touching the top road and the other two hanging over the mud road we planned to land on.

Immediately people from the village had joined force with large pieces of wood to lift the bus off the concrete. Patiently, all tried different tools and approaches. A long line of cars developed on both sides. It was peak hour around five or six o'clock. Each time in a new attempt all of us had shown up to push, when finally, the fourth time, the front wheels plunged forward onto the mud road below. Taking a risk and with several pieces of wood shoved under the back tires the driver set his bus in motion. Terrible sounds surrounded us, but the bus came to a halt on all fours one level below on the murky road. There we drove against traffic for about three kilometers until we were on a two-way street again.

I had observed a people working together, who smiled and not judged, and who relentlessly focused on the solution. Unsure I tried to pinpoint if this related to their Asian culture or Buddhism. My life at the temple and this experience traveling on the bus with the nuns had shifted me.

—◆◆◆—

Spoiled and purified here in Vietnam, the meaning of my life had changed. I became ready to leave the temple, go home and start a new chapter of my life. I intuited a new path: One of a deeper belief in myself. I explored, "Ingeborg, how often do you have to be reminded to believe in yourself? You have worked on this concept for many years now, ever since your husband died. Why do you forget all the time and fall into uncertainty? You followed the needed reflection, the tough and honest appraisal of your life to come to a focus."

"Maybe it's a lifelong process and I needed to come to Vietnam and get another reminder," I answered myself.

Nervous about the mold in the room, the uncertainty of my passport to extend my stay, I took the steps to leave. After the trip into the mountains, I had been in pain after a fall I took.

"My flight with Singapore Airlines is this Friday. I'll be leaving straight from the temple to the airport," I told Hang Tinh.

It had been hard to utter these words, to believe in myself that it was the right decision to leave earlier than anticipated. But once pronounced I had a sense of relief and began packing and saying my goodbyes to the people I came to love and laughed with a lot.

"The master wants to see you before you leave." Hang Tinh announced. That evening we tracked up the mountain road to his residence.

Again, we spoke about karma with, as a compass, the minimal I knew about it. The cyclic event of it caused by deeds sunk in deeper. The dialogue became a meeting of the spirits, the spirit of the master and mine. It embarrassed me to fire back each time he said something. I couldn't help myself. I came from another culture, another belief system—Christian and Native American, and fought his all the way. "But what about love Master, what about love? It cannot be all karma. I just won't have it."

The master interrupted these moments by getting up. He entered his residence. Soon he'd come back with a gift of a large book with Buddhist teaching. He'd highlighted authors for me like Edward Conze, Heinz Bechert and Nārada Mahāthera to check out once back in the US.

A round of tea followed with delicious cookies and sweets. Then he'd continue about karma and Hang Tinh patiently sat through it all translating his and my words. After an hour or so I got exhausted.

"Master, I think my spirit is fighting yours," I said. "I'm sorry about that, I will reflect on that later, when I'm alone."

I didn't expect his response: "I wouldn't want it any other way; I don't want you to just accept my teachings."

After these words I became more relaxed, better able to respond and again this power of Love rose like a strong beacon. "What about love, what about love," pounded in my head. No, it cannot be all karma." Again, the master rose and went into his residence. He returned with a plastic bag and filled it with green tea, cookies, and fruit for my journey on the plane the next day. This happened several times and all the while his gifts and cares expanded in size in front of me. While I'd stay in my head, he, the master, entered a deeper level of practical giving from the heart. His big heart unfolded in front of me, and I couldn't receive it, I didn't see it with the closed heart that pulsed in my body ruled by the head.

"Keep up the daily meditation and watch your emotions." His last words hooked me. Mulling over my emotions and how to watch them became an invitation to a new perspective beyond emotional intelligence.

After three hours I left, not really remembering the karma he taught. However, all had been said. My being contained his teachings somewhere. Emotions flash-flooded my space; the reality of leaving, of life, decisions and uncertainty had set in.

The next morning monks and nuns came to say their goodbye. I had packed the book the master gave me on Buddhism, a copy of compilation of Buddhist teachings worldwide that had been presented to the United Nations. I planned to begin reading it on the plane.

The master had arranged for his driver to take me to the airport. As many nuns that fitted in the car joined with their goodbye. In the car driving to the airport of Hanoi, we sang English and some Chinese songs.

At the airport I waited for the return journey to begin. Soon I sat down in my assigned seat for the flight from Hanoi to Singapore. Then karma hit the core of my being.

The truth of the master's words at the beginning of my stay at the temple entered my heart. "We have known each other for many lifetimes," his words that I had responded to flippantly at the time. "Let's makes some pictures of us now, in this lifetime." A flood of sadness of separation, of loneliness of … of … hit me all at once. I couldn't contain it. It resulted in sobbing from a depth I hadn't known before. I had left a friend, a karmic friend of many lifetimes, no doubt about that. And as for Hang Tinh and the others, they were part of *Duyen* a part of the serendipity of life. That relationship didn't feel Karmic, not yet.

"I'll bring you some water," a kind flight attendant said. And much in the mode of life in the temple I responded to her with my hands folded and bowing them forward in a "yes." Soon I regained composure. An integration process of my experience in Hanoi had started.

Again, I'm convinced of the value of spiritual direction, the need to reflect and the process of forgiveness, compassion, sharing and interacting. Many years ago, Sister Margaret's unconditional love and untired presence raised this awareness, together with my studies to become a spiritual director. I'd like to bring the identity process into focus for others—making it fun while not losing sight of the symptoms of missionary zeal. It needs to be rooted in love, a softened heart, my thoughts ran. I had to include balance and flow of an inner and outer world.

"You don't want to be too holy," rings my mind. You love the mischief, the encounters with others that have some magic. You like romance and want the companionship of a man; your being craves it. It's the best way to learn, to value—fall in love with a person, with a people and their culture.

A good teacher doesn't fall in love, Standing Eagle once mentioned. I wrestle with my thoughts. But there must be some exchange, energy, and tension. You fall in love with the other, the other way of doing things, the other way of seeing, the other way of eating, believing, laughing, and dancing. You follow; follow like a dog follows its master, I summed up in my head. That's how I lose myself with the people, with the culture, and occasionally with a fascinating man or woman. That's what happened with the photography teacher in Hanoi the first round of my visit. I loved his way of seeing, seeing the people, his sense of discovery and risk taking, the tea-drinking gatherings and muddy excursions. That's what happened with medicine men who taught me. Childlike, I learn fast that way.

Sr. Margaret peaked it all. She had the experience and wisdom to love me unconditionally for thirty-plus years. Where does she find her strength? Let alone the commitment. Or medicine people who over a longer period teach me complex possibilities of energy, the Oneness in the world. They are gifted karma.

But then it happens… I get hungry for my own food and draw back. Go back to where I came from. Who am I? What happened here? How am I integrating all this? My moods go up and down with the chaos that dwells in my head. How do I integrate and become whole once more? I'm changed now.

What do I do with it, these countless gifts? How do I give back? That nagging to want to give back drives me mad. Again, I need to surrender ... until the mischief wells up like the tide of a thousand oceans. I cannot be that holy. It must be my Dutch genes, the ones of my dad; I can see the mischief in his eyes just before he'd tell a joke. I'll pass my experiences on to the next generation, rooted with a good dose of faith in them.

My relationships in the past, my husband, important men like my dad and the strong men I had encountered in my life, all karma? Instead of encountering them I had *fallen* in love with each of them ... these meetings had been destiny. And I was unaware, just like I didn't realize that thoughts were things. I'd focused on romance instead of exploring the mysterious bond in front of me. I had known these people in other lives. Had I been raised as a Buddhist with thoughts of previous incarnations; we could have happened upon each other in a different way.

This blindness had excited my life. It had steered it in a way that only Providence can. It held a gift, a stone for the journey, one that I could not see yet. The artery of individuation in my life had been the spiritual, the experiential and the integration of the academic as well. Toby's death demanded a life from my head to my heart. It became a deep longing, but then, this longing may have been there all along. From the time I entered love relationships as a young woman, I felt a bigger love than for just one person. "When I die, I can love everyone," I used to think.

Only during my life with Toby, experiencing our deep love, but especially after Toby's death when I was thirty-four, I invigorated this path. The thirties stir a bigger awareness for many, they embrace a sense of responsibility for the future. Humanity and the planet cocoon through centuries of wars, natural catastrophes that force us to shed naiveté, just like I did at Toby's death. Will we choose a consciousness of interrelatedness and interdependence, a consciousness of cosmic Oneness? Catastrophes on a personal or collective level carry a weight that can spiral us up to a new way of knowing.

My motto, "I still have more to give," crashed with my life and Toby's running amuck. My breakthrough came when I began to surrender in that psychiatric hospital. I had surrendered to a G*d or Light or Love whatever you want to call it. This had derailed my own suicidal thoughts and propelled a brand-new life. I began to recognize love and experience joy.

Nonetheless, it is tough for me to bow, to bow to the Buddha, the Holy Spirit, the Muse within. As if in war I battle two forces, those of doing and those of receiving. Most of the time the doing, my controlling, wins.

But I'm gaining ground with silence, with meditation, with exploring the love. My capitalization demands to step out in faith and trust this universal existence of love that's bigger than I ever can imagine…and I recall the monks, the nuns prostrating in front of the Buddha. They bow with respect to inner and outer love. A free Buddha lives within me too. It demands bending my knees daily as a conscious encounter with my own dominance. Yet will I do that? Deep inside there is a knowing that only then, can I step into a world with various degrees of control like my own. "Identity grows with taking responsibility," Sr. Margaret reminded me. I need to balance that act of doing. Balance it with the other side of me, that maybe is called the Feminine side. This part calls me to surrender to having faith and to <u>receive</u> a loving mystery.

RE-AWAKENING THE HEART OF TOLERANCE

W HILE I SHARE MY PERSONAL search for identity in these writings, I discover that this new territory requires different boundaries. Living amid a tumultuous world in constant transition, new approaches in communities and countries are needed. The Dutch in the Netherlands, my origins, have encountered the fluctuations of tolerance and intolerance since the 15th century. A few years ago, their tolerance demanded re-adjustment.

Initially Holland didn't realize the change brought by people who came in the 1960's from Spain, Morocco, Turkey to find work. Many of the needed laborers didn't have a high level of education. They were welcomed by the Netherlands, Germany, Belgium, and others in the region, often doing jobs some Dutch didn't want to perform anymore. Hard working, they too brought their own history, religion, culture, and value systems.

Attracted by good and free healthcare, education, and prosperity they stayed and eventually their families joined them from abroad. Through proximity to their country of origin including television programs and computer access their culture could be maintained. They continued their original language within the family. Even marrying one of their own, often young brides considered under the legal age in Holland, be it in Morocco or Turkey, could be arranged during vacations to their homeland. Therefore, immigration expanded and continued. The flow of families from countries where separation of state and religion are ill-defined became renewed and strengthened on a regular basis. Some values such as free speech and behavior were in direct opposition to the Dutch system.

After the baby-boomers, the Dutch had smaller families in contrast with new immigrant Dutch who had larger ones. It came about that the number one boy's name in Amsterdam, the Dutch capital, was Mohamed, a Muslim name. Especially in the south of the Netherlands, some towns had many people speaking a different language and carrying an atypical cultural identity. Many Dutch in these towns felt like strangers now.

While the Dutch allowed the use of street drugs like marijuana, be it strictly controlled, the immigrants did not accept Dutch norms of sexuality which included gays, monitored prostitution, dating and freedom of speech. Honor killings and moral monitoring through control of the whereabouts and actions of women and girls were not a part of the Dutch belief system. Anger and seeking a solution became urgent when Pim Fortuyn, a politician, and later Theo van Gogh, a filmmaker, were brutally murdered for their opposing expressions on Muslim women and religion professed by people who immigrated into the Netherlands. Tolerance and intolerance demanded to be looked at again.

This population shift not only happened in the Netherlands, but it also surfaced in other parts of Europe and the world as well. Close to the Netherlands in Denmark worldwide reactions, even killings, occurred when a newspaper's cartoon depicted the prophet Mohamed negatively. This added to the examination of free speech and choice. As a positive the word "respect" is increasingly heard in schools and around the globe. I believe September 11, 2001, with the destruction done in the US through Muslim extremists began to shift free speech for many in the US.

Dealing with my own anger when destruction or injustice happens is the hardest to do. Where your energy goes, you go, I know that much. My biggest challenge is to examine both the positive and the negative in a balanced way. I salute people who can carry two opposing opinions simultaneously while not getting emotionally triggered. After the initial blow I'm called to emerge in a bigger way with something new, something innovative and creative, something that is life giving. The pandemic and large worldwide migrations both for people and animals are insisting on yet another approach of what it means to be part of the whole. The healing and return to balance worldwide need each of our wisdom, strength, potential and collaboration. Out is the time we lived in that aimed personal welfare without seeking the collective. We need rare leadership that can be flexible enough to handle this bag of toys. Pandemics point to smart thinking of the viruses among us. No need for borders/boundaries of the old kind. You and I must let the old thinking die. These are outdated insight we need to let go of. Old belongs to the ancient and becomes a steppingstone for daring and testing new ideas. New tolerance is a component.

I used to get together with a group of improv drummers in Houston. Some of us were taught by drummers from Africa, some played in orchestras and longed for freedom of musical expression. Others were doing their best to keep the beat. It was a muddling sound and after a while our friend Annette would yell "Let go you all" and soon a sound of drummed harmony filled our space.

I admire people like Elie Wiesel, the political activist and holocaust survivor and Peter Catches, the Lakota medicine man, who embrace others that have deeply wronged them in the past, even embracing their different religions.

Master Thich Nhat Hanh from the Vietnam Buddhist temple links tolerance with forgiveness. Margaret Byrne, a Catholic Cenacle sister, speaks of a stream of consciousness that moves from forgiveness to compassion, followed by a desire to share and interact.

These are spiritual perspectives. Many of us independent to the core search on our own. I submit to a knowing that everything is interrelated from the tiniest atom and cell, therefore the "I" in me must change to "We," a bigger consciousness.

"Consciousness is one thing, but don't forget it is strongly influenced by the unconscious," teaches Carl Gustav Jung. "The personal shadow is the bridge to the mass shadow."

Education is called to address these issues. Which schools teach about treaties with Native American tribes? Which history books contain and explore the truth of the Guatemalan war in the 80's or more recently the war in Iraq? Which universities are shifting from a business model to true research and innovation serving the student's own directives as well?

Which causes will you and I pursue, after today's man or woman on the moon? Will our cause include a global healthcare with different forms of medicine? Will our cause include the right relationship with the earth and new interactive research in science, new expressions of music, poetry and other forms of art?

Integration of cultural values is complex. Many countries are seeking their identity in the global transformation. The United States moved away from a country defined as closed and seen in isolation by the rest of the world. The unethical lobbying in business, (for example, the government's support of certain pharmaceuticals, economics based on Monsanto and the sorts, petrochemical strategies, and gun laws) call up the tolerance of part of the US population while the opposing ones express their intolerance.

How do I process these contradicting views? Acting under the influence of emotion could prove disastrous. These society emotions trigger elements of insecurity and domination that leer at you like a mountain cat. With no limits and a misplaced tolerance, an outpouring of collective anger can suck the energy out of you.

How can groups that use the political or religious arena to control large groups and resources that run the world be stopped? In my opinion they can't. New ideas formed by passion, not by mania could help us thrive. What can be done is to create an environment that supports reflection, generational healing, growth, and freedom to explore new thoughts: A core freedom where people can evolve and are only stopped at the point of endangerment to others. You and I need to revisit our tolerance and intolerance in the context of coming together for the sake of the earth and humanity.

Boundaries need to be set though, and in the Netherlands, I know some communities are controlled differently by police than others. Hopefully, a balance can be found honoring different cultures. Sex, the birds and the bees, the flowers all creation is involved in this energy—we must not hinder it. National domination and religious fundamentalism contribute to the problem of exploring social values and tolerance. "The educated have as poor a record for tolerance as the ignorant because it is as easy to be infected by intolerance as by the common cold," says Theodore Zeldin, former dean of St. Anthony's College, Oxford. Older people in the West could reach a hand to the young and vice versa to get a more realistic vision.

One example is that higher education has stepped into the world arena since 1964 through yearly collaborations of university presidents and executives around the world. The International Association of University Presidents echoes shared goals and expansions toward international relationship and peace. All the while we, as a society, are responsible for a free and safe environment that assures tolerance so we may grow and explore.

Populations in various countries seek to develop a new identity forced maybe by fundamentalism, huge immigrations yet also through massive international student exchanges across the world. Middle Eastern countries, Saudi Arabia, Palestine, Iraq, are tied to a variety of identities. Some like Jordan, the United Arab Emirates, and perhaps Egypt, Libya, and Tunisia, may explore their own model of democracy. Australia maybe uncertain whether it will throw out its anchor in Asia, or, as always, remains aligned with Britain. Mass world migration will challenge our old views fast. A new value system will emerge there were the heart is and whole system thinking prevails.

For us in the 20th century, this storm can lead to an appreciation of delicate cultures such as those of Tibet, the Mayans, and the Native American nations, which took thousands of years to build. They now gain support in preserving their valuable languages, stories of relationship and their identity.

These times require that I testify to my generational wrongs as well, such as my naiveté when as a young woman I came to live in Guatemala. Toby, my husband, directed the building of a Canadian nickel mine in a small Mayan village. Its construction damaged the earth, and upon completion it polluted the air for the population of El Estor. Unknown to me at that time, the Mayan Indians who lived on the land that contained the nickel had been violently removed to make space for the mine several years before I arrived there.

However, the low price of nickel was on the side of the local people and the mine closed after a brief start up. It had been dormant for decades now. Houses built for employees are standing and rotting behind a wire fence. Maybe a fierce jungle growth will take over. Unfortunately, the Guatemalan government collaborated with a Russian company and presently the mine is not employing any locals and spewing toxicity into the waters and air for the locals living there.

That we had maids cleaning the house and caring for the children was a given. In the 70s it was part of the dominant culture in Guatemala to pay a person, many of them Mayan Indians, twenty to twenty-five dollars a month for tending the house. Yes, they received living quarters and food, and I did take in a child for a year, helped at the local school, and helped build a library. But are these mining operations and their toxic effects, right? These entitled situations remain today in South and Central America, the Middle East and Asia.

Besides the robbing of the land the notion of paying someone such a low salary was and is morally wrong.

However, the very poor living on dirt floors had the same system going. They too had people working for them or raising their children. Was it begun in the fifteenth century with the Inquisition, or did it exist earlier when the Quetzalcoatl brought together cultures like the Toltec and the Mayan in the Americas? How did agriculture, mathematics and astronomy come together for that many people then? What transitions did they apply? Which G*ds did they pay homage to?

How can we talk about tolerance and intolerance, as defined in the Western world, when we don't take the time to know who we are, where we are going and what we value on a personal level and as a culture?

Despite the deep imperialistic and dominant nature in the world I observe myself getting tired of attacks against my culture of origin. I seek a balanced view of identity of the people I'm part of. I do not want to be an island with loose emotional anger toward immigrants, political, and other groups. Intolerance can force people into hiding. It shuts you up, could feed the inner reservoir of emotion.

History shows us that often the truths of delicate cultures are sacrificed to the financial or cultural benefit of a dominant society. Bagdad once was a cosmopolitan center of knowledge where both male and female contributions thrived. Who and what is the driving force behind the next dominant society? We are called to step up in knowing who we are and to go beyond our definition of relationships up till now.

What are the ingredients of tolerance? To me it is a healthy dose of respect, reflection, curiosity, risking opening my heart and expand my thinking. The word "tolerance" is heavy. It is unpopular not to tolerate certain things. Some say tolerance is a discipline. If that is so, tolerance needs to be part of education. Tolerance is part of my identity and a gift of my country of birth, of course healthy boundaries are part of my identity as well. Boundaries must be part of the collective identity too. Frustrations are signaling that boundaries need to be set. I'm an evolving person, part of an evolving species who integrate new situations, environments, and reflections. I'm part of the cosmos always changing always moving.

Most importantly it requires reflection on how and what not to tolerate in this world we all form a part of: Who am I, how do I want to grow and how can this serve humanity and future generations. However, what is good for one person, one country, may not benefit the whole world. People in each country carry unique gifts.

In my mind tolerance creates a state of happiness in relationships. When I'm happy I reach out to others and feel connected. Unhealthy intolerance, as acted out in control, dishonesty, and religious fundamentalism, creates negativity and therefore isolation. Tolerance seeks a just and fair diverse society where people can explore and grow.

However, one views it through the mirror of pain, or through a prism of progress, future generations are at stake. This "all of us together" thinking is coming in sight like a beacon of hope. May a flexible and wise leader emerge, one who senses the whole of creation.

ONENESS

I wonder, is it our human self-importance and inner fire wrongly purposed? Leaders around the globe have focused on power and economic gain for millennia now. The heart of humanity in the East, the West, North, South and in the Middle ticks slowly away while our planet, the earth that feeds us, mirrors the consequence of our created imbalance. Despite this, soldiers, men, and women fighting, continue to be sacrificed away in harm's way away from their family.

We are conditioned to think in opposites and have a dualistic mindset. Few can hold one thought, two opposites or multiple ideas without judgment. A good listener can create a container of Oneness and discern the common denominator of what's required to come together as one. Martin Luther King handled very strong beliefs of millions and brought our brokenness together into the Oneness of "I have a dream." Religion and belief systems influence our perspectives. Cultural backgrounds inform us as well. Worldwide our perspective has long been focused on possession and dominance. Our predominant focus on competition and economic gain imprisons us. Our society cries out for balanced male/female living in right relationship with the planet.

THE INDIGENOUS, I NOTICED, FIRST focus on a "personal relationship" with respect for the land, the animals and all of creation and the universe we live in. Most of their land and waters still have intact ecosystems.

Each of us pronounces *"Mitakuye Oyasin"* on our way into the sweat lodge. It's the Lakota word for "all my relations." To speak those words feels strange. It takes time to fathom what's meant by it. Maybe it will even take all my living years to grasp this Oneness with all of creation.

I need to do this, I'm ready. My mind has been restless for too long. I need to go to the center of who I am. Lately, I get irritated a time too many, taking things personally and shooting back with sarcasm. This center is pivotal for me and for my family and my friends. My relationships must evolve in a loving and centered way. I do my best as a human but rising and falling is happening too often lately.

Books written by Dr. John C. Lilly, M.D., like "The Center Cyclone" remind me that relationship is at the core of everything, my cells, and my presence in the world. He alerts me that I overlook the importance of relationship above all. I fail in communication with people, let alone with other parts of creation, the animals, the plants, water, fire, earth and sky. I would like to become more open to this as I don't even remember or know how to boost my understanding of communication. What I do know from previous experience is that a "sweat" moves me forward in all of this.

I'm grateful for the woman who shares her land here a few miles outside of Houston. She tends the dome-like skeleton made of willow branches built a few years ago. This morning we covered it with blankets.

My shoes are on a pile with those of the others. I feel the soggy ground between my toes. The pine trees smell fresh from last night's rain. Together with others, I wait to proceed. My impatience ebbs away as I enter a different kind of time, one that the medicine man directs us into. Slowly, I approach the sweat lodge where a thick piece of cloth flapped open shows the small entrance.

The *inipi*, this earthy ceremonial space, helps me to go inward, to purify. The *inipi* is where I find my center and where my ego evaporates. My mind becomes second now.

I wish I could do this at least once a month. I ponder how it could ever become ethical to integrate this Indian ceremony, absent in the Western Dutch culture I'm from. Peter Catches (*Zintkala Oyate*), the Lakota medicine man leads people in the *inipi* through the spirit world. As a trained spiritual director, I lack the expertise needed for a sweat. One must earn that right, I'm told.

Grateful for the opportunity to have sporadic experiences with people from a culture close to the earth, I embrace Peter's visit to Houston.

It's late in the afternoon. Days before, others split wood for the fire and gathered the stones. Barefooted, crawling with one hand holding my traditional long dress above my knees, I move forward through the small opening into the dark. I smell the earth. My eyes adjust to the dark. I feel for my spot next to the person entering ahead of me. The anticipation of Oneness and surrender lead me. My body recognizes the crumbling of my fragmented mind into the present moment.

I'm sitting now, cross legged. Others follow and the space begins to feel compressed. The presence of the medicine man, who I have known for several years and whom I trust to lead me in spirit, generates calmness. His words are sparse. Each direction he gives weighs in. I observe him as entering a different world. I have been waiting for him to guide me toward this core of my being. His communications with the fire keeper outside the lodge are direct. These two men tune into each other. "Stones please... that's enough. Water..." The flap to the entrance closes. Peter's drumming and gentle singing in Lakota indicate the beginning.

What's happening here is a timeless knowing I don't understand but want to surrender to. Together with other people from around Houston, I'm entering this unification with something larger than myself.

I wonder how Peter will lead the sweat. I look forward to more Lakota songs. Some songs in his book "Sacred Fireplace" (*Oceti Wakan*) by Peter S. Catches—edited by his son Peter, over time helped me gain depth and meaning. I expect gentleness in his guidance. I trust. Simultaneously my body knows about the heat of the stones, *tunkas*, in the middle pit of the sweat. I pull my legs back a little, especially when the fire keeper brings in more red glowing rocks each round. No, I wouldn't want to burn myself.

If this is going to be any good, I'll have to go to that deep part inside of me, that space I have tried to avoid far too long. That space that's blocked by my self—importance, ice cream addictions, yes, half a gallon at one sitting while watching TV, and my ego that wants to have success on the job.

I'll have to endure the hot steam that transforms like sacred alchemy. All these graced experiences work together to get me there, each person's prayers, the songs, the earth, the darkness, the steady drumbeat, the fire, and fire keeper who pitches red hot stones into the pit each round, followed by water changing into hot vapor. The sacred pipe, songs, sage, and the authentic participation of those around me form a synchronic unfolding beyond under-standing: Something good and loving.

The need to surrender pulls on my anxiety. Will I make it through all four rounds? Will I come to the point of deliverance where, as in the past, energy flows through me and images emerge of those in need?

This is me; this is who I am, a part of the whole. Where does this part of me go in the day to day living when I bite off my own wings with ego and self-importance?

People from the Indian Nations that now are helping me to return to my essence with their ancient language, songs and wise presence, the ones whose treaties have been trampled upon, are leading me. For the sake of the whole, the Oneness, they the Indigenous keepers of experiential teachings lead me to my core once again. As a part of the dominant society, I feel humbled to learn a different relationship with the earth. I'm an integral frag-ment of a whole. I believe, they, the Lakota, understand that my centeredness is important for all, especially the future of life and humanity on this earth. This forgiveness, their love for me, gives me hope; it invokes a different longing, one of nurturing and love for my children and grandchildren, and whatever tribe, nation, or civilization I'm from. It narrows my gap between head and heart. .

In contrast to this Indigenous experience in Texas, my life began in a major city in the Netherlands. It's a busy place and a tough spot to connect with the earth though it can be done, especially with the Northern Sea close by.

Rotterdam, my city of birth and a world harbor in the Netherlands, today consists of almost fifty percent immigrants.

And while Oneness is happening all over the world, I, together with most of the world's population, don't see it, don't remember. Like many I fall prey to my own and others control and domination. Sometimes when I consciously slow down and follow a different beat, I see glimpses of what could be.

That happened not long ago, while I was in Mexico. The dolphins communicated with me mind to mind. This surprised me; a dormant capacity of communication awoke in me again, one I, together with other humans fail to remember. "Many animals, through the void, forgot too," Eugene Black Bear, a Southern Cheyenne Medicine man told me.

These dolphins woke me up one night with their clicking sounds. In my nightgown I stepped out onto the balcony above the reservoir where the dolphins stayed. The area below, an encased body of water connected to the sea, was as big as a soccer field. The dolphins were active, not asleep. Watching them in anticipation of their jumps, I found the dolphins instead begin to communicate and refer to the human control issue: *El pecado del mundo*, the sin of the world—they said. To my surprise that communication came to me in the Spanish language. Then they jumped. Their jumping in the dark night expressed liberation from the daytime when their every trick and directed move was controlled and rewarded with fish. Now at night they frolicked, their self-directed leaps showed freedom.

The dolphin's capacity for communication and relationship had stunned me. My curiosity would lead me to books by Dr. John Lilly and his experiences with dolphins.

Many dolphins in the world are captive. They exist on human terms. Many are slaughtered for consumption in the Japanese area. And with our warped mind on war, I learned they are trained by the military in the US, Russia, and possibly even Iran. Their jobs as you can imagine are not pretty. How could I communicate with dolphins again without need of their captivity, in freedom? I wanted their freedom.

The dolphins are a tough reminder and lesson to realize of how I live my life with control and how this control finds an entry through fear, judgment, and untamed emotions. Do I ever learn this lesson of allowing things to happen?

"Are you saving the world again?" Johnnie, my brother-in-law frequently asked. Naturally, with the international programs I created for the university I wanted to make a difference, wanted to bring some awareness of the interrelatedness of everything. But hey, did I know what direction would be good? This earth moves fast enough as it is without me doing anything. Edward Hays, in his book "Prayers for a Planetary Pilgrim" takes my balloon down quickly: "Grant me patience, then, as I plod slowly toward wholeness and holiness. But also, make me eager to achieve a largeness of heart, a generosity of giving, and a greater depth of humble service." Now, if that isn't about relationship, I tell myself.

At the end I bow down to the fact that everything is interrelated from the tiniest atom and cell. I find it exciting when this awareness of Oneness flows and a growing number of people unite to reduce war and promote a just interaction with humans as part of nature across the world; focused, for example, on clean water and air, food distribution and health issues.

Because of the teachings in process theology at the pastoral center in Antwerp, Belgium, I became aware of being an integral part of a universal happening in space and time. Everything was interrelated. That invitation to study there by a local pastor after I moved to the Netherlands after Toby died, had opened the gate of an infantile G*d image. The final punch came several years later through learning more about quantum theology taught at the Jung Center in Houston by my Jungian analyst Jim Aylward. I'm making a difference. My minute thoughts and actions make a difference? "Relationships," it echoes in my mind—*Mitakuye Oyasin*—I believe it. I'm part of the big bang over and over again. It's what Jim Aylward, helped me to own up to.

My life unfolds with the unfolding of my cultural and spiritual identity—a never ending search for a deeper sense of authentic being. With experiential learning of Oneness by the Indigenous I delve into the mystery of relationship with the earth, the animals, the water, the sky and more. Learning now becomes an integral part of my cultural and spiritual identity—my relationship with the sacred. I feel my place as part of the universe. Christianity, my roots, and foundation, teaches love and forgiveness. Exercising love and forgiveness keeps me centered. Through my experience with the Buddhists, I awaken to the concept of karma, their Zen meditation and endless compassion. The deep notion of a new beginning each day at their temple *Truc Lam Tai Thien* in Vietnam refreshes and renews my existence. And while I just separated these religious orientations, I'm very aware that each religion points in the same direction to Oneness and loving communication. This orchestra of life with creation and destruction in and outside of me is all about relationship and communication.

There are many times and ways to come to stillness and grow my understanding of what "all my relations," that *Mitakuye Oyasin*, means. This Oneness might be infinite and timeless. Oneness is a joyous promise. There is also the hidden element of choice, the option to what I'm committed and called to in this partaking of relationships within the Oneness. I recall a saying by a Dakota Indian, "Don't walk in front of the pipe." It puts me in my place.

The sweat lodge experience brings me to this place of who I am and who I am not. I'm challenged by the increasing heat; my mind becomes more focused. I sweat. I sit uncomfortably. The drumbeats by the medicine man carry me. I mumble and join into the Lakota prayers. From people across and beside me I hear prayers, prayers of gratitude and prayers for help. Their gratitude and prayers touch mine and decrease my ego. The presence of the others supports me. A deep knowing inside feels they are on my side, they join my requests for help, my prayers.

I focus on my breath which tries to find a relationship of a comfortable in-breath of the hot air in the dark that surrounds me. I'm part of nature, a minute part of a loving miracle. I matter in the whole. Ingeborg Standing Bear Woman has more to give... and to receive.

AUTHOR'S NOTE

REMINISCING, I TRULY MISSED CONNECTING with my dad, having an exchange of thoughts. Generational trauma for both of us prevented our true essence to connect. I shall most recall Dad's love for Mom. His patience with the symptoms of Alzheimer surrounded her with dignity and joy throughout her decline till the very end. Each day Dad made her smile and experience joy, never giving in to despair. Quite the contrary, he created her favorite music tapes, made her laugh, and visited her every day, after care at home was physically impossible. And if that was not enough he surrounded all his grandchildren with joy, connection, and presence. They adored him and rightly so. Who can say during the days shortly before Dad left us: "I have loved enough?" You have! And that includes the love for me, my brother Henk, my sister, and the grandchildren with later great grandchildren.

I also want to give tribute to Peter V. Catches, and his wife Cindy. Without them in my life and the opportunity to share Peter's and at times Cindy's teachings at the university and on a personal level, who would I be? I still recall Cindy saying: you must give until it hurts.

The closeness in spirit with Peter Catches helped transform my childish interpretation of falling in love into learning about *Ocety Wakan* the sacred fire of Oneness.

Gratitude overflows when thinking of all Indigenous people I encountered in the US and Guatemala. To this day I keep growing this *Ocety Wakan*. I daily make mistakes in my relationships and am smoothing out the pain-bodies floating around. Yet my trust and feeling of belonging in relationship and Oneness evolves.

I balance my Muse with respect for the Creative Spirit in others, so I may receive what others can teach me. Excited and grateful I call the child forth from the essence of my being, now and always. I'm capable, often innocent, and courageous, like the rat slag (cartwheels) I did as a seven-year-old child over and over again; the mystery and potential of my own core being: Together with the Rotterdam Dutch, I sing the Feyenoord soccer anthem "Not words but deeds."

SELECTED REFERENCES AND BIBLIOGRAPHY

Andrews, Ted. *"Animal Speak,* The Spiritual and Magical Powers of Creatures Great and Small,"* 2002.

Beck, Don, PhD. *"Spiral Dynamics integral,"* certifications 2003 and 2005.

Brooke Medicine Eagle. *"Buffalo Woman comes Singing,"* 1991.

Brown, Joseph Epes. *"Animals of the Soul,* The Sacred Animals of the Oglala Sioux,"* 1993.

Catches, Pete Sr., Edited by Peter V. Catches. *"Sacred Fireplace (Oceti Wakan),"* 1999.

Horst, Han van der. *"Rotterdam Bruid Van de Maas, Van Prehistorie tot Nu,"* 2017.

Lilly, John, M.D. *"The Center of the Cyclone.,"* 2007.

O'Murchu, Diarmuid. *"Quantum Theology,"* 2004.

Thich Thanh Tu, Zen Master. *"Keys to Buddhism,"*

Young Eisendrath, Polly and Florence Wiedemann. *"Female Authority, Empowering Women Through Psychotherapy,"* The Guildford Press, 1987.

Whitney, Michael. *"Matter of Heart, The extraordinary journey of C.G. Jung into the soul of man,"* 1986.

RECOMMENDED READING

Cajete, Gregory. *"Native Science. Natural Laws of Interdependence,"* Clear Light Publishers, 2016.

His Holiness the Dalai Lama and Archbishop Desmond Tutu, with Douglas Abrams. *"The Book of Joy, Lasting Happiness in a Changing World,"* 2016.

Susag, Dorothea M. *"Roots and Branches, A Resource of Native American Literature—Themes, Lessons, and Bibliographies,"* National Council of Teachers of English, 1998.

Van der Kolk, M.D. Bessel. *"The Body Keeps the Score,"* 2016.

www.ingramcontent.com/pod-product-compliance
Lightning Source LLC
Chambersburg PA
CBHW070900120626
46546CB00001B/71